十二月十四日對面

御代官

Russia's Japan Expedition

of

1852 to 1855

俄使赴日记

Адмиралъ графъ Е. В. Путятинъ. † 16 (28) Октября. Съ фотогр. грав. Ю. Барановскій.

ADMIRAL EVFIMII VASIL'EVICH PUTIATIN

Russia's Japan Expedition
of
1852 to 1855

by
George Alexander Lensen

University of Florida Press
Gainesville
1955

To My Family

A UNIVERSITY OF FLORIDA PRESS BOOK

COPYRIGHT, 1955, UNIVERSITY OF FLORIDA

Library of Congress Catalogue Number: 55-8081

MANUFACTURED BY ROSE PRINTING COMPANY, INCORPORATED
TALLAHASSEE, FLORIDA

Acknowledgments

PERMISSION TO QUOTE COPYRIGHTED MATERIAL IS GRATEFULLY ACKNOWL-edged to publishers as follows: Barnes and Noble, Inc.: *Americans in Eastern Asia* by Tyler Dennett (New York, 1941). The University of California Press: *Japanese Expansion on the Asiatic Continent* by Yoshi S. Kuno, volume 2 (Berkeley and Los Angeles, 1940). The University of Chicago Press: *Western Influences in Modern Japan* by Inazo Nitobe and others (Chicago, 1931). Kelly and Walsh, Ltd.: *The International Relations of the Chinese Empire* by Hosea Ballou Morse, volume 1 (Shanghai, Hong Kong, Singapore, and Yokohama, 1910). Alfred A. Knopf, Inc.: *The Western World and Japan* by G. B. Sansom (New York, 1950) and *Black Ships Off Japan* by Arthur Walworth (New York, 1946). McGraw-Hill Book Company, Inc.: *Japan Since Perry* by Chitoshi Yanaga (New York, Toronto, London, 1949). Kegan Paul, Trench, Trubner and Co., Ltd.: *A History of Japan* by James Murdoch, volume 3 (London, 1926). Princeton University Press: *Yankee Surveyors in the Shogun's Seas* by Allen B. Cole (Princeton, 1947). G. P. Putnam's Sons: *Bushido, the Soul of Japan* (New York and London, 1905). Acknowledgment is further made with thanks to Mr. Clarke H. Kawakami and family for permission to quote from *Japan in World Politics* (New York: The Macmillan Co., 1917) by their late father K. K. Kawakami.

[V]

I SHOULD LIKE TO TAKE THIS OPPORTUNITY TO EXPRESS MY SINCEREST gratitude to my teachers and friends at Columbia University: to Professors Hugh Borton, Philip E. Mosely, C. Martin Wilbur, and Henry F. Graff, who read through the whole manuscript and made valuable suggestions; to Professors L. Carrington Goodrich and Chi-chen Wang, who stimulated my study of Chinese; to Mr. Ryusaku Tsunoda and Dr. Osamu Shimizu, who helped me hurdle some of the more difficult passages in the Japanese sources; to Sir George Sansom, under whose guidance I did some of my earlier research in Russo-Japanese relations; and to Mr. Howard Linton, Miss Miwa Kai, and Mr. Philip Yampolsky of the East Asiatic Library, who did much to expedite this project. I am thankful also to Dr. Lewis F. Haines and Mr. Phil Stough of the University of Florida Press for their generous assistance in preparing the manuscript for publication. Last but not least, I am greatly indebted to my wife, Bobbie, who spent many lonely hours during the years that I worked on this dissertation in my "spare" time and who patiently typed the whole original draft.

All translation, whether from Japanese, Chinese, Russian, German, or French, was, of course, done by myself.

Any errors that may be found in this book are solely my own responsibility.

GEORGE ALEXANDER LENSEN

Preface

THE CENTENNIAL OF THE OPENING OF JAPAN BY THE UNITED STATES HAS refocussed attention on our most colorful and undaunted Commodore Matthew Calbraith Perry. Ever since Pearl Harbor, there has been an increasing interest in his exploits. Perhaps as much, if not more, has been written about Perry in the last thirteen years as during the preceding eighty-seven.[1] His name has become a historical landmark, as evidenced in such titles as *Japan since Perry* and *From Perry to Pearl Harbor*.[2] But, preoccupied with Perry, we have lost sight of a man whose name had been on the lips of many Japanese in the 1850's: Vice-Admiral Evfimii Vasil'evich Putiatin.[3] "Putiatin" became in fact synonymous with "foreigner" or "foreign" in Japan, and there is a record of an old samurai who went by the name of Yamato-Putiatin because he was versed in such Western accomplishments as the fabrication of matches.[4]

Putiatin was in command of the Russian squadron that visited Japan at about the same time as Commodore Perry — and for more or less similar purposes. This Russian expedition had been scheduled to start out as early as 1843.[5] It had been postponed for financial and diplomatic reasons until news of the imminence of an American Japan Expedition persuaded Tsar Nicholas I to delay no further.[6] And so it happened that the "red devils" (akaoni), as the Russians were then called by the Japanese — either because their hair appeared

red or because they wore red uniforms — reached Japan only about six weeks after the Americans, and assisted Perry, though indirectly and against his will, to pry open the door the Shogunate had slammed shut over two centuries before.

Our study is a description of the activities of this Russian expedition in Japanese waters. It is not an analysis of the mission itself. For that, there is not enough material available. Both Putiatin and Ivan Aleksandrovich Goncharov, the former in his report to the Admiralty, the latter in his diary, specifically stated that they were excluding information dealing with the negotiations, Putiatin because he had set it down in a special note to the Ministry of Foreign Affairs, Goncharov because he wished to save it for use in a separate book.[7] Neither source is at our disposal.[8]

The instructions issued to the admiral have not been made public.[9] We can infer some, if not most of them, from Putiatin's reports and a Japanese translation of a Russian state paper, but such deduction can serve only as an adjunct to a description of the mission rather than as a basis for an analysis of the mission itself.[10] Japanese records contain a considerable amount of material concerning the negotiations, but in the absence of Russian accounts against which the Japanese sources can be checked, not enough reliance can be placed on the latter to justify final conclusions.

Russian documents have been handed down to us in Japanese translation. But what the Russians had written and said may not have been identical with what the Japanese thought they had written and said. There is reason indeed to believe that the Japanese sources are inaccurate. The language problem was very great. The negotiations were conducted sometimes in Dutch, sometimes in English or Chinese. With each step the danger of mistranslation or misinterpretation increased. The official Japanese reply to the Russian state paper, for example, had been written in Chinese. Although three members of the expedition had lived and studied in China for years, they were unable to decipher it. When it was returned to the Japanese, their own interpreters could not understand it either. One of the plenipotentiaries, a Confucian scholar, had to translate it into Japanese before the Japanese interpreters could render it into Dutch to be retranslated into Russian.

The various interpretations did not always agree. As Putiatin noted: "To prove Chinese [version], not prove Dutch [one]."[11] Nor were all mistranslations accidental. The Russians complained that the interpreter Nishi Kichibee would purposely distort, modify, and soften many of their statements.[12]

There is also evidence that recorded conversations had often been prearranged. The Japanese officials feared their own government more than they feared the Russians. They were less afraid of opening their country than of being suspected of not having exerted enough effort to prevent it. As the records were "proof" of their actions, the records must be favorable. To illustrate: After the departure of most of the Russians from Japan, the remainder, under the command of Aleksandr Musin-Pushkin and Nikolai G. Schilling II, sought diversion in rowboat trips to neighboring little bays. The local daimyo (feudal lords) would at once complain to Edo (modern Tokyo), the seat of the Tokugawa Shogunate, Japan's *de facto* government, about every infringement of their territory, and the officials assigned to the Russians would have to explain these transgressions. Their reports usually stated that the mariners had received permission from Nakamura Tameya, the official in charge, to row out and see whether Russian vessels were coming to pick them up, and had been forced by strong winds to seek shelter in the particular bay. Whenever such reports were due, the interpreter Hori Tatsunosuke would visit the Russians and ask them to explain their excursions in this fashion. Nakamura would thereupon appear with a retinue of officials and secretaries and sternly ask a string of questions, mutually agreed upon beforehand, and listen to answers, also prepared beforehand. Every word would be carefully recorded. The investigation completed, a smile would brighten Nakamura's good-natured face and he would stalk away contentedly.[13]

It is evident, therefore, that a narrative of Russo-Japanese negotiations demands the careful perusal of both Russian and Japanese sources so that one can be checked against the other. In the absence of sufficient Russian material to justify a detailed chronological account of the negotiations, we have summarized the points at issue in a separate chapter (Chapter X: "The Treaty of Shimoda").

Limited in scope though a narrative of Putiatin's mission must be — without consideration of Russian policy and motives, of the impact of the expedition on the Japanese administration, of the negotiations, and of the degree to which Russian aims were achieved — it seems valid nevertheless. The expedition differed from all previous Russian ones to Japan in size and genre, and ushered in a new and political phase in Russia's own *Drang nach Osten*. It furthered the opening of Japan. It stimulated Russo-American rivalry. Our study adds a chapter to the history of Russian navigation and exploration as well as the expansion of European civilization. It introduces us to personages that remained on the scene of Russo-Japanese relations for years to come. It throws light on the extension of the Crimean War to Pacific waters. It lays the foundations for a more detailed analysis of Russo-Japanese negotiations in the 1850's, for it is our hope that, as more material in Russian and Japanese archives becomes accessible, others will help to round out the narrative.

Our study is based primarily on five fundamental sources: the official reports of Vice-Admiral Putiatin, commander of the expedition, the diary and letters of Ivan Aleksandrovich Goncharov, his secretary during the first part of the mission, the memoirs of Nikolai G. Schilling II, participant in the second part of the mission, the diaries of Kawaji Toshiakira, main Japanese plenipotentiary, and the diaries of Koga Kinichiro, plenipotentiary and Confucian scholar. The reliable main report of Putiatin served as the skeleton for our narrative because it alone deals with the whole period under discussion. The diaries proved complementary in information. They fitted together like the pieces of a picture puzzle.[14] Their entries could readily be checked for accuracy. As it was, their authors were men of known integrity.[15] And there were opinions of great interest in the diaries, particularly in those of Goncharov and Kawaji. The letters and diary of Goncharov, embodied in *Fregat Pallada,* and the Nagasaki and Shimoda diaries of Kawaji have been published and widely read in Russia and Japan respectively. Written at a time when little information was available in either country about the other, they played a considerable part in formulating Russian ideas about the Japanese and Japanese ideas about the Russians.[16] Viewed in this light, it can be seen that a description of the Japanese as childish, effeminate, and militarily incompetent, for example, could have led to the impression that the Japanese were a people whose military prowess need not be taken seriously, an attitude prevalent in Russia at the turn of the century.

Additional information has been sifted from numerous other reports and letters printed in the *Morskoi Sbornik,* as well as from *Bakumatsu gaikoku kankei monjo,* Tokyo University's important compilation of foreign affairs documents.

One secondary source deserves special mention. It is Martin Ramming's excellent German article concerning the role of the Russians in the opening of Japan to intercourse with the Western powers. To our knowledge, it is the only attempt made heretofore to give an account of the Russian Japan Expedition as a whole. Its only limitation lies in the fact that it is but thirty-four pages long and thus confined to a survey in relatively broad terms.

Such Western histories of Japan as do make mention of the Russian expedition, James Murdoch's *A History of Japan,* for example, treat it as incidental to the American expedition.

We do not wish to detract from the well-deserved fame of Commodore Perry, but do want to portray the Russian Japan Expedition in its proper perspective. Few Western historians have done that. Such an excellent textbook as Sir Bernard Pares's *A History of Russia* contains nothing about the expedition. Perhaps the clue to Russian lack of interest lies in the outbreak of the Crimean War, which overshadowed the events in the Far East in importance and absorbed the attention of students of that period. One of the outstanding characteristics of early Russo-Japanese relations in general is the fact that, whereas Russian policies in the Far East were of utmost importance to the security and national existence of Japan, they were subordinate in Russian eyes to European affairs.

A hundred years after the opening of Japan we are struck by the similarity of world conditions. Once more Japan has bowed to American and Russian might, once more her only real weapons are those of diplomacy, her opportunity is rivalry between the two powers. Will she pursue the old policies of trial and error, of seeking immediate gains without consideration for consequences, or will she draw upon the lessons of the past century and carefully chart a new course, a course of enlightened self-interest and peace?

Introduction

In 1639, JAPAN CONSCIOUSLY EMBARKED UPON A POLICY OF ISOLATION.[1] Her doors were closed to all foreigners except a handful of Chinese and Dutchmen. All Japanese were forbidden to leave the country and, if already abroad, forbidden to return. The building of vessels of ocean-crossing capacity was prohibited.

For almost a century, Japan had dealt with Portuguese and Spaniards, for over a generation, with Dutchmen and Englishmen. The intercourse had brought her no economic advantages; if anything, much of her currency had been drained. Of Christian love and brotherhood she had learned little, for but little had been brought to her shores. Manifold only had been the stories she had heard about Europe — frightful tales of the Inquisition, religious fratricide, imperialism, and slave trade. When the missionaries began to dabble in politics and when Western merchants failed to confine their sale of firearms to government-controlled ports and supplied potential enemies of the state, the Japanese government saw little reason why it should not rid itself of the foreign menace.

Sir George Sansom well points out that it was no ordinary conservatism but fear — fear not of the contamination of national customs, but of domestic uprising against itself — that forced the Tokugawa Shogunate to close the doors of Japan.

By 1615 Ieyasu, the first Tokugawa Shogun, had after long struggle imposed the authority of his family upon all his feudal rivals. But neither he nor his successors felt entirely secure for several decades, and it was a cardinal feature of their policy to take every possible precaution against rebellion by one or more of the still powerful western feudatories. The legislation of the Tokugawa shows a constant preoccupation with this danger, which was by no means imaginary. The Mori family in 1600 ruled thirteen of the sixty-six provinces, the Shimadzu family were strong in Kyushu, while there were other feudal houses that also chafed under Tokugawa rule. Any of these singly or in combination could have seized a favorable opportunity to revolt, as indeed in the long run they did in 1867 when the Shogunate was overthrown largely by an alliance of the clans of Satsuma (Shimadzu) and Choshu (Mori) with other anti-Tokugawa forces. It is significant that this alliance enjoyed the moral and material support of Western powers.

In 1637 the Tokugawa government had good reason to fear that one or other of these great families might conspire with foreigners — Spanish, Portuguese, or Dutch — trade with them for firearms, get their help in procuring artillery and ships, and even call upon them for military or naval support. The leaders of the ruling house, firmly established as it was, did not feel strong enough to face this risk; and they took steps to remove it by closing the country to foreign influence, so far as that was possible.[2]

Only a number of Dutch and Chinese traders were permitted to stay; and they, almost completely isolated from the Japanese people. The Dutch had denied their Christianity and had proven their trustworthiness by a naval bombardment of the antigovernment forces during the Christian Rebellion of Shimabara (1637-1638). As it was to the advantage of the Shogunate to keep open some avenue of information about developments in Europe, particularly those that might affect the security of Japan, the Dutch were permitted to stay. But they were confined, almost imprisoned, on Deshima, an artificial, little fan-shaped island in the harbor of Nagasaki.

The island of Deshima was surrounded by high wooden fences. Several yards distant from the shore, high wooden pillars were set up in the water, and under no circumstances were ships allowed to sail beyond the bounds marked by these poles. Deshima was connected by a long, narrow, stone bridge with the city of Nagasaki. At both ends of this bridge guardhouses were erected, and the guards stationed therein never permitted the Dutch to cross. With the exception of licensed prostitutes and Buddhist priests from the Koyasan monastery, no Japanese were allowed to visit Deshima. The Dutch traders and men from the ships of Holland were privileged to enter Deshima only after they had trampled on the images of Christ and the Virgin Mary as evidence of the fact that they were not Christians. The Dutch who resided in Deshima were allowed to cross the bridge and to visit the city of Nagasaki only once a year – on New Year's Day and the six days following. And before entering the city, they were required to trample on the images of Christ and the Virgin Mary as proof that they had not embraced Christianity. A refusal to do so would mean either death or expulsion from Japan.[3]

Japan's balance of trade with the Dutch and the Chinese was unfavorable. Gold, silver, and copper flowed out of Japan in such quantities that the Japanese government found it necessary to restrict foreign trade more and more. By 1715, it was limited to only two Dutch vessels and thirty Chinese junks a year.[4] Whereas commercial transactions devoid of cultural imperialism and subversive activities had proven to be without danger from a political standpoint, the Japanese government had become completely disillusioned about the potentialities of foreign trade. When difficulties in the Netherlands led to the dissolution of the Dutch East India Company (1798) and necessitated the chartering of foreign, primarily American, ships, the Japanese remarked that "if the Company for any reason whatsoever was no longer in a position to carry on its trade with Japan itself, then all reason for the stay of the Hollanders in Japan disappeared."[5] But the Dutch remained, though more restricted than ever in their movements.

Meanwhile, Western interest in Japan was renewed. England, which had voluntarily withdrawn from Japan in 1624, desired the re-establishment of trade relations with Japan "in order to buy tea and silk and to encourage trade competition with a view to lowering the price of Chinese products."[6] The *Argonaut* (1791) was only the first of a series of English vessels to attempt the reopening of Japan.[7]

The two nations most concerned with the reopening of Japan, the United States and Russia, had had no previous dealings with that country. Not until the eighteenth century had Russian and American merchants approached Japan. It is beyond the scope of this book to review early Japanese-American intercourse, but a few brief comments may be of assistance to the reader.[8] The *Lady Washington* and the *Grace* (1791) were the first American vessels to visit a Japanese port. They had tried to dispose of sea-otter peltries, en route to China.[9] It was the rapid development of the Pacific Northwest fur trade that brought the first Americans to Japan. In the 1820's, whaling added to their number in the Pacific. Upon the conclusion of the Sino-American treaty of Wanghia (1844), increased trade with China led still more Yankees through Japanese waters. Shipwrecks were common. Japanese treatment of American sailors was often harsh. Steps for the protection of American lives thus became more and more urgent and provided a rallying point for the forces of trade, evangelization, and Manifest Destiny.[10] One other important factor came into play: steam navigation.

The application of steam navigation to the trans-Pacific routes by American vessels met with the almost insuperable obstacle of lack of coal supplies. Steam navigation on the coast of China had been attempted with success during the Anglo-Chinese War, and had been taken up for mercantile purposes, but the coal was brought out from England and was very expensive. . . . The needs of American shipping companies were imperative. Japan was believed to have large supplies of coal, and her ports in the days of uncertain steam navigation were absolutely essential to the proposed line of American trans-Pacific steamers.[11]

Two unsuccessful pre-Perry American attempts to establish commercial and diplomatic relations with Japan merit our attention. One of these attempts was that of the *Morrison*. This vessel entered Uraga in 1837 to repatriate Japanese waifs and, taking advantage of this opportunity, to discuss trade and missionary work. When Japanese officials discovered that she was unarmed, they had their shore batteries open fire. The other attempt (1846) was that of the *Columbus* and *Vincennes,* under the command of Commodore James Biddle. When the latter was boarding a Japanese junk to receive the official reply of the Japanese government to his proposals for trade, a Japanese soldier deliberately pushed him. Instead of cutting the man down, as a samurai would have done, Biddle rested satisfied with an apology and the assurance that the man would be punished in accordance with Japanese law. It was not long before it was learned in Washington that word had spread throughout Japan that Americans accepted insult with complacency.[12]

The person most responsible for the opening of Japan was, of course, Commodore Matthew Calbraith Perry, commander of the American Japan Expedition of 1852-1854. Not only did he carry out the instructions issued to him by the State Department, but because of the illness of Secretary of State Daniel Webster actually drafted the instructions himself. The story of his success is well known and need not be repeated here. We shall touch upon his activities as they bear on our study.

It is with Russia's part in the opening of Japan that we are concerned, and a brief survey of Russian activities prior to Vice-Admiral Putiatin's expedition seems apropos.[13]

Russia learned of Japan's proximity to the Kuril Islands around 1700, but information was scanty and Peter the Great instructed the Siberian Command to gather more facts. In 1713, 1714, and 1719, unsuccessful attempts were made to reach Japan.[14] In 1732, Captain Vitus Bering and his assistants, Captain Aleksei I. Chirikov and Lieutenant M. P. Spanberg, began outfitting another expedition, authorized by Empress Anna. Bering and Chirikov were to sail to the shores of North America, Spanberg to Japan. It was very time-consuming to prepare such an expedition in the inhospitable region of eastern Russia, and Spanberg was unable to leave until 1738.

Spanberg and his assistants Walton and Shelting led the *Arkhangel Mikhail,* the *Nadezhda,* and the *Sviatoi Gavriil* past Uruppu Island to latitude 46° N, where Ezo (modern Hokkaido) was believed to be situated, but did not sight land. Forced to discontinue their search because of the approach of winter, they returned to Bolsheretsk, where they built another ship and completed further preparations. The next year (1739) the expedition once more followed along the Kuril Islands toward Japan. A heavy storm separated the *Sviatoi Gavriil* from the squadron. But all vessels reached Honshu (the main island of Japan), the three that had continued as a unit establishing contact with the Japanese at Tashiro Beach (Ojika County, Mutsu Province) at approximately latitude 38°20′ N and near Amatsu Village (Nagasa County, Awa Province) at approximately latitude 35°10′ N, the *Sviatoi Gavriil* sailing down the coast of Japan as far south as approximately latitude 33°30′ N. The northern route to Japan had thus been found.

In 1742, Spanberg once more set out with three ships, but fog and brisk winds separated the vessels and not one of them reached Japan.

Meanwhile, a department of Japanese studies had been founded (1705) at the Academy of Sciences in St. Petersburg to develop linguists for future expeditions. Japanese waifs served as teachers, children of Russian soldiers as pupils.

Between 1745 and 1772, Russian activities were confined to the Kuril Islands, by way of which, the Russians hoped, trade could be conducted with Japan.

In 1772, Catherine the Great instructed the commander of Kamchatka to make arrangements for another mission to the Kuril Archipelago and the islands of Japan. The merchants Lebedev-Lastochkin and Grigorii Ivanovich Shelekhov (founder of the Russian colonies in North America) agreed to sponsor the expedition. They purchased, equipped and sent out the *Nikolai* (1775), but the vessel got only as far as the eighteenth Kuril island (Uruppu?), where it was shipwrecked. The brigantine *Natalia,* a government vessel, was thereupon put at the disposal of the two merchants. The ship reached Uruppu

(1777), where it remained for the winter. In June (1778), thirty-four of the Russians proceeded in canoes from Uruppu to the twenty-second island (Atkis), where they met and conferred with men from a Japanese vessel. The Japanese gave the Russians letters addressed to the Russian government in which they expressed their desire to trade with Russia. Russians and Japanese agreed that for the time being they would exchange goods in the harbor on the northern side of Kunashiri Island. The Russians were to come to that place the following year (July 31, 1779) to confirm details of trade procedure.

Unfavorable winds prevented the Japanese from keeping the appointment, but they caught up with the Russians on Atkis, whither the latter had continued. Two officials from Matsumae arrived in September and put an end to the discussions. They informed the Russians that they must not come back again to Kunashiri or Etorofu. If they needed food, they could send the Kurilians after it; if they wished to trade, they must go to Nagasaki to discuss the matter.

In 1787, a squadron of five three-masters was readied for an around-the-world expedition to protect Russian rights in territories discovered by Russian seafarers, carry out geographical investigations in the Pacific Ocean, establish trade relations with Japan, and bring various nautical and military supplies to Siberian ports. But the outbreak of war with Turkey and the expected break with Sweden intervened, and the voyage was cancelled (November 8, 1787).

On September 24, 1791, Catherine the Great issued a ukase to the Governor General of Siberia to send another mission to Japan. Professor Erik (Kirill) Laxman was asked to plan the expedition, and his son, Lieutenant Adam Kirillovich Laxman, to command it. A commercial representative of the merchants Shelekhov and Solikov accompanied the mission. Japanese waifs were taken along to provide an excuse for the voyage.

On September 24, 1792, the *Ekaterina* left Okhotsk. Passing through Nemuro Kaikyo, the strait between Kunashiri and Ezo, she entered Nemuro Harbor on Ezo on October 20. From here Adam Laxman notified the governor of Matsumae by letter that he had come as envoy to the Japanese government. He wrote that he intended to proceed directly to Edo and there hand over a state paper and gifts, as well as the waifs he had brought back. The governor communicated this to the Shogunate, adding that the Russians had consented to wait for an official reply until May or June; should none be forthcoming by then they would sail on to Edo. The Shogunate replied that the Russians should be detained in Nemuro and be treated with friendliness and attention, the waifs accepted and sent to Edo.

The Russians never wanted for anything. Barracks were built for them and they were permitted to live on shore. They were not allowed to trade, but "mutual gifts" were exchanged. Various officials arrived from Matsumae and Edo. Their comments led Laxman to believe that his mission would be crowned with success.

Finally (February, 1793), Laxman was asked to proceed to Matsumae. He agreed to do so, but not on land and under guard, as proposed by the Japanese. He insisted on sailing to the harbor nearest the meeting place. On July 15, the *Ekaterina* reached Hakodate. There Laxman was received splendidly. The governor's bath was put at his disposal and a big party was given in his honor. On July 24, Laxman and his retinue left for Matsumae under heavy escort.[15] Four days later they entered the festively decorated city where a house, furnished Western style, had been prepared for the Russians.

The negotiations lasted from July 28 to August 3, inclusive. Laxman's credentials were returned, as was the letter previously transmitted. The Japanese officials informed the envoy that in accordance with their national law all vessels of countries with whom Japan had no relations must be attacked and captured if they ventured into Japanese waters. The Russians could this time return in peace, allowance being made for the fact that they may have been unfamiliar with the laws of Japan. But they must not come again! At the same time, however, Laxman received a certificate of entry to Nagasaki Harbor, as well as a whole list of gifts: one hundred bags of rice, one hundred bags of wheat, three long swords, eggs, and venison. The Japanese even accepted counter-presents, though not without protest. Letters written by Professor Laxman to scholars in Edo, together with three thermometers and various natural specimens were also turned over at Matsumae for further delivery. On August 6, 1793, the Russians started back, boarded the *Ekaterina* (August 16), and returned to Okhotsk (September 19).[16]

In 1803, the Russians attempted an around-the-world shipment of supplies to their American colonies. Captain Ivan Fedorovich Krusenstern had originated the plans for the voyage as he had felt that the usual two-year round-trip shipment of furs of the Russo-American Company (formerly the United American Company) by way of Okhotsk and Kiakhta was too time-consuming and that the transportation of essential commodities to the colonies through Siberia was too difficult. Advantage was now taken of the opportunity thus offered to send along an embassy to Japan. Chamberlain Nikolai Petrovich Rezanov — son-in-law of Shelekhov, and since his death, head of the board of directors of the Russo-American Company — was named envoy. His instructions expounded the theory that propinquity creates special privileges, and that Russia as a neighbor of Japan had more right to trade with her than had any other country.

The around-the-world expedition, consisting of the *Nadezhda* and the *Neva*, left Kronstadt in August, 1803. At the Sandwich (Hawaiian) Islands the vessels separated, the *Neva* heading for the colonies, the *Nadezhda* for Kamchatka and then Japan. On October 8, 1804, Rezanov approached Nagasaki, but though he presented the permit Laxman had brought back, he was not admitted to the port until December 24, 1804, and even then only upon surrendering Russian ammunition for "safekeeping." Negotiations began in April (1805). Although Japanese etiquette was not observed so far as extreme bowing and prostrating is concerned, Rezanov did have to remove his sword and boots and squat on the floor. He conferred with Japanese officials again and again, but to no avail. They accepted neither documents nor gifts, and reiterated that Russian vessels must not approach Japan again. Rebuffed, Rezanov left in great anger (April 30, 1805).

In September, Rezanov instructed the director of the colony of the

Russo-American Company to send two men-of-war under the command of Lieutenant Nikolai Aleksandrovich Khvostov and *Michman* Gavriil Ivanovich Davydov to the shores of Japan to avenge the insult he believed to have been hurled at Russia and cow the Japanese into trading with his country. Rezanov altered his instructions to Khvostov and Davydov a number of times and finally seems to have decided against the expedition, at least for the time being.[17] But Khvostov and Davydov marauded the northern possessions of Japan just the same (1806-1807), spreading fear and hatred of Russia throughout Japan.

In 1811, Captain Vasilii Mikhailovich Golovnin was sent by the Russian government to make a thorough survey of the southern Kuril Islands. He went ashore at Kunashiri Island, accompanied by only seven of his men. The Japanese, desirous of avenging themselves for the raids of Khvostov and Davydov, lured the Russians into their fortress, pounced on them, tied them up, and sent them to Hakodate. For over two years, the Russians were held prisoners and released only after written assurance was given by Russian authorities that the Russian government had had nothing to do with the raids on Japan's northern possessions and harbored but friendly feelings toward Japan.[18]

Failure of repeated Russian attempts in 1814, 1815, 1816, and 1817 to maintain contact with the Japanese authorities who had freed Golovnin led to a temporary discontinuance of expeditions to Japan. For about a generation, Russia seems to have lost interest in Japan, but by mid-century her activities were renewed.

Eighteenth- and early nineteenth-century Russian attempts to establish relations with Japan had been primarily economic in motive. Stories of tremendous riches in Japan had called forth the first expeditions. As the colonization and development of Siberia progressed, increasing quantities of supplies had to be provided for that region. To ship them from Europe by land or by sea involved much time, hardship, and expense. A further incentive was therefore given to attempt trade with Japan, if possible, directly in Japanese harbors;

if not, then indirectly — legally or illegally — by way of the Kuril Islands. Russian acquisition of Alaska emphasized the potentialities of northern Japanese ports as havens of refuge and supply, and further stimulated interest in a Russo-Japanese *rapprochement.*

By the middle of the nineteenth century, however, Russia's economic desires were supplemented, if not supplanted, by political considerations. The government had concluded that the establishment of a strong Russian position in Eastern Asia presupposed good relations with Japan and that neither England nor the United States could be permitted to gain as much influence in Japan as they had obtained in China.[19] And so the Russian Japan Expedition of 1852 to 1855 was born.[20]

Adjutant-General Vice-Admiral Evfimii Vasil'evich Putiatin was appointed commander of the squadron and ambassador to Japan. For both positions Putiatin was well qualified. He had served under the famous Admiral (then still Captain) Mikhail Petrovich Lazarev (1788-1851) on his around-the-world expedition (1822-1825) and belonged thus to the elite group of mariners of the "Lazarev school." He had participated in the battle of Navarino (1827) and other campaigns. He had successfully handled a diplomatic mission to the Shah of Persia (1842-1843) to secure Russian trade and fishery on the Caspian Sea.[21] Last but not least, he had repeatedly advocated closer relations with China and Japan.

The impact of the arrival of the Russian squadron was great. It forced a decision upon the Japanese. They had not answered Perry's demands and had hoped to evade the issue further. But the appearance of the Russian men-of-war made it clear that the days of Japan's seclusion were numbered. As Tokutomi Iichiro comments: "No matter how much you chase [away] flies on food they will gather the same [way]. [This is] a pattern [that is] manifested in associating with foreigners."[22]

Ever since the latter half of the eighteenth century, the Shogunate had been forced to review and revise its policies as more and more foreign vessels ignored its decrees. As Sir George Sansom notes, "the strict legal position was that ships might enter Nagasaki for purposes of trade provided that their presence was not inconsistent with the anti-Christian edicts...."[23] But upon the arrival of Rezanov, the Shogunate had decided, after prolonged deliberation, that to permit the Russians to trade would be to permit them to spread their heretical religion, to seize Japanese territories, and to exchange useless foreign goods for useful Japanese ones, and that it was in Japan's interest, therefore, to reject Rezanov's proposals.[24] The Shogunate had instructed all seaboard daimyo to deny landing to foreign ships that arrived under the pretext of returning shipwrecked Japanese, but to assist vessels in distress, supply them with provisions, and peacefully send them on their way.[25]

The raids of Khvostov and Davydov and the aggressive behavior of the Englishmen aboard H.M.S. *Phaeton* in 1806 had spurred the Shogunate to strengthen Japan's coastal defenses. "Yet so irresolute were the Shogun's counsellors," notes Sir George Sansom, "that within a few years they had relaxed their precautions and had to submit to a number of incursions by ships in search of water and fuel, which the local forces could not cope with."[26]

Further acts of violence by English seamen had resulted in the issue of a new edict, the *Ni-nen-naku* (No-second-thought) Expulsion Order (1825). "It enjoined all local authorities to destroy any foreign ship that should come close inshore and to arrest or kill any members of its crew who might land. There was to be no hesitation, no discussion."[27] It was this new policy that led to the shelling of the *Morrison* in 1837. But by 1842, Japan had once more relaxed her vigilance.

This vacillation in the policy of the Shogunate reflects the diversity of opinions held and expressed by Japan's leading military men, scholars, and publicists.[28] When Commodore Perry presented his demands, the Shogunate did not act with resoluteness. Instead, it communicated the American demands to all daimyo and officials above the *fui* class and requested their advice. Of the sixty-one clans whose answers have been handed down to us, twenty-two argued for the opening of the country and eighteen emphasized the im-

portance of averting war, while only nineteen suggested that American demands be rejected. Two remained undecided. Of the officials
above the *fui* class whose replies are extant, thirteen advocated the
opening of Japan, many more the avoidance of war, and only three
opposition to the Americans. A similar preponderance of opinion in
favor of appeasement can be found in the writings of the publicists.
But the expressed desire for peace was not a declaration of sympathy
for America; it was a confession of weakness.[29] Disagreeing with
the contention of Tokugawa Nariaki of Mito that "if we do not
drive them [the Americans] away now, we shall never have another
opportunity,"[30] most officials followed the line of thought of Abe
Masahiro (Ise-no-kami), president of the Supreme Council:

...as we are not the equals of foreigners in the mechanical arts,
let us have intercourse with foreign countries, learn their drill and
tactics and when we have made the nation as united as one family,
we shall be able to go abroad and give lands in foreign countries to
those who have distinguished themselves in battle; the soldiers will
vie with one another in displaying their intrepidity, and it will not
be too late then to declare war. Now we shall have to defend ourselves against these foreign enemies skilled in the use of mechanical
appliances, with our soldiers whose military skill has considerably
diminished during a long peace of three hundred years, and we
certainly could not feel sure of victory, especially in a naval war.[31]

The arrival of the Russian squadron added strength to the antiwar
arguments. It was obvious that Japan could not successfully combat
the combined forces of the United States, Russia, and other Western
countries. But, at the same time, a new opportunity was offered to
Japan, the opportunity of seeking protection in the time-honored
Chinese game of "fighting barbarians with barbarians." The idea
of letting the stronger one (at that time, Russia) protect their country
in return for commercial concessions suggested itself at once to the
Japanese.

The conclusion of treaties of amity and friendship with the United
States, Russia, and other countries by no means put an end to Japanese ambivalence. In 1859 and 1862, Japanese feeling ran high against

Russia. Friendly relations were resumed in 1875, only to give way to renewed hostility in 1895 and 1896. In 1901, Japan strove to limit Russian penetration of Manchuria and Korea by an alliance with Russia. Rebuffed, Japan turned to the United States and England for support. By 1904, Japan was at war with Russia. As Japanese successes threatened to upset the balance of power in the Far East, President Theodore Roosevelt's enthusiasm for his erstwhile protégés dampened quickly. Three years after the outbreak of hostilities between Russia and Japan, a Russo-Japanese entente blocked American financial expansion and an American financier (Jacob H. Schiff) complained not much later:

It can certainly not give any satisfaction to the American people, when they find Japan, to whom they had lent their unreserved support in her desperate struggle for self-preservation hardly more than a decade ago, joining hands, under the protection of England, with her erstwhile foe who sought to crush her, and thus combine against the forces of civilization, who wish to see established a strong, self-reliant China, rather than an impotent vassal state, a second India. America will be the last to deny Japan's dearly purchased right to work out her manifest destiny on the Asian continent, but Japan must not seek to do this in unison with Russia, whose methods of government are not such that its blessings ought to be permitted to be extended beyond its own borders.[32]

In 1907, 1910, 1912, and 1916, ties between Russia and Japan were tightened. But, in 1918, Japan intervened in Siberia in the hope of fishing in troubled waters. Three years after her withdrawal from Russia, she recognized the Soviet regime (1925), eight years before the United States did so. In 1934, she signed the Anti-Comintern Pact, in 1941, a nonaggression pact with Russia. In 1941, she attacked the United States. Truly this was a road of trial and error and one of irony, for all the Japanese government had wanted in the 1850's was to be left alone in peace. Little did Perry and Putiatin realize that some day "that locked coffer with the lost key" would be a Pandora's box for their descendants.

Contents

"An uninvited guest is worse than a Tartar."

— AN OLD RUSSIAN SAYING

"The miseries of the world are begun by thieves and barbarians, but completed by degenerate officials."

— AN OLD ORIENTAL SAYING

1

Destination Japan

ON OCTOBER 19, 1852, THE FRIGATE *Pallada,* FLAGSHIP OF THE RUSSIAN Japan Expedition, left Kronstadt and headed for Portsmouth, England. Adjutant-General Vice-Admiral Evfimii Vasil'evich Putiatin, who had hastened ahead on a private steamer in August, awaited her there. He had purchased another vessel in England, the iron screw-schooner *Fearless,* built originally for the Mediterranean fruit trade and outstanding in speed and seaworthiness, had her converted into a warship and renamed *Vostok* (East).[1]* At the same time he had acquired four sixty-eight-pounders for the frigate, as well as sixty Lancaster and Wilkinson carbines, plus gifts for the Japanese, to supplement those taken along from Russia.

The *Pallada, Fligel'-adiutant Kapitan-leitenant* Ivan Semenovich Unkovskii[2] commanding, reached Portsmouth on November 12, 1852, with twenty-two officers (not counting Unkovskii) and four hundred and thirty-nine men of lower rank aboard.[3] Of these, six officers and thirty-seven men came as ship's complement for the schooner purchased in England.[4] Aboard were also Archimandrite Avvakum of the Aleksandr Nevski Monastery, who knew Chinese well, and two officials of the Ministries of Finance and Foreign Affairs, one to serve as interpreter of Chinese and Manchu (Collegiate Assessor Iosif Antonovich Goshkevich),[5] the other as secretary of the Admiral (Collegiate Assessor Ivan Aleksandrovich Goncharov).[6]

* *Note section begins on page 161.*

[1]

The *Pallada's* voyage had been not without mishap. Off Cape
Dragör (near Copenhagen), she had run aground on a sandbank,
though only lightly and for a short time, and in the Gulf of Finland
one of her crew had fallen overboard and drowned and three others
had died of cholera before reaching England.[7]

As the most insignificant damage in the submerged part of the
vessel, such as for example the loss of one strip of copper sheathing,
could breed serious complications on a two-year-long voyage, Putiatin sent the frigate into dock for a thorough check-up. At the same
time, he had a water-condensing machine installed.[8] Although a careful examination of the ship failed to disclose any damage to the lower
part of the hull, there were signs of rotting in the upperworks and
much of the calking had to be changed and new pieces put in the
wooden sheathing. It was evident that, in spite of her many admirable
features, not the least of which was speed, the *Pallada* would be of
doubtful reliability during prolonged sailing.[9]

The repairs and alterations of the frigate, preparations of the
schooner, and strong unfavorable winds detained the Russians in
England beyond expectation.[10] Putiatin originally had planned to
sail past Cape Horn, but as the unexpected delay in departure would
have brought him there during a most unfavorable and dangerous
season he decided to proceed around the Cape of Good Hope into
the China Sea where he could utilize the favorable monsoons that
blow by the end of April. He duly informed the Ministries of the
Navy and Foreign Affairs of his change in plans and sent word to
the commanders of the corvet *Olivutsa* and the Russo-American Company vessel *Kniaz' Menshikov*, then at the Sandwich (Hawaiian)
Islands, that they join him at the Bonin Islands.[11]

On January 18, 1853, the *Pallada* and the *Vostok* finally weighed
anchor, but high seas and strong winds detained them in the channel
for several days more. Sailing on, the frigate reached Madeira ahead
of the schooner, took on supplies and continued south, having left instructions for the *Vostok* to proceed to the Cape of Good Hope. By
February 6, the frigate cast anchor at Praia on São Tiago Island, one

of the Cape Verde Islands. Here it was found necessary to overhaul the rigging that had been weakened by the strong winds and high seas the frigate had battled throughout her passage from England.[12]

In Praia, the frigate met a United States squadron of two corvets and a schooner, supervising the discontinuance of the slave trade along the shores of Africa. Shortly before the arrival of the Russians, the Americans had seized a vessel with Negro captives. Praia served as a base for this United States squadron, all supplies being kept on shore under supervision of the American consul.

It was at Praia also that Putiatin first learned that another American squadron, under Commodore Matthew Calbraith Perry, was already at the shores of China headed for the same destination: Japan.[13]

The remainder of the voyage on the Atlantic was "a prolonged pleasant excursion." "The beautiful coloring of sky and water, the fresh air and clear calm days, one like another, and magnificent nights, all ... sustained among the officers and men of lower rank vigour, a gay disposition, and the desire to continue the voyage."[14] Their time was well spent. When not occupied with immediate routine duties, the officers busied themselves with the study and translation of nautical information pertaining to their voyage; the midshipmen made astronomical observations with the excellent sextants, purchased in England, and the crew engaged in daily gun practice and other drill.[15]

The Russian squadron was fully provided with supplies. Such provisions as salted meat and biscuits, which kept relatively well, had been taken on in Kronstadt, all others in England. They were replenished on the way as need arose.[16]

On February 15, 1853, the *Pallada* crossed the equator at longitude 15°20′ W. On March 22, she sighted Africa and proceeded to Simon's Bay on the Cape of Good Hope, where she was joined by the *Vostok* later that month.[17] It was found necessary to calk the frigate anew, both inside and out, and generally prepare the ships for further sailing. The local British authorities were very obliging. They sold the admiral coal and other supplies from government stocks at relatively moderate prices. This came as a great relief to the Russians, as prices on the open market had skyrocketed because of the large number of ships that came to the Cape as a result of increased emigration to Australia.[18]

Anxious to give the members of his expedition a maximum of training, Putiatin took advantage of this stopover to send a reconnaissance mission into the interior of Cape Colony. "Such a voyage," reported he, "... will serve as experience for exploring similar but less known places which we are about to visit."[19]

One of the sailors (Karmanov) failed to return aboard ship. A search was organized, but the man was not found. The next day his body was washed ashore. There was no trace of violent death, and it was decided that he must have fallen from the pier at night and drowned unnoticed.[20]

By the latter half of April, both vessels were ready to continue on their way. The admiral, well-satisfied with the seaworthiness of the schooner, sent her ahead to Hong Kong via the Cocos (Keeling) Islands and Java, while the frigate remained at the Cape tarrying for instructions from St. Petersburg. These duly arrived two days later on an English mail steamer.

Putiatin learned, among other things, that two couriers, bearing additional instructions concerning his mission to Japan, had been sent out by the Ministry of Foreign Affairs via America. He therefore dispatched orders to the couriers to meet him at the Bonin Islands, which had already been designated as rendezvous for the four vessels of the Russian Japan Expedition: the frigate *Pallada* and the schooner *Vostok,* as well as the corvet *Olivutsa* of the Kamchatka flotilla and the transport *Kniaz' Menshikov,* a Russo-American Company ship.[21]

On April 24, 1853, the frigate weighed anchor and headed toward Sunda Strait. On April 26, the vessel weathered a heavy storm. Leaks on all decks and other damages offered definitive proof that the *Pallada* would be unable to complete satisfactorily the long and arduous voyage yet in store for the Japan Expedition. Putiatin decided, therefore, to send *Leitenant* Ivan Butakov as courier to St. Petersburg to request replacement of the *Pallada* with the newly constructed frigate *Diana* of the Baltic Fleet. Since mail steamers came to Batavia (Java), the admiral decided to take the courier there, letting him return to Russia via the East Indies and Egypt.[22] But, while at anchor in Sunda Strait at the Malayan settlement Anger (Java) on May 29, 1853, Putiatin learned that the Dutch mail steamer, on which he had intended to send Butakov, made the East Indies run rather irregularly. He thus proceeded to Singapore, which had constant mail communication with Europe.[23] He reached Singapore on June 6. Having assured himself of Butakov's departure and having replenished the supplies of the frigate, Putiatin sailed on to Hong Kong (June 13). Upon his arrival (June 25), he found the schooner *Vostok* waiting for him. The local British authorities showed him every courtesy.

Putiatin visited Canton Harbor on the schooner (June 30). He sent a letter to the Chinese governor-general to the effect that the Russian government had no doubt that both Russian men-of-war and merchant vessels would be well received in the five Chinese ports opened to Europeans. The governor-general replied that because of the Russo-Chinese overland trade in the north he could not permit Russian merchantmen to enter these harbors. He made no mention of warships. Meanwhile, the schooner cast anchor near the city itself. She did not salute the Chinese flag "as the Chinese do not have the custom of replying," but exchanged salutes (fifteen shots each) with the English brig *Rapid*. The Chinese official hence could not help knowing that a Russian man-of-war had entered the harbor, but he filed no protest. "And as in this region," reported the admiral to the Navy Ministry, "it requires but a precedent to affirm any new custom, I consider the question of the unhindered visiting of the five Chinese ports by our warships already solved."[24]

In Canton, Putiatin not only received "authentic news" about the progress of the Taiping Rebellion but learned also that Commodore Perry's squadron, consisting of six vessels,[25] had already left the

Liu Ch'iu Islands and was steering toward the shores of Japan. This information hastened the *Pallada's* departure from Hong Kong (July 8) to the Bonin Islands, rendezvous of the Russian Japan Expedition. The schooner had already been sent ahead.[26]

On July 21, 1853, the *Pallada* ran into a typhoon and once again showed dangerous signs of age and weakness.[27] One of the sailors (Ian Laria) was fatally injured during the storm and died five days later.[28] Delayed by calm that followed the typhoon, the frigate did not reach Port Lloyd (Peel Island) until August 7.

The other vessels were already there. So were couriers *Leitenant* Aleksandr E. Kroun and *Kollezhskii Sekretar'* (Collegiate Secretary) Bodisko, who had arrived on the *Kniaz' Menshikov* with supplementary instructions.[29]

Contrary to expectation, there were almost no provisions available at Port Lloyd. The local English and American settlers had sold all the victuals they could spare to a number of whalers as well as to Commodore Perry's squadron, which had visited the harbor before the Russians (June 14 to June 18).[30] Putiatin, therefore, stayed at Port Lloyd only long enough to make the necessary repairs on the frigate. He did find time, however, to send some of the junior officers and midshipman on a training mission aboard the *Olivutsa* to the southernmost group of the Bonin Islands.[31]

On August 16, 1853, the four vessels of the Russian Japan Expedition weighed anchor and set sail for Nagasaki.[32]

2

Nagasaki: First Visit

AFTER TEN MONTHS AT SEA, THE RUSSIAN JAPAN EXPEDITION APPROACHED the shores of Japan (August 21, 1853).[1] Here was "that locked coffer with the lost key," the country where a crowded little heap of humanity "dexterously avoids the ferrule of civilization." Here was that "ant hill," the inhabitants of which "presume to live by their own mind and laws," "stubbornly reject the friendship, religion, and trade of the foreigners," and laugh at Western attempts to "enlighten" them. "Will it remain this way long?" queried the Russians, caressing their sixty-pounders. If the Japanese would only let them study the natural resources of their country! They might find there not only copper, diamonds, gold, silver, and topaz, but even "the dearest mineral of the nineteenth century": coal.[2]

The squadron was now near Nagasaki, but it had become dark and the vessels did not enter the unfamiliar roadstead.[3] They had been sighted by three Japanese guard posts which speedily relayed news of their arrival.[4]

In the morning (August 22), the *Pallada* hoisted the banner of the Imperial plenipotentiary and sailed toward the outermost roadstead of Takahoko offing.[5] "We were entering," wrote Goncharov, "with a somewhat compressed heart, at least myself, with the feeling with which you go into a prison, though there be trees planted in that prison."[6]

7

A boat with four scantily clad Japanese appeared within some twenty feet of the frigate. After much waving and gesticulation, the men were persuaded to come aboard. Here were the first Japanese guests of the Russian expedition. They were invited into the captain's stateroom and there served liquor, tea, and sweets. While still in their boat, the Japanese had pointed at the piece of white cloth that fluttered from the frigate's foretop-gallant mast. On it was written in Japanese: "Oroshiya kuni no fune" (Vessel of the Russian Empire). Now, they had the inscription copied down and hastened back to the city to report what they had seen.[7]

The Russians were still several miles outside the harbor when Japanese officials boarded the *Pallada*. They posed various questions and presented a document, drawn up in French, English, and Dutch, instructing the Russians to proceed no further than the outer roadstead on pain of "great unpleasantness."[8] "But it could be seen from the caution and apprehension with which the Japanese transmitted these questions," commented Putiatin, "that they were only carrying out an old custom, prescribed by law and applied to all foreign vessels, and that the sight of four men-of-war had filled them with fear and perplexity."[9]

The arrival of the Russian squadron took the Japanese government by surprise. True, on August 3, 1853, eighteen days before its appearance, Donker Curtius, the Dutch factor, had turned in to the Nagasaki *bugyo* (governor or magistrate) his yearly report concerning world developments, and had stated in this survey that a Russian naval unit under the command of Vice-Admiral "Puraraten" was about to sail for Japan, apparently, "to follow the movements of the American fleet." But by the time the report was forwarded to Edo (August 28), the Russians had already cast anchor.[10]

The Russian vessels had not yet reached the unprotected outer roadstead when permission arrived for the use of the next one, nearer the city. The few foreign vessels that had been suffered to enter Japanese harbors during the period of seclusion had been admitted to the inner roadsteads only after considerable delay. The expedition was thus off to a good start! The governor did not know whether the Russians would stop at the roadstead as requested, hence hastened to legalize their possible approach. "In this hurried dispatch of the invitation," noted Putiatin, "lay apparently the apprehension lest the men-of-war violate the established rules and thereby bring to the attention of the people the weakness of their government in the face of an armed foreign power. This hypothesis was confirmed time and again later on by similar measures of the Nagasaki governor."[11]

The governor's message had been brought by Japanese interpreters. "There is a whole group of interpreters here," wrote Goncharov. "During a short time some thirty visited us.... They know only Dutch[12] and are used to communicate with the Dutch, who sitting here year after year could of course themselves learn Japanese. But who will teach them? It is prohibited on pain of death."[13]

In the captain's stateroom, the interpreters unrolled a document containing a multitude of questions. The Russians had been forewarned that this would happen, and had arrived prepared to answer the queries without evasion. The Japanese inquired when they had come, how long they had been at sea, how many men there were on each of the four vessels, and how many guns the ships carried. When the Russians announced that they had brought a letter to the governor of Nagasaki in which the purposes of the expedition were laid out, the Japanese asked them the same question they had posed to the Americans: Why had it been necessary to dispatch four vessels to deliver one letter? "This ironical question," commented Goncharov, "reflected their childish [sic] distrust of our arrival and the suspicion lest we harbored some hostile stratagems."[14] Perry had parried the question like an accomplished diplomat. Noted Spalding: "Commodore told them that it was a greater compliment to their emperor — probably!"[15] The Russians hastened to reassure the Japanese that their aims were peaceful and friendly, but they could not help smiling at "these soft, smooth, white effeminate faces, the cunning and intelligent physiognomies, the little topknots and curtsies."[16]

It did not take long for the interpreters to become acquainted. They drank wine, ate cake, smoked cigars from the wrong end, and generally enjoyed themselves. At the same time, however, they examined everything with great curiosity. They did not feel too secure. "How they would prick their ears when there was some noise on deck!"[17]

The interpreters accompanied the Russians on the *Pallada,* the Japanese oarsmen stayed in the boat at the guess-rope.

A calm delayed the expedition at the first roadstead but, at 4:00 P.M., the squadron lined up in battle formation, the band struck up *"Bozhe tsaria khrani"* (the Russian national anthem), and the vessels ceremoniously sailed past the batteries of Nagasaki where crowds of Japanese onlookers had gathered. By 6:00 P.M., the squadron cast anchor at the inner roadstead.

The voyage was in its eleventh month. The men were tired of preserved food, they were tired of being aboard ship. In Java and at Singapore their vessels had been met by boats laden with fruits, sea shells, monkeys, and parrots. They had been beckoned ashore. But not here! Would they succeed in at least seeing women? In vain they sought among the naked figures in the boats "one not so red and rough as those of the oarsmen."[18]

The interpreters departed. It was night, and among the stars a comet appeared. The squadron lay surrounded by guard boats with brilliant multicolor fish-skin lanterns. Watch fires studded the coast and the summits of hillocks beyond. "One could not purposely have lit a better illumination in honor of the guests." Guard-calls echoed through the night. Boats went back and forth. "It was apparent," wrote Goncharov, "that men had been posted everywhere, that we were being watched by thousands of eyes and our every movement guarded."[19]

The next day (August 23), two city elders, their interpreters, and retinue were received by Vice-Admiral Putiatin and staff. Their arrival aroused great interest, for everything was still new and fascinating. The officials were shown to the afterdeck and there seated on chairs.

The other Japanese refused to sit down, respectfully motioning toward the elders. Tea, liquor, biscuits, candy, and pastry were served. The Japanese took out little pieces of paper and wrapped up some of the candy to take home. A piece of bread and a biscuit were also hid in their bosoms. The liquor was consumed with great enjoyment.

The question as to what had brought the officials aboard, as well as all subsequent conversation, was relayed with cumbersome ceremony. A fat, pock-marked interpreter stepped before one of the officials, bowed deeply and, thus bent, transmitted the query. The official, with a similar bow, replied in a whisper-like voice, while all the other Japanese listened in the same respectful position. When he had finished, the interpreter took a deep breath, straightened up, and in an ordinary voice retold the answer. The other interpreter remained silent: the senior interpreter would translate, the junior interpreter quietly check his effort. "This system of mutual espionage," commented Goncharov, "is somewhat similar to that of the Jesuits."[20]

"Why were we told on the frigate," inquired the Japanese, "that the corvet left Kamchatka in May, and on the corvet that she left in June?" (The corvet had left Kamchatka in May, but had stopped over at the Sandwich Islands. The commander of the vessel had misinformed the Japanese in the vain hope of escaping an additional torrent of questions.) "What business is it of yours where we have been?" asked the Russians. "All that is of importance to you is that we have come."

The Russians could not understand why the Japanese wanted to burden themselves and others with those questions. "We must send them to Edo," the Japanese replied. "And everything must be sent to Edo?" "Everything."

The Russians showed the Japanese a map of the world. They pointed out Russia and Japan. "Seeing how small the latter was they [the Japanese] began to laugh good-naturedly."[21]

The officials were informed that the admiral had brought two letters from *Graf* Nesselrode, State Chancellor of the Russian Empire, one addressed to the governor of Nagasaki, one to the *Roju*, Japan's Supreme Council. They asked that a meeting be arranged with the governor at which the letters could be transmitted.[22]

The officials left. There had been no friction. "The Japanese are no longer what they were forty or fifty years ago. They were very kind. They asked for the names, ranks, and duties of every one of us, and wrote everything down...."[23] The Japanese met Putiatin's wishes with an obligingness which, judging from older records, had theretofore been unknown.[24]

On August 24, the Russians requested use of a place on shore and permission to purchase provisions. The Japanese sent some supplies aboard as a gift, but stated that no landing permission could be granted without special instructions from Edo.[25]

The assistant to the Dutch factor visited the frigate. He came accompanied by a flock of Japanese interpreters, who refused to budge from his side. When the Russians opened the conversation in French, the Dutchman, "fearing the Japanese," quickly requested that only Dutch be used. He stated that the factor himself would pay his respects the next day. But the factor did not come. When, upon return of the transport from China, the admiral sent the latter half an ox — a rare treat in a semivegetarian community — the factor expressed his gratitude in a brief note, stating that he was happy that the "true reason" of his "impoliteness" had been understood.[26] Japanese officials, meanwhile, believed that Donker Curtius had been unable to visit the admiral because of their great difference in rank, the more so since the wife of the king of the Netherlands was the daughter of the Russian tsar.[27]

From August 25 on, every night toward eleven or twelve o'clock, the men on the Japanese guard boats would suddenly begin to yell at the top of their voices, as if bewitched. Speculation arose on shore whether Russian magic might not be the cause. The matter was about to be reported to Edo when one of the officials (Baba Gorozaemon) declared that this clamor was probably due to fear; frightened, the Japanese guards shouted to give each other confidence.

After a heavy storm, everything would stop by itself. To prove his contention, the official spent a night on one of the guard boats. He had been right. The Japanese beat drums to break the ghastly silence that enveloped the little craft at sea after dark. Nothing supernatural took place. A rainstorm on August 31, put an end to this phenomenon, just as he had predicted.[28] The guards had become accustomed to night watch at sea. Yet, in spite of this incident "indications are that worry did not exist in Nagasaki to the extent that it prevailed in Uraga" after Commodore Perry's arrival.[29]

On August 26, Baba Gorozaemon and Oi Saburosuke visited the *Pallada*. Baba appeared good-natured, lively, and communicative. "Don't think," wrote Goncharov, "that there was anything that was strange or amazing to the European in the conceptions, words, and manners of the Japanese (except perhaps that they blew their noses in little pieces of paper and hid candies: but keep in mind how two-thirds of the Russian people blow their noses and how recently our gentlemen discarded the reticule, which they would fill with sweets at other people's dinners and parties). Positively nothing: only the dress and the really clumsy hair-do catch the eye. In all other respects they are a people — if one does not compare them with Europeans — who are fairly developed, free, and pleasant in intercourse and extremely entertaining in the uniqueness of their upbringing."[30]

Baba and Oi were entertained in the admiral's cabin. They were seated in massive easy chairs, while some of their retinue occupied chairs behind them. The admiral sat vis-à-vis the Japanese on a sofa; four other officers, Goncharov included, on a long divan near the portholes. The Japanese interpreters remained standing, though respectfully bent. Their faces could not be seen. Only the ends of their swords stuck up. They would remain in this position until ready to face the Russians. Then they would straighten up and interpret.

The governor would not and could not meet Putiatin without permission from the Shogunate. He requested that the letter addressed to himself be forwarded through the officials, but as for the letter to the Supreme Council, its transmission entailed ceremonial which he was not empowered to determine. Special instructions must be obtained from Edo. When *Kapitan-leitenant* Pos'et[31] stated that an answer should be received within a fortnight, Baba objected that the matter required serious deliberation and that a reply would take some thirty days. The admiral agreed to wait, but urged greater haste. One of the interpreters promised that the courier would "fly like a bird." Putiatin declared that he had taken into consideration the distance between Nagasaki and Edo as well as the slowness of the means of transportation, and warned that, if the answer would not arrive within thirty days, he would take his squadron up to Edo and there personally negotiate with the government.[32]

Baba accepted the letter for the governor. He unwrapped a lacquer box, untied and opened it, placed it on the table, received the letter with both hands, respectfully raised it to his forehead, and put it into the box. The box was carefully rewrapped into a *furoshiki* (a Japanese wrapping cloth) bearing the governor's crest. Around the knot of the *furoshiki* a cord was tied, and this cord stamped with Baba's seal. The letter was ready for delivery.

Now the Japanese were wined and dined. (The admiral retired, leaving the entertainment of the guests in the hands of his staff.) Once more the officials examined, tasted, and sampled everything. Now a candy would be wrapped up in paper, now a piece of cake, now some jam — and candy, cake, and jam all disappeared in the folds of their kimonos. A music box that played *"Grâce, Grâce"* from *Roberta* failed to impress them. Baba had two at home, which the Dutch had brought. When Baba complained of constant headaches, the Russians offered medical assistance, but Baba declined it politely.

After dinner, the Japanese were shown all kinds of pictures, including illustrations from Philipp Franz von Siebold's work on Japan. Later on they asked to be shown about the frigate. They looked at all the equipment and attentively listened to explanations. "Everything interested them," recorded Goncharov, "and in this curiosity there was much that was naive and childish, even though the Japanese held back lest they display it too much." The retinue wandered up and down the deck, their mouth half-open with astonishment. The pattering of their straw sandals and the rustling of their silk skirts reminded the Russians of women. "You look up and are disappointed," complained Goncharov.[33]

It was almost evening when the Japanese left. As a parting gesture, which no doubt many a Russian sailor and orderly appreciated, they promised to have the laundry of the Russians washed in the Dutch factory.[34]

Later that evening, officials returned to report that the letter had been transmitted, a fact about which the Russians had had no doubt.[35]

Time went by. The Japanese continued their visits almost twice a day. They would come to bring provisions, to ask more questions, or to show the vessel to some official or friend who had not yet seen it. They watched military drills of all kinds with great interest. Not all appeared dumfounded or self-satisfied; some were pensive and modest, seemingly conscious and desirous of better things than those that surrounded them. "In these men," wrote Goncharov, "lies the future of Japan — and our success."[36]

"After about three days" (August 30?), Baba returned and reported that the governor had seen the letter "with pleasure" and had understood it well, but that without permission he could not receive the admiral. He had dispatched a special courier to Edo and an answer could be expected soon.

As already mentioned, Putiatin had sent word to the governor of Nagasaki (Osawa Bungo-no-kami) that he wished to purchase supplies. The latter had replied that he could not accept Russian payment without approval from Edo. The admiral had insisted, however, that he would not accept any goods for which he could not reimburse the Japanese. In the end, Osawa had sent a small shipment of poultry and greens, asking Putiatin to accept it as a gift. The latter had done so under the condition that a counter-present would not be refused.[37] But this gift had not solved the Russian supply problem. Putiatin decided, therefore, to send the transport *Kniaz' Menshikov* to Shanghai and the schooner *Vostok* to the Straits of Tartary.[38] He requested the governor to readmit the vessels without interference.

On this occasion [Putiatin reported], the governor of Nagasaki in spite of all his wariness made a serious blunder, which later on he could no longer correct. He asked us not to send the transport after provisions, offering to supply our vessels by way of the Dutch factory, which, having permission to trade in Japan, could purchase the Japanese provisions and resell them to us. I hastened to accept this favorable proposal, and throughout our stay in Nagasaki we constantly received poultry, fish, and fresh greens through the good offices of the Dutch factor Donker Curtius who readily rendered this service. But since it is impossible to obtain meat in Japan, as religious beliefs interdict the slaying of cattle, and since I also had to send papers to the postal station, I was unable to comply with the governor's request . . . and the two vessels departed as planned.[39]

Conscious of this slip, the Japanese became more vigilant. They had refused the Russians permission to come ashore. When the latter mentioned that they planned to check their chronometers on a nearby bare rock, they quickly stuck a tree on the rock so as to make it resemble the shore on which the Russians had promised not to go.[40]

Time began to weigh heavily on the Russians. "We worked and were bored, did not work and still were bored," noted Goncharov.[41] One day seemed like the other. At 4:00 A.M., the sailors would rise and begin to wash the deck with sand and stones. Between six and seven thirty, the officers would get up as well, go to flag raising, have their tea, and then settle down to work.[42] In addition to their regular duties, they busied themselves with the translation of nautical foreign-language material, the charting of Nagasaki harbor, and the study of the coastal fortifications.[43]

On September 14, at about 2:00 A.M., a fierce wind transformed the whole roadstead into one big whirlpool. The *Pallada* cast her third anchor.

Nishi Kichibee, the new senior interpreter, a round-faced, very alert and restless Japanese, boarded the frigate for the first time

on September 17. He had come to discuss the etiquette which was
to govern the reception of the admiral and the transmission of
the state paper. Goncharov was instructed by Putiatin to draft the
necessary ceremonial.[44]

On September 18, Nishi came to inform the admiral that an answer
had arrived from Edo. When Pos'et summarized for him in Dutch
the ceremonial Goncharov had drawn up, Nishi objected to the size
of the retinue, pointing out that that of Rezanov (in 1805) had been
smaller. "But I replied," reads Putiatin's report, "that the present
embassy had been undertaken on a larger scale than the former."
The admiral demanded and received further concessions. "I considered it necessary," explained he, "to act in that case with a certain
amount of persistence and talk them out of as many rights as possible,
since according to the customs of this people a precedent serves as
the rule of the future."[45]

Throughout the next day (September 19), negotiations concerning
the ceremonial continued.[46] "You over in Europe," Goncharov wrote,
"worry whether 'to be or not to be,' while we spend whole days
struggling to determine whether 'to sit or not to sit,' 'to stand or
not to stand,' then how, and on what...."[47] The Russians would not
sit on the floor and the Japanese would not sit on chairs. Irritated,
the Russians finally declared that they would bring their own chairs.
As for the governor — he could sit on what he pleased. The admiral
had withdrawn to his stateroom and did not participate in these
discussions except indirectly through his subordinates.

Nishi stated that Osawa wished to have the officers as guests for
breakfast. After the negotiations he would retire to his room, and
the Russians to another one. There they would eat. "Alone?" asked
the Russians, "...in Europe this is not done." But this was Japan,
and so the arguments raged on and on.[48] The Japanese wanted the
Russians to go ashore in Japanese boats, but the Russians insisted
on using their own. It goes without saying that the Russians would
not consider parading around in full-dress uniform without boots.
But the Japanese remove their footgear when entering a building.

The Russians finally decided to sew special covers for their boots to protect the Japanese floor mats.

In the evening, the Japanese returned once more to ask the Russians to reconsider their refusal to dine without the governor. The Japanese were given to understand that they might serve tea, as was their custom, but nothing else. As regards the procession, the admiral persisted that *norimono* (palanquins) be provided for all officers. Contrary to Russian expectation, no objection was made to the use of the band. Concluded Goncharov: "Probably all, including the governor, wanted to hear it."[49]

On September 20, officials returned to the frigate to rehash questions of ceremony. In vain they urged the Russians to land in Japanese boats. But the latter felt that the Shogunate wanted to show its subjects that the Russians were not coming on their own, but were being brought ashore, and thus remained adamant in their refusal.

A Dutch résumé of the ceremonial was sent to the governor through the interpreters. The latter had announced that the meeting would take place the following day. The official next in rank to the governor and two gubernatorial secretaries would come to notify the Russians when all was ready for their reception. The Russians asked that they be sent at 10:00 A.M.[50]

"The eagerly awaited morning has arrived," Goncharov wrote on September 21, 1853. "We have been here for a whole month. We know everything about Japanese pigs, deer, and even crawfish, not to mention the Japanese themselves, but as yet nothing about Japan."[51]

At 10:00 A.M., the officials duly arrived aboard the *Pallada*. As one man, they took a deep bow. The two old secretaries then stepped forward, their gaze fixed steadily before them. They were led to the captain's cabin, as were the other officials and their retinue. Later on, upon their own request, they were shown into the admiral's stateroom. There they accepted tea, but declined everything else, announcing that they had come only to report that his excellency the governor was expecting the admiral. They asked that the Russians do not follow them immediately as they were both members of the reception committee and thus had to get ashore in time to meet them, and departed. The other officials remained aboard ship.

After a brief religious service conducted by Archimandrite Avvakum, the Russians began to file down into the boats. The instant that the admiral's cutter pushed off, the flags of all nations were unfurled on the *Pallada* and *Olivutsa* while the first notes of the national anthem were momentarily drowned out by three thunderous hurrahs. For a minute, the Japanese on the hundred odd boats, that had been milling around the frigate since morning, were stunned; then they in turn raised their voices in a loud cheer.⁵²

There were nine boats in the Russian procession. The band played almost continuously. The parade uniforms of the Russians and the colorful kimonos of the Japanese spectators on the boats and along the shore added to the festive atmosphere.

The Russians enjoyed the view of the excellent coast line past which they travelled, but some felt that here, where "nature had done everything on her part" to give man the opportunity to realize wonders by the application of his creative hand, "man has done nothing." Their European eyes missed a white colonnade, a country villa, a church with golden domes — the stuff that Russian dreams are made of. "And what if we were to take Nagasaki away from the Japanese?" queried Goncharov. "They do not know how to use it. What would there be here if others were in possession of this port? Look what places [they have]! The whole Pacific Ocean would become alive with trade."⁵³

Putiatin praised, in his report, this "in all respects superb" harbor. Its shores were easily accessible and formed an excellent anchorage for vessels of all nations. Its heights offered strategic positions for an effective defense of the city. He added that the Japanese, however, had failed to erect proper fortifications. "These shores would not have withstood an attack from the sea by the most insignificant power."⁵⁴ A special study that *Kapitan* Konstantin Losev had made under his direction pointed out that the thirty-eight batteries and one hundred and thirty-seven guns that defended Nagasaki were impressive on paper only, as the Japanese had "no conception" of the science of gunnery. The batteries had been placed in such a way that they could not support each other, that their guns and crews were left not only unprotected but wide open to flanking fire. Japanese fortifications seemed confined to those places past which foreigners sailed in normal times or where anchor was cast. Little three-wall huts had been constructed above the guns to protect them from inclement weather. Now the Japanese could shoot when it rained, but not only did their batteries present easy targets, their own line of vision and fire had been greatly impaired.[55] In all fairness to the Japanese we must add, however, that they seem to have been not unaware of the shortcomings of their defenses. Wrote Koga, later on, about the guns in front of Kawaji Toshiakira's house: "They are big but not newly made. Their...implements are all secondhand. In case of an emergency, they are better than nothing."[56]

The Russians were surprised to see so many grey and "insignificant" houses with covered windows. "Everything has been curtained," complained Goncharov, "the houses, the boats, and the streets, while the people, whom it would not in the least hurt to curtain themselves, walk around already too unbuttoned."[57]

The boats landed. On shore, the guard-of-honor lined up in two ranks on the right side, the officers on the left. A crowded mass of Japanese gathered behind them, and yet it seemed that relatively few had been permitted on the beach. They watched from roofs, from behind curtains, from terraces, from mountains, from everywhere.

As the admiral set foot on land, music filled the air and officers and guard presented arms. But there was no reception committee in sight. Only the ever-present interpreters were there. The Russians demanded an explanation and the interpreters scattered in search of the proper officials. Finally an old, well-dressed man with "sleepy eyes" appeared with his retinue. He faced the Russians lifelessly. "It was difficult not to laugh when looking at these skirt-clad figures with little pigtails and bare little knees," wrote Goncharov derisively.

The Russians were led to the Western Government Office,[58] where

Osawa was to receive them. *Norimono,* some of them borrowed from the nearest Zen temple, had been prepared for the Russians, but the latter found them too uncomfortable and walked to the rendezvous.[59] As Koga later noted: "The Russians really cannot use palanquins, but request them because of face."[60]

The road was lined with Japanese soldiers. Before long, the Russians arrived at the government office. There Putiatin ordered guard and band to remain in the courtyard while he and the other officers and their orderlies, twelve persons in all, prepared to enter the building. Nishi was standing at the entrance and beckoning them inside. The Russians pulled the specially sewn protective covers over their boots and went in.[61]

The mariners passed through halls lined with row after row of human figures, sitting motionlessly on the white floor mats like porcelain dolls. Not an eyelash moved. Not a glance followed the Russians. "And they haven't had this for forty years!" recorded Goncharov in amazement, "and almost none of them had ever seen a foreigner."[62] Everything was quiet. Only the footsteps of the visitors resounded through the hall. Many of the Russians had trouble with their boot covers. They just would not stay on. Time and again, an officer had to retrace his steps and pick up the covers. The Japanese would still be sitting there, as rigid and as quiet as when the ambassador had first passed.

The Russians now came to a room lighter and more spacious than those they had seen. A large golden bow graced the *toko-no-ma* (alcove). Thirty more motionless figures were sitting in this room. As the Russians entered, Osawa also appeared. He seemed a man of about fifty, with an important, stern, and rather clever expression on his face. Both sides bowed. Goncharov inadvertently glanced at his boots — the "cursed" covers were gone. After a few civilities, the governor requested that the Russians place the letter from their state chancellor to the *Roju* into a lacquered box that stood on a nearby table. This done, he asked them to take a "rest"—"God knows from what exploits," as Goncharov commented — and disappeared.

The delegation was led into another room, where the chairs from the frigate had been set up. The five senior officers sat down, while those for whom no chairs were left remained standing. No longer did everyone seek to protect the meticulously clean mats from the coarse boots. Goncharov, for example, tired of picking up the covers at every other step, had hid them in his hat, "and there the matter rested." The interpreters entertained the Russians. Twelve attendants appeared — one for each guest. Holding a cup of yellow tea with both hands, they deftly fell on their knees, bowed, and placed the cup on the floor mat before the visitor, and withdrew. They soon reappeared, each with a set of Japanese smoking utensils — a lacquered stand, a burning charcoal-filled brazier, an ash tray, a pipe and tobacco. The Russians sat on chairs, clad in tight, full-dress parade uniforms. If it had been "terribly awkward" for them to stretch out now one hand, now the other to reach the tea, it was almost impossible — and hardly dignified — to take the pipe, stuff it, light it with charcoal, sit up to take the one or two puffs that a Japanese pipe offers and then bend down again, shake out the pipe, and repeat the procedure. It was just like Aesop's fable of the Fox and the Stork.[63]

Nishi asked whether the musicians could be offered refreshments. Approval was given but, at the same time, an officer was dispatched to instruct the sailors to drink not more than one wineglassful.

Meanwhile the Japanese put simple but beautiful boxes of confectionary before each guest. The sweetmeat was not bad. As Goncharov sarcastically reasoned, if, on the basis of a well-known Russian saying, one can eat a sugared shoe sole, why not a sugared carrot?[64] Finally, Nishi returned and announced that the governor would receive them if they had "rested." The group returned to the conference hall.

The first part of the meeting had been held standing, as agreed upon in advance. Now seats were provided for the senior officers on both sides. The Russians sat on chairs that they had brought along — servants had quickly carried them from the lounge[65] to the conference hall — the governor on a small platform. The interpreters were prostrated at the feet of the Russians. The remaining Japanese officials sat on the floor, Japanese style.

The governor took a document out of a lacquer box and read it in a clear, though hardly audible, voice. When he finished, an old official rose, stepped up, fell on his knees, and with a bow accepted the paper, rose, went over to Nishi, once more fell on his knees, and this time without a bow handed over the document, rose again, and returned to his place. Nishi, in his harsh voice, offered a Dutch translation. The governor had read to Putiatin the orders that had come from the *Roju* authorizing acceptance of the letter from *Graf* Nesselrode to the Japanese Supreme Council.[66] A second document was duly read and translated. It stated that "the letter will be accepted, but a speedy reply is impossible."[67] Putiatin objected, but the governor insisted that the importance of the issues (clarification of boundaries, opening of Japanese ports to trade), plus the fact that they had been raised so unexpectedly, precluded an early decision. Furthermore, Edo was far away and communications were slow. "Then I asked the governor," reads Putiatin's report, "whether he did not agree that it would be better if, to speed the matter up, I myself proceed to Edo with the squadron and deal directly with the Supreme Council. The governor, who hitherto in his speeches and receptions had maintained the dignity of his position, suddenly changed countenance ... and objected in a soft voice that 'to the extent to which my action [sailing to Nagasaki and not to Edo] had been pleasing to the government, to the same extent it would pain the Japanese eye to see foreign vessels in the capital.' "[68] With what "cold importance and sternness" the governor had tried to "support his truly Japanese worth," and now this sudden change! "What happened to him?" mocked Goncharov, "whither did his solemn, dry, and important tone and proud bearing disappear? His Japanese Excellency has been thrown off balance."[69] "I took advantage of this circumstance," continues Putiatin's report, "and remarked that it would be up to the Japanese government to keep me in Nagasaki by promptly answering the letter I had brought."[70]

Official business taken care of, renewed civilities were in order. Both sides insisted that they were happy to make each other's acquaintance. "We did not lie," commented Goncharov, "we really had been curious to meet the governor, the more so since we had not gotten off the frigate for a month and . . . saw in it a diversion. But as for Osawa, you could vouch that at that very moment there sat within him the father of lies himself, the Devil, to whom, of course, he also sent us in his thoughts. They say that an uninvited guest is worse than a Tartar; in this sense we Russians were really worse than Tartars to him. . . . When we arrived, Osawa had only two more months to serve before leaving [for home]. . . . Our arrival is of such importance to Japan that the government considered the presence of both governors in Nagasaki essential.[71] Is it not true that Osawa Bungo-no-kami had reason to grieve our arrival?"[72]

The governor withdrew and the Russians started back. As they were returning through the lounge, the interpreters blocked their way and asked them for dinner. Putiatin repeated his previous demand that Osawa join them. As the latter would not do so, the Russians ignored all further pleas of the interpreters and walked on, past the richly laid out table with its Western dishes and bottles of all shapes — probably taken from the Dutch. The Russians stepped out of the building. The band struck up a march, the guard presented arms, and the procession marched back. That same day, Baba set out for Edo with the Russian letter.[73]

On September 26, 1853, the transport *Kniaz' Menshikov* returned from Shanghai with the first news about the expected break with Turkey, France, and England. This information forced Putiatin to reconsider his plans. The Chinese port in which he had intended to supply the needs of his fleet would become inaccessible in the event of war because of British and French military superiority in those regions. Putiatin judged that his ships would be safest in San Francisco "where the English would not have dared to violate neutral rights." As the outbreak of hostilities did not appear to be imminent yet, however, he decided to send the transport back to Shanghai for more information, and to follow there with the rest of the squadron upon receipt of a decisive answer from Edo and upon arrival of the schooner *Vostok* from Tartary Bay, in order to make repairs and take on supplies before undertaking the long passage to California.[74]

On September 27, the Russians hoisted a red flag — the signal that they wished to talk to the Japanese — and two officials came aboard the frigate. The Japanese were told that their boats were too close to the vessel. The Russians would not permit their actions to be hindered. They would disperse these boats by force.

The transport was also boarded by Japanese officials, who asked such questions as where she had been and how long. Then the officials crossed over to the frigate, had Pos'et called from the dinner table, and inquired whether they had been told the truth. Pos'et got angry and told them not to ask this again. They misused Russian "indulgence"!

That day, Mizuno Tadanori (Chikugo-no-kami), the new Nagasaki *bugyo*, arrived at his post.[75] With him there came also another interpreter: Moriyama Einosuke.[76]

The next day (September 28), Japanese officials informed the Russians that the governor permitted them to enter the inner roadstead — but not too close to shore, lest they interfere with the movements of Japanese vessels.

On September 29, the Russians were busy writing reports to St. Petersburg. They had no time for visitors, yet the Japanese came again, once more inviting the Russians to enter the inner roadstead. When the Russians told them that they wanted to go closer to shore than the officials had suggested, the latter hastened back to ask the governor and promised to return the following day with an answer. "Still no word about shore," wrote Goncharov. "They are waiting [to see] whether we might not leave. The governor has probably been ordered not to assign [us] a place until the letter from Russia has been read in Edo and it has been learned why we have come, in the hope that perhaps it might be necessary [for us] to go ashore."[77]

On September 30, officials and interpreters revisited the frigate.

Goncharov made the acquaintance of Moriyama. "He speaks English only very little, but understands almost everything. He learned [it] from the Dutch, some of whom know English. Moriyama has also studied some French. He said that he has many books, mostly Dutch; there were also French ones. According to Pos'et he knows Dutch well."[78]

The Japanese made an important concession. They told the Russians to anchor any place they wished along the roadstead. In fact, they urged them to take the frigate from the second roadstead to the fairway leading to the roadstead nearest Nagasaki. But the admiral wished to spread out his vessels as much as possible. He wanted the corvet to stand at the entrance to the inner roadstead, the schooner and transport in the passageway itself, while the frigate remained at the second roadstead. Were the frigate to leave the second roadstead, reasoned the Russians, the Japanese could so line up their boats in back of the frigate as to deny the Russians use of that roadstead.

When Japanese boats "took it into their head" to hinder Russian ones from moving about freely, the Russians called the officials aboard again and informed them that any Japanese who came too close would be driven away by force. The Russians had come to Nagasaki and not to Edo, they had not gone ashore; they had done their best to please the Japanese. As the Japanese showed no appreciation of Russian indulgence, the Russians would continue to ride about as they pleased.[79]

On October 1, the Russian vessels took up their new positions. One hundred and eighty boats had gathered to tow them. Some laid by the frigate. The Russians threw bread and money to the oarsmen and offered them rum. Many of the Japanese climbed onto the guns and into the portholes. "Yelling, noise," complained Goncharov. The corvet moved, then the transport, and lastly the frigate, but under power of her own sails, without any assistance from the Japanese. Now the Russians were closer to shore and could observe life on land through their telescopes.[80]

The following day (October 2) toward evening, a heavy wind

rose and another anchor was cast. No Japanese came aboard. Nor did they come the next day or the day after. As Goncharov recorded on October 6: "There was nothing and really nothing. The Japanese are apparently angry at our persistence in travelling along the roadsteads in spite of their guard boats, and perhaps because of the cold reception."[81]

October 7 was the first anniversary of the Russian Japan Expedition, as the *Pallada* had entered the roadstead of Kronstadt on October 7, 1852. It was duly celebrated with a *Te Deum* and a big dinner. Officials were invited aboard. "Again the heads of the Japanese were stroked," narrated Goncharov, "they were called into the admiral's cabin, served liquor and tea, and asked about a place on shore." They replied that they expected instructions from Edo shortly. The Russians told them that they would not mind moving the frigate into the fairway, as suggested by the governor, if only the string of Japanese guard boats were removed. When the officials began to justify their actions by referring again to their laws, Pos'et told them the constraining laws against foreigners were after all not eternal, but had existed for only some two hundred years, and that it was time to give in to circumstances and to change them. "Moriyama answered very intelligently and soundly: 'You understand why our laws are this way (here he showed with his own hand how they were, i. e. constraining, but did not dare to say it). There is no doubt that they must change. But European vessels have begun to visit Nagasaki persistently and in large numbers only during the past ten years, and, therefore, there had not been any need to change [them].' "[82]

On the evening of October 9, there was a theatrical performance aboard the *Olivutsa*. The officers of the corvette and of the frigate acted out Gogol's *Wedding* and *Lawsuit*. All had a good time.

On October 10, officials arrived to say that the governor could not remove all Japanese boats from the fairway. On the morrow, they further reported that he wished to close the center of the passageway and instead open it near the shore by removing one boat on each side. But the admiral replied that any craft that dared to block the middle passageway to the corvet would be driven away by force. The interpreters did not stay for tea.[83]

Meanwhile, the members of the expedition were kept busy. Putiatin would not let anybody "die of boredom." Reported Goncharov: "The admiral cannot see an idle person. The moment he notices anybody without something to do he will suggest something immediately...." The officers spent much time in reading, research, and translation of nautical material.[84]

On October 12, the officials were called but did not come. They seemed annoyed at Russian threats. As Goncharov notes, the Russians had begun to deal with the Japanese more firmly. On the 13th the Japanese stayed away as well. By the 14th, the Russians had tired of waiting. A note was sent to the officials warning them that, if they would not appear, an officer would be sent to town after them. In the evening, an interpreter arrived to announce that the functionaries would come aboard the following day at noon. One of the long-threatened "removals by force" occurred that day when Russian cutters approached two Japanese boats near the frigate, pulled up their anchor and towed them farther away from the frigate.[85]

The next day (October 15) at 11:00 A.M., three officials, among them Oi, came aboard, but had nothing new to offer. They were still expecting "daily" an answer from Edo concerning assignment of a place on shore. Provisions were taken on as usual. They consisted of various greens, fish and lobster, and even a small deer. The Russians asked that fans, lacquer boxes, and the like be sent also.

On October 16, the Japanese interpreters finally informed the Russians that the Japanese boats would be removed farther. They requested, however, that the Russians do not participate in this. The latter had stated that, as the governor's orders to remove the craft were not being carried out, they themselves planned to assist His Highness by towing them away for him. The next day (October 17), two Japanese guard boats with guidons and pikes ordered their own boats to withdraw much farther. Putiatin meanwhile decided to say no more about these craft and simply ordered his men to take into tow and pull along any Japanese boat that might trail the cutters again.[86]

On October 21, a somber group of Japanese officials boarded the *Pallada* and asked to see Putiatin. They were so unusually downcast and solemn that the Russians realized at once that they bore bad tidings. In the admiral's stateroom, they announced gravely that the Shogun (Tokugawa Ieyoshi) had died on August 26, four days after the arrival of the Russians. To receive a speedy reply was thus impossible. They pointed out that the burying of the late Shogun and the investiture of his successor involved such ceremonial that nobody in Edo would have time to answer the Russians.[87] "But what about a place on land?" inquired the Russians. "No reply has yet been received from Edo." The Russians were angry. Putiatin told the officials that they did not know how to appreciate politeness and consideration; others would have landed already. He noted that the Russians now saw that Nagasaki was simply a trap into which foreigners were lured to be deceived. There, far from the capital, negotiations would be dragged out more and more in the hope that the foreigners would tire and leave. "But all Europe will learn of this," threatened he, "and not one vessel will come here, but [will sail] to Edo — you can be assured of that.... Ask the governor: does he or does he not intend to give us a place? There must be an answer tomorrow."[88] The official meeting was over. The Japanese were served tea and liquor. They cheered up to such an extent that the Russians began to wonder whether the information they had received was true, whether the Shogun had really died, whether he had died as recently as August 26, as claimed, or whether he had died considerably earlier and the announcement of his death was now made to delay negotiations further.[89] The Japanese had stated that the Russian letter to Edo and the announcement of the Shogun's death from Edo had by-passed each other. The Shogun had thus died before receipt of the Russian state paper in the capital.

Putiatin sat down and wrote two notes. In one, he expressed the Russian government's grief at the loss which Japan had suffered; in the other, he pointed out that "this event [the Shogun's death] occurred before the receiving of our first papers and did not prevent them [the Supreme Council] from ordering them accepted, as well as determining the ceremonial for the meeting between the Russian plenipotentiary and the governor, etc., and consequently will not hinder further orders also, as the course of government affairs in such a large empire cannot stop regardless of circumstances." "Therefore," he wrote, "we shall wait for an answer from the *Goroju* [*Roju*] and ... will not leave the shores of Japan without a definitive settlement of the business that brought us here." He warned that should the requested reply be further delayed, he would proceed to Edo![90]

Later that day, the gubernatorial answer was brought in response to the admiral's demand for a place on shore where chronometers could be checked. "It was the same story: No word had as yet been received from Edo...." On October 22, Nishi called for the the Russian reply; on the 23d, he returned to say that he had delivered it to the governor. There was still no news from Edo.

The Japanese came daily, primarily to learn whether the Russians might not be contemplating landing by force. They requested that the Russian cutters not travel too far, as the slower Japanese boats could not keep up with them. "But why do you follow?" the Russians demanded. "Orders," the officials replied. And a tall old man added: "We ourselves too would like the change to come sooner."[91]

On October 30, Putiatin invited the Japanese officials to continue visiting the frigate even though they might not have any business to discuss, so that they could familiarize themselves as much as possible with Russian ideas and the Russian way of life. The junior interpreters misinterpreted the message and two officials hastened aboard to ask what the Russians needed.[92]

On October 31, Oi arrived "with a little request from the governor." The daimyo of Chikuzen was to proceed the next day from one wharf in the fairway to another one in order to inspect his troops and their quarters. He would be accompanied by up to one hundred vessels. The governor felt that the frigate lay in their way and requested that she be moved aside. But Putiatin replied that it was a great deal easier for the boats to go around the vessel, than for a man-of-war to change positions.[93]

On November 2, the Russians were informed that word had finally been received from the capital. Everybody was excited. *"Grande nouvelle!"* wrote Goncharov, "... we expected impatiently that we would be called to Edo or would be told this or that. ..." But all that the communication from the *Roju* contained was an acknowledgment of the fact that the Russian letters had arrived safely.

When the Russians had arrived at Nagasaki, they had found a Dutch vessel in the harbor. Now she was about to depart for Batavia, and the Russians wished her to take their mail along. They ignored Osawa's plea not to visit the Dutch. A gubernatorial request to communicate with the latter on the open sea — out of the sight of the Japanese people — and threats to block passage to the Dutch ship were of no avail. The Russians notified Osawa that they did not understand how the thought of interfering in the dealings of two European vessels could have gotten into his head.[94]

The Russians began to worry about the *Kniaz' Menshikov* and the *Vostok*. Two months had already passed since the transport had left for Shanghai after letters, newspapers, and provisions. Yet, she had been instructed to be back within seven weeks. On November 4, she finally rejoined the squadron. On November 15, the schooner also returned from the Straits of Tartary, mission accomplished. Japanese guns announced her arrival. "How much news!" exclaimed Goncharov.[95]

Putiatin had come to Nagasaki, the port to which the Japanese had confined their limited intercourse with the outside world, in the hope that his action would be appreciated as a friendly gesture and rewarded by concessions. As Japanese officials procrastinated, Putiatin threatened to expedite matters by proceeding directly to Edo, the seat of the Shogunate. In the middle of November, he actually decided to carry out his threat, but unfavorable winds delayed

his departure. On November 17, he informed Oi and another func-
tionary — the officials always appeared in pairs — that he was about
to leave Nagasaki. They were delighted. He had not told them,
of course, that he intended to visit the capital, but had only requested
that they come back the next day for papers as well as gifts for the
governors and interpreters and send aboard as much water and
provisions as possible. "Little do they know that we are planning
to feed ourselves with these provisions en route to Edo," remarked
Goncharov.[96]

But Osawa and Mizuno were alarmed. The next morning (November 18), senior officials came aboard the *Pallada* and announced that
the governors had decided to accept the papers for consideration.
Then they inquired why, when, and where the Russians were going.
But the latter would not tell. "We mystified them," wrote Goncharov,
"skillfully avoiding to answer [their] questions."[97]

The Japanese refused farewell gifts, reiterating that under no circumstances could they accept anything without special permission
from Edo. The Russians retorted that then they too would never
accept any presents. When the officials left, they were no wiser about
the admiral's plans. Even their request that the Russians give them
one day's advance notice before sailing had been rejected. Considering the fact that the Japanese had theretofore persistently evaded
or at least delayed answering any and all Russian requests with a
view to tiring out and turning away Putiatin, it would have seemed
that the prospect of his departure should have pleased them. Instead,
they displayed considerable anxiety. This paradoxical change in
Japanese attitude gave rise to speculation among the Russians that
an answer must finally have been received from Edo.

In the evening, the officials returned to the frigate. This time they
brought Moriyama as interpreter, apparently in the hope that he
might get more out of the Russians than Nishi, who had questioned
them in the morning. But the conversation continued in the same
vein: "Whereto?" "Wherever the wind will carry [us]." The Russians
did make it clear, however, that, as previously stated by the admiral,
they would not leave the shores of Japan without having completed

their mission. "But you will receive the answer in Nagasaki," argued the officials. No comment. "Put yourself in our place," pleaded Moriyama. "We were ordered to find out [your plans], but shall return with the same [amount of information] with which we departed." "And put yourself in my position," replied Pos'et, "the admiral does not tell me another word about his intentions, and I do not know what to tell you."[98]

Early in the morning (November 19), Japanese officials arrived. They declared that, as the admiral was determined to leave, they would not try to detain him, but they did wish to note for his consideration the fact that the governor knew for certain that the long-awaited answer would arrive "in about ten days, certainly in not more than eleven and perhaps even in seven." The Russians replied that, after a three-months-long wait, seven days would not make much difference. But they must have a place on land to make repairs on the vessels, check the chronometers, and perform other tasks. Then, if the reply would advance matters, they would remain; if not, proceed wherever necessary.

Throughout these discussions, now one now another interpreter or junior official left the stateroom to tell something to the Japanese who waited in their boats. The officials were just promising that they would bring the admiral's statement to the attention of the governor, when their words were drowned out by loud voices outside the cabin. Moriyama went to the door and reported that two messengers had arrived, but could not get past the guard. Admitted, they produced a document. Trying hard to appear very surprised, Nishi announced that mail had arrived from Edo. The note, addressed to both governors, had been signed by Abe Masahiro, president of the *Roju*. It stated that "four plenipotentiaries, *groote Herren*, important dignitaries, are coming from Edo to meet and negotiate with the admiral." As to when they could be expected in Nagasaki nothing was said.[99] The officials began to point at the paper and gesticulate: What a miracle — no sooner had they mentioned it, than it arrived. The Russians could no longer suppress their laughter, and the Japanese themselves joined in.

The Japanese left, but returned after dinner and announced that, although the governor had not received permission, he would assign them a place on land. In the evening, they came again and offered the Russians Kibashi-ura, the bay which Chamberlain Rezanov had occupied before.[100] But the officers whom Putiatin sent to inspect the place found it completely unsatisfactory.

While the Russians had now decided not to proceed to Edo, Putiatin still planned to leave, if only temporarily. "As it was impossible to expect the arrival of the persons earlier than in a month, I deemed it useless to remain any longer in Nagasaki," he reported.[101] He wished to go to Shanghai to learn how things stood in Europe, to provide the expedition with fresh supplies for several months, to change his letters of credit, and to repair some damages on the recently returned schooner *Vostok*.[102] When the Russians informed the governor that the place he had assigned them was unacceptable, he replied that there was no other. The Russians pointed out other spots and threatened to leave. In fact, they asked him to send the necessary provisions. The governor refused, telling them to obtain the supplies, little by little, from the Dutch. Evidently he hoped to be able to detain the admiral this way. "We'll go without provisions," retorted the latter.

When the governor finally prepared another place, it too proved unacceptable. He told the Russians that the area they had pointed out belonged to the daimyo of Omura and was outside of his jurisdiction. He had informed them of the appointment of the plenipotentiaries, he had assigned them a place on land — if they left, it was not his fault.

The admiral sent ashore a note to the governor, as well as papers to be transmitted to the plenipotentiaries upon their arrival in Nagasaki. He informed Osawa that he would return to Nagasaki before long. If upon his arrival he would not find either the plenipotentiaries or an answer to the state paper, he would immediately proceed to Edo.

On November 23, 1853, the Russian squadron weighed anchor, having spent three months at Nagasaki.[103]

川路聖謨肖像

（安政元年十二月廿四日露人撮影）

KAWAJI SAEMON-NO-JO TOSHIAKIRA
(From a photograph taken by members of the
Russian expedition)

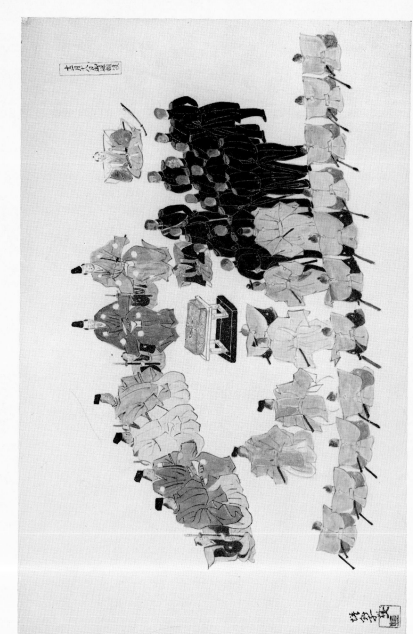

TRANSMITTAL OF THE JAPANESE REPLY TO THE RUSSIAN STATE LETTER. (After a drawing in *Bakumatsu gaikoku kankei monjo*, vol. 3)

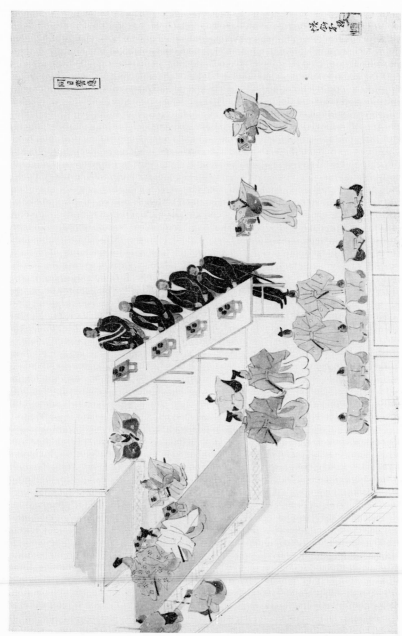

ENTERTAINMENT OF THE RUSSIAN AMBASSADOR AND STAFF BY THE JAPANESE PLENIPOTENTIARIES, JANUARY 12, 1854. (After a drawing in *Bakumatsu gaikoku kankei monjo*, vol. 3)

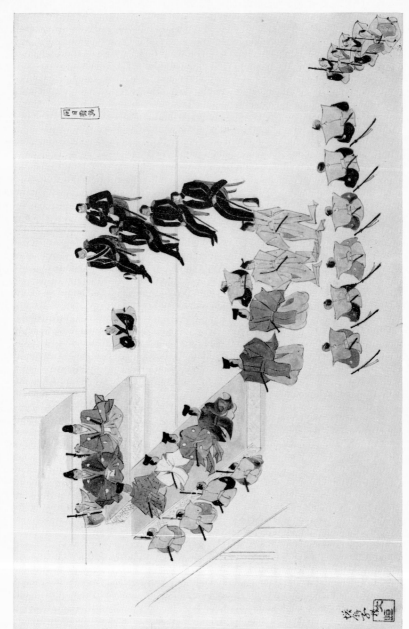

RUSSO-JAPANESE NEGOTIATIONS. (After a drawing in *Bakumatsu gaikoku kankei monjo*, vol. 3)

3

Nagasaki: Second Visit

On November 26, 1853, the *Pallada* cast anchor at the Saddle Islands, the northernmost group of the Chusan Archipelago. From there Putiatin proceeded to Shanghai on the schooner. It would have required the help of a large steamer to tow the frigate up the narrow fairway of the Yangtze River.

At Shanghai, the admiral learned through communication received from the Ministry of the Navy by East India mail that the frigate *Diana* had been assigned as replacement for the *Pallada*. She had left Kronstadt in October and was now en route to the Sandwich Islands, where she planned to join the expedition. But intelligence about an English squadron off the western shores of America, dissuaded Putiatin from sailing to the New World. European newspapers obtained in Shanghai had informed him about the commencement of hostilities between Turkey and Russia and the expected break between the latter and France and England. Consequently, he sent instructions through the United States consul in Shanghai to the skipper of the *Diana* to be at De Kastri Bay in the Straits of Tartary by spring.[1]

While in Shanghai, Putiatin was witness to clashes between adherents of the Small Sword Society and Manchu troops.[2] "Every day," he reported, "from morning to evening both sides kept firing, without harm, by the way, to either side. The troops of the pretender were

superior, looked more vigorous, and were better dressed, while the
troops of the Chinese emperor were composed, so far as I could see,
of a mob of ill disciplined, pitiful riffraff."[3] The imperial camp resembled a "noisy and motley bazaar," the soldiers a "crowd of good-
for-nothing tramps without any military appearance." Discussing the
effects of the rebellion on commerce with China, Putiatin wrote:
"The opium trade continued: within sixteen miles from Shanghai
there stood a whole fleet of English and American vessels with car-
goes of this poison. . . ."[4]

The European and American merchants, taking advantage of the
disturbance, offered the admiral a poor exchange rate on his London
letters of credit. He purchased, therefore, only the most essential
supplies from them. "Due to the obligingness of Commodore Perry,"
Putiatin reported, "a certain amount of coal" was released to him
"at a reasonable price" from the stock of the American men-of-war.[5]

It was unlikely that Putiatin would soon again be in a position
to communicate with St. Petersburg and, therefore, he sent back
reports, studies, and maps by courier (*Leitenant* Kroun) via Hong
Kong and the East Indies.

Upon the completion of necessary repairs, the *Vostok* returned to
the Saddle Islands.[6] On December 29, the four vessels of the Russian
Expedition once more set sail for Japan. On January 3, 1854, they
were back in Nagasaki.[7]

The squadron slipped so quietly into the harbor during darkness
that it was not sighted until already casting anchor.[8] "Our present
arrival was so unexpected," wrote one of the Russian officers, "that
the Japanese had made no preparations to receive us, as they had
done in the past. They did not have time to gather at the entrance
batteries and to post gunboats and other guard boats at various
places. . . . The frigate was met by only an interpreter without the
natural pride and haughtiness of the Japanese, on the contrary, with
full respect and modesty. It was apparent that the Japanese wanted
to conceal that they had been surprised by our early arrival, but the
moving of small and large boats soon thereafter, when we cast

anchor at the roadstead, proved that they had not expected us at all."[9]

Later in the day, officials led by Oi came aboard the frigate to welcome the Russians. Their amiable chatter was cut short by the inevitable question: "Are the plenipotentiaries here?" "They will be," replied Oi. "If they won't be," warned the admiral, "we shall go to Edo as planned. Time is precious and we shall not waste it. The plenipotentiaries may already be here and you just do not want to tell us." Insisting that the plenipotentiaries had really not yet arrived, the officials withdrew.[10]

In the afternoon they came again. The Russian raised the same question: "Are the plenipotentiaries here?" No, they were not, and would not be in three days — as previously stated by mistake — but in about a week. "If they do not arrive by Saturday [this was Wednesday]," threatened Putiatin, "we shall leave."[11]

That morning, the Russians had already demanded enough water and provisions to last for an extended trip to Edo. The officials now brought aboard poultry, pigs, vegetables, fruits, and whole chests of candy. Gifts from the governor, they explained. But the Russians replied that they had previously refused to accept presents because the governor would take nothing from them. If these provisions were to be considered gifts they did not want them. The junior interpreters hastened back ashore to consult the governor, while the Russians did their utmost to entertain the remaining officials. They showed them pictures and played a little organ. The pigs squealed, the hens cackled....[12]

Moriyama interrogated Goncharov. He was anxious to learn whether there had been any contact between the Russian and American forces, how much the former knew about the activities of the latter, and where Perry was. Realizing fully what Moriyama wanted to find out, Goncharov decided to have fun at his expense and make his task as frustrating as possible.

Moriyama's voice was low and wheedling. He inquired in broken English where the Russians had been.

"In China," replied they.

"What did you see?"

"A lot; among other things the war between the rebels and the imperial forces."

"And what else?"

"What else? ... Also some Americans."

"Whom?!"

"Commodore Perry...."

"Commodore Perry?!?!"

"Commodore Perry we did not see, but we did see the captain of the American corvet *Saratoga*."

"*Saratoga*?! But where is Perry? In the United States?"

"No, not in the United States, but in Amoy...."

"In Amoy?"

"Or in Ningpo...."

"In Ningpo?"

"Perhaps in Hong Kong...."

Half an hour later, Moriyama reported the conversation to a senior official. The latter noted everything down carefully.[13]

Goncharov told Moriyama he ought to visit at least Shanghai, a European-style city. Moriyama agreed and added that he would very much like to take a trip around the world.

"Well, let's go to Russia," said Goncharov. "What cities, shrines, and palaces, what an army you will see there...."

"To Russia — no!" Moriyama interrupted lively. "They have no women there!"

"Who told you that?" queried Goncharov. "What do you mean there are no women there? Plenty!! But you are married?"

"Yes, I have a ten-month old daughter. A few days ago she was vaccinated against small-pox."

"Then what do you want with women?" asked Goncharov. Moriyama just smiled. "What a Japanese Don Juan!"[14]

Finally, word was brought that the governor agreed to accept the gifts.[15] At the same time, he requested that the admiral change the time limit from Saturday to the following Thursday (January 12).

The plenipotentiaries were coming with a retinue of about six hundred men and in four separate groups, hence could travel only slowly. The admiral replied that if the governor would guarantee that a meeting would be held on the 12th he would wait; otherwise, he would sail to Edo. The Japanese seemed very pleased.[16]

On the whole, the officials seemed much friendlier than before. Open hostility had never been shown, but suspicion and mistrust had been apparent. "Now, however," wrote one of the Russian officers, our relationship has changed considerably.[17] Goncharov felt the same: "The governors seem to do everything in their power to please us, or at least to give the appearance of pleasing us. It is the very opposite of what was three months ago.[18]

The supplies the governor had sent were now quickly taken below and Russian counter-presents prepared. That same evening, gifts for Osawa were sent ashore through the officials. There was a malachite clock, a group of bronze figures, and two crystal vases, as well as liqueur, sherry, and sugar.[19]

On January 6, the Russians once more asked for a place on shore. The request had been expected, for one of the officials produced a sketch of a piece of land set aside for the Russians. The site contained an "idol temple" and one or two other buildings. These would have to be cleared before the Russians could take over.[20]

Christmas (January 5 and 6) passed with due celebration aboard the vessels. Moriyama asked why everybody was dressed up. "Although we avoided talking to them about Christian religion," wrote Goncharov, "I told him." "One must after all accustom them by and by to everything that is ours," added he in parenthesis.[21]

On January 7, 1854, the plenipotentiaries arrived.[22] Two days later (January 9), the Russians were informed of this. The admiral told the officials that as he had gone ashore to deliver the state letter, it was now the plenipotentiaries' turn to come aboard with the reply.[23]

The diary of Koga, the Confucian scholar and plenipotentiary, gives a vivid description of the "endless" trip from Edo to Nagasaki.

Only when we realize that the plenipotentiaries walked most of the way,[24] stopping at every scenic spot, admiring every lovely spring and every famous temple, and attending numerous banquets, can we fully understand why their arrival was delayed so long.[25]

Meanwhile, Pos'et, Rimskii-Korsakov,[26] Losev, and Iugan Kh. Furugel'm went to inspect the area the Japanese had assigned to the Russians on shore. They found it satisfactory (it was situated at the entrance from the fairway to the inner roadstead) and the admiral decided to bring the frigate closer to shore so as to make the spot more readily accessible. Much discussion ensued. On January 11, the Japanese requested a three-day delay in the use of the area, as preparations had not yet been completed.[27] On the fourth day, and many a day thereafter, apologies were offered, but the place remained "unprepared." When the governor finally sent word that it was ready, he set so many conditions that the admiral told him he no longer needed it. "And that is what the Japanese wanted," commented Goncharov. "They must avoid giving foreigners any reason to go ashore. Had they given a place to us, they would have had to give one also to others; but they hoped either to escape this necessity altogether, or limit it as far as possible [or] finally postpone this event as much as can be."[28]

Squabbles continued as to who was to visit whom.[29] As Koga recorded, "the barbarians finally gave in,"[30] but they posed certain conditions: that one of the plenipotentiaries meet the admiral at the entrance of the conference building, that the plenipotentiaries be present at meals given in honor of the Russians, and that the guard of the latter be allowed to consist of forty men, not counting the band. Putiatin promised, in turn, to receive the Japanese plenipotentiaries aboard the frigate with due respect and greet them with a gun salute, if but desired. The officials agreed, but said that they would further communicate with the admiral concerning the gun salute. Meanwhile, however, Putiatin decided to salute his flag the moment the Russian cutters pushed off.[31]

As already mentioned, the date for the first meeting between the admiral and the Japanese plenipotentiaries had definitely been set for January 12. The Russians were to leave the frigate at 11 A.M. "But it is understood," wrote Goncharov, "that an hour is only set so that one knows how much later than the appointed time to come — such is the custom in good society. And we, as people of good society, pushed off at half past one."[32]

At 10:30 A.M. the official next in rank to the governor had arrived with a whole string of retinue to announce that the plenipotentiaries awaited the Russians. He had drunk a cup of tea, gulped down two glasses of sherry, and hastened back ashore.[33]

The Russian procession was led by Pos'et on the admiral's gig. His was the duty of meeting and lining up the guard that followed on the longboat. Then came a cutter with the band, another cutter with chairs and servants, two more with officers from the various vessels, the admiral's cutter with the admiral and the commanders of the four vessels (Unkovskii, Rimskii-Korsakov, Nikolai N. Nazimov, and Furugel'm), *Leitenant* Baron Kriudner, the Chinese language interpreter (Goshkevich), and Goncharov aboard, two whale boats, and another gig.

The sailors were lined up on the yards. A threefold "ura!" from their lips filled the air. Multicolored flags unfurled and, like strewn flowers, bedecked the rigging. The band struck up the national anthem and the guns thundered in salute.[34]

As the Japanese officials had been leaving the frigate, Putiatin had sent Pos'et to tell them through the interpreters that their boats should go as far as possible away from the frigate, as a gun salute would be fired. An official had hastened back to dissuade the Russians, but in vain. He had warned that a misunderstanding might result, as the Japanese batteries, not informed about this, might also open fire.[35] "This is a barbarian custom," Koga had jotted down, "but our laws do not permit it. They must not fire the cannons. If the sound of the cannons be heard, the soldiers of the two clans will come and attack from both sides."[36] But the Russians had only remarked that "that is how it should be — to return a gun salute." Told that the cannoneers had already taken their positions, the Japanese had disappeared hastily.[37]

The Russians had followed. No sooner had they passed the bow of the frigate when the cannons thundered the first salute. "The mountains awoke suddenly and resounded as if some giant were rolling with laughter." A second shot from the frigate, one from the corvet, the frigate, the corvet.... "The laughter of the mountains continued." Shot followed shot; now they would roar on both sides simultaneously, now they would overtake each other. "The mountains were beside themselves and the governors probably more than they."[38] The frigate and the corvet each fired twenty-one shots.[39]

If it had "hurt the Japanese eye" to see foreign vessels in the harbors of Japan, how much must it now have hurt the Japanese ear. But nothing happened. The Japanese did not return the fire.[40] "...White smoke rolled and rolled," recorded Koga, "and almost created a big disturbance. Fortunately [it did not]."[41]

The boats quickly approached the shore. A multitude of little Japanese craft hastened along. All wanted to land at the same time as the Russians. The result: chaos and confusion. Wrote Goncharov: "Had they been ordered not to let us ashore, they could not have done better than they did now in order to let us."[42]

The Russians landed. "They came up with a brass band giving the appearance of Takashima-style maneuvers."[43] Everything seemed to be as on the first visit. The Russian band and guard lined up at the same place, and so did the Japanese troops. "These same soldiers," mocked Goncharov, "with the cardboard caps on their heads, and guns, or quasi-guns in [their] cases, with their feet asunder and their knees forward." The same officials were there, the same *nori-mono* — everything was identical, except that now the junior pleni-potentiary "with a strange hair-do" stood on the flight of steps.[44] "As my position was the humblest," noted Koga, "I was charged with this duty. Alas!"[45] When the Russians approached, Koga folded his arms in salutation, turned around, and led the way to the office. Thought he to himself: "This is really like opening the door and receiving robbers."[46]

As the Russians entered the conference room, the screens at the other end moved apart like scenes in a theater, and the plenipotentiaries stepped forth slowly, one at a time. First came Tsutsui Hizen-no-kami Masanori, then Kawaji Saemon-no-jo Toshiakira, third Arao Tosa-no-kami Narimasa, and last Koga Kinichiro Masaru, who had led them to the Western Government Office.[47] The four Japanese lined up and exchanged bows with the Russians. On the right side, at the elbows of the plenipotentiaries, stood both Nagasaki *bugyo;* and on the left four more important figures, among them Nakamura Tameya[48] and Kikuchi Taisuke. Behind the plenipotentiaries sat their attendants with precious swords in their hands. At the left, near the windows, other officials were seated in a row.[49]

For a minute, both sides silently sized up each other. Tsutsui seemed "a somewhat stooping old man; from old age his mouth was always a little open." Kawaji appeared "about forty-five years old [he was fifty-two], with big brown eyes and an intelligent and energetic face," Arao "very elderly," "thin-bodied and swarthy" with downcast eyes "as if he had spent his whole life in reclusion," and with a "somewhat bird-like face." Koga appeared "middle-aged, with a very common face, of which there are many, which expressed nothing — like a shovel." "One can readily tell from such faces," mused Goncharov, "that they think little about anything beyond [their] daily working day problems."[50]

Kawaji glanced at Putiatin. The latter had removed his hat, "the shape of which had the narrowness and end of a small bucket, was adorned with gold, and had feathers attached to the top." He very much resembled Nagai Noto-no-kami. "His tea-color hair measured three *sun,*[51] his whiskers the same." Kawaji had heard that the admiral was only thirty-one, but he looked like sixty (he was fifty-one). He wore long epaulets. "On the *haneri* [fold of the kimono] there were *go* stones[52] of gold."[53]

Osawa, who but recently had received the Russians "with such dignity and pride," now stared before him. But now and then he would stealthily scowl at the Russians. "And he had a reason for it," admitted Goncharov. "He had only a month or so left to serve before going to Edo and now, thanks to our kindness, he has been sitting [here] for a year and a half, and God knows how much longer he will continue to sit here." As for Mizuno Tadanori, the other governor, he seemed no sage, but a man of angry countenance.[54]

The plenipotentiaries made a sign that they wanted to speak, and in the twinkling of an eye Moriyama and Nishi "crawled up to their feet like two snakes," touched the floor with their foreheads, and, remaining in this position, listened, "barely breathing." Tsutsui began to talk. He spoke quietly and slowly. He congratulated the admiral on his arrival and wished him good health. Putiatin returned the salutation. Tsutsui then addressed a similar formal welcome to the captain of the *Pallada*. "But these official expressions of feeling," wrote Goncharov, "very good from the mouth of Osawa, somehow did not become Tsutsui. He looked at us so kindly and benevolently, as if he wished to say something else, something more sincere."[55] Tsutsui next greeted Pos'et, who acted as Dutch interpreter, and then all the other officers, one by one. Thereafter, Moriyama moved to the official next in rank and translated the latter's greetings to all the officers in the same order as before. The remaining two plenipotentiaries and the two governors followed suit. Putiatin then thanked the Japanese in his own name, as well as that of all the others.[56] The plenipotentiaries narrated how difficult their trip had been, explaining thus their late arrival.[57]

All this had been said and done standing.[58] Civilities completed, the officials asked the Russians to rest in the lounge. Very fine powdered tea was served. The hosts explained that it was set aside for use by only the highest officials. "The tea is excellent, strong and aromatic," wrote Goncharov, "but to us it appeared not altogether tasty, because it was without sugar. Nevertheless, we extolled it to high heaven."[59] Japanese pipes and tobacco, as well as sweetmeats in beautiful boxes, were placed before the guests. The officials, who in the presence of the governor had ignored the Russians, now were full of attention and courtesy. Perhaps, as Goncharov observes, "they did not respect us very much until plenipotentiaries were sent from Edo to give us a festive and honorary reception."[60]

After a while, Nakamura came to announce that dinner was ready. He apologized that there was not enough space for all of them to dine together, and that they would have to eat in different rooms. Putiatin, Unkovskii, Pos'et, and Goncharov ate in the lounge together with only the two senior plenipotentiaries, Tsutsui and Kawaji. The Russians sat on chairs brought along from aboard ship, the Japanese on *tatami-dai* (platforms with Japanese floor mats).[61] The Japanese had consulted the *Engi-shiki* (a collection of regulations concerning the ceremonies of the palace, audiences of officials, and so on, published during the Engi era [A.D. 927]) and the *Oritaku-shiba-no-ki* (the autobiography of Arai Hakuseki, a famous man of letters and historian [1656-1725]) as source books of ceremonial. They had actually intended to use chairs and tables themselves, but, unable to obtain any, had had to adhere to the old custom.[62] Six attendants — one per diner — appeared and humbly put individual low Japanese stands with bowls of food and a pair of chopsticks before each person.[63] "As for the serving," states Kawaji's diary, "we intended to use officials in Nagasaki for the Russians, and our retainers for Tsutsui and myself, but the officials of that place were so terribly afraid that they were very unskilled at the time of practice, and the retainers Shibazaki Hidesaburo and Yasui Tsukumo and the retainers of Tsutsui had to wait on the barbarians."[64] To the great relief of the Russians, forks and spoons, taken from the Dutch factory, were brought in. "To prove to you that everything that has been served is used as food," remarked Tsutsui, "we shall start first. Won't you uncover the bowls and eat whatever you may like?"[65]

Dish by dish, the Russians explored Japanese cookery. They did not fully appreciate *sashimi* (raw fish), nor did they care to quench their thirst with plain hot water at the end of the meal; but all in all they remained quite satisfied, quite satisfied except for one thing — a clove had been served in their tea. "What barbarism!" thought Goncharov, "and in the land of tea to boot!"[66] But neither were the Japanese to be in ecstasy over Russian tea. Commented Koga after a reception aboard the frigate: "The leaves [of the Russian tea] are coarse and boiled dark, and [taste] like medicine."[67]

Tsutsui looked at the Russians "friendly and affably." "We have come from beyond many hundreds, you from many thousands of miles," noted he. "We had never seen each other, were so far apart, and now have become acquainted, sit, chat and dine together. How strange and pleasant this is!" The Russians felt the same way about it. "We did not know how to thank him for his friendly expression of the then mutual feeling. We too had the same thoughts, the same impressions about the strangeness of such *rapprochements*."[68] They did tell their hosts that in Russia the Japanese were considered first among the peoples of the Far East in knowledge of living and refinement of manners, and that now they had seen it at first hand.[69]

After dinner, the admiral announced that he wanted to ask the plenipotentiaries two questions concerning the matter that had brought him to Japan, and he wished an answer the very same day.[70] Tsutsui blew his nose in a little piece of paper that he then hid in the sleeve of his kimono and objected gently that Japanese custom did not permit talking business during the first meeting at which one made somebody's acquaintance. "Propriety and the laws of hospitality demand this." Although the admiral commented that these questions could hardly damage their friendship and would require no more than a simple "yes" or "no" answer, it was obvious that it would have been fruitless to talk shop. "In general," narrated Goncharov, "both the important and unimportant dignitaries expressed themselves after dinner more in interjections which it is impossible to transmit in words. Pectoral sounds came from all corners. To discuss business is unseemly, but this — *nichevo!*[71] Commented Koga: "The barbarians are cunning. When about to leave, they must raise a difficult question and pretend it is a small matter, and afterwards you know [that it was not]. The two old men [Tsutsui and Kawaji] are experienced persons; therefore, can act accordingly."[72]

Putiatin agreed to hold the two questions until the following day, provided the plenipotentiaries would then answer by evening. The

Japanese asked how they could promise this without knowing the questions, but the Russians replied that they themselves did, and knew that they could be answered by then. "They promised to do whatever possible," concluded Goncharov, "and we parted great friends."[73]

It was New Year's Eve (Russian style). Recorded Kawaji: "I wonder if there is a celebration aboard ship. On the three masts there are many kinds of flags, just like on a *tanabata-dake*."[74] During the night, Japanese guards reported much yelling that sounded like the "*katsuo katsuo*" (bonito bonito) of Japanese merchants.[75]

4

The Visitors Entertain

ON JANUARY 13, 1854 (NEW YEAR'S DAY, RUSSIAN STYLE), JAPANESE officials went aboard the *Pallada* to discuss various minor matters. The Russians, all in full dress, offered them champagne. Soon the faces of the Japanese became flushed and Moriyama began to apologize in a mixture of English, Dutch, French, and Nagasaki dialect that he had drunk too much. "He had learned from the Americans how to drink champagne," noted Goncharov. "And how quickly: they had stayed only six days!"[1] But then as Sir George Sansom has pointed out, the officials who negotiated with the Americans "needed no lessons in conviviality, once their business on board was done and they were offered refreshment. In the alcoholic world, there was a complete meeting of minds as between East and West."[2]

The Japanese scheduled the next meeting for the 15th. Putiatin agreed and insisted that it be held aboard the *Pallada*. Moriyama thereupon requested that the Russians dispense with gun salutes.[3]

The Russians busied themselves selecting presents for the invited guests. It was no easy task. They knew the names of the more important officials, but not of the minor ones. Remembering the latter by sight only, they had to refer to them in their list as "the pock-marked one," "pig-tail," "skinny," or by names of Russians whom they resembled. (The Japanese used similar appellations. Thus, while Goshkevich, for example, was calling one of the interpreters "the

[48]

pock-marked one," he himself was known to the Japanese as "the pock-marked barbarian.")[4]

Mizuno received a pier glass, a little carpet, and two multicolored lamps; the other officials, a mirror each and broadcloth and other material.[5] Not a person who had been of service was forgotten, not even the lowly officials under whose supervision water and provisions were transported.[6]

So engrossed were the Russians in planning a splendid reception for the Japanese, that it never dawned upon them with how much trepidation the latter were anticipating the meeting. On the 13th, Kawaji had called on Tsutsui and voiced his misgivings: "If we go aboard ship, the Russians may press upon us saying rough things. Perhaps they will make us determine Japan's boundaries."[7] Matsudaira Mino-no-kami, who was also at Tsutsui's, agreed as to the existence of such a threat. The Russians dried their sails daily and were liable to take off without notice. Their ships were fast, and the Japanese shore batteries would not have time to stop them. Why not include, therefore, among the retinue of the plenipotentiaries nineteen of his retainers "who do not care about dying" and add to the boats that accompany them a powder-laden *yakibune*?[8] Should the Russians start to sail away with the plenipotentiaries aboard, these men could set fire to the boat and then board the frigate, swords drawn.[9]

After Matsudaira left, Kawaji told Tsutsui that the proposal had been reasonable. And yet, gratifying though it might be for the plenipotentiaries to know that their capture would be avenged by the burning of the Russian man-of-war, this would mean that a great country would be made the enemy of their government. The plan must thus not be sanctioned. "Truly I, Saemon-no-jo, having been charged with this duty, think of life as but one day," Kawaji added. "I would gladly sacrifice my life in any way, were it for the benefit of my country." But under the prevailing circumstances, he believed, he could best serve his nation, in case of capture by the Russians, by proceeding to Russia and there talking to the "king."[10]

Much discussion followed. Nakamura Tameya pointed to the importance of Kawaji and Tsutsui and asked that he be sent to Russia in their stead, but Kawaji protested that this was contrary to his samurai spirit, while Tsutsui argued that he was so old that he would not be throwing away his life. Tsutsui wished to go, but Kawaji insisted: "I, Saemon-no-jo, will go." Even Koga, the Confucian scholar, joined in: "Everybody says such things. Shall I only remain? No, never! I, Kinichiro, will go."[11]

When Kawaji questioned Moriyama later in the day, the latter assured him that there was no cause for alarm. "If I have failed to see any trouble," he exclaimed, "and trouble should arise, I, Einosuke, shall be the first to jump the ambassador in recompense. I shall be the first of the soldiers."[12]

Kawaji returned home very late. In his diary he jotted down: "These days we do not go to bed before about midnight."[13]

The Japanese did not give an answer to the two questions Putiatin had sent ashore that day.[14] They announced instead that a reply to the Russian letter had been received from the *Roju* and that perusal of this document might provide the desired information. There was little the Russians could do but wait.[15]

Early the next morning (January 14), Matsudaira called on Kawaji. The latter received him in his own room and personally served *noshi*.[16] He politely declined the services of Matsudaira's retainers, but noted that, in the event of a mishap, Matsudaira must act in accordance with governmental orders and may even have to destroy the Russian vessels. Kawaji would not object. After much flattery, Matsudaira left. By nightfall, a letter in Matsudaira's handwriting reached Kawaji. He wrote that throughout the day he had observed the movements of the Russian vessels through a telescope. They had approached the shore by some twenty *cho*.[17] Their crews were busy cleaning the ships, and all indications were that the Russians really planned to invite the officials aboard. Matsudaira concluded that he had taken many retainers to a detached mansion near the Russian ships. From there they could secretly guard the Japanese vessels.

Kawaji could thus visit the Russians without worry. Kawaji sent thanks for Matsudaira's thoughtfulness. In his diary he noted: "Such troubling with kindness for us on the part of a 540,000 *koku* daimyo[18] must be due to the glorious influence of *Tosho-gu* [Tokugawa Ieyasu]."[19]

By the day of the meeting (January 15, 1854),[20] the frigate had taken on a festive appearance. The meticulously scrubbed deck seemed white as linen; "it was as clean as after a rainstorm."[21] The copper glowed brightly in the sun. The Russians wore full dress. On the poop deck, a tent had been constructed out of signal flags. In it, carpets were folded into seats for the plenipotentiaries, while chairs were set up for their retinue. A similar arrangement was made in the admiral's cabin, except that here tables were also provided: one for the plenipotentiaries, one for the admiral and three officers, and one for the Japanese master of ceremonies. Chairs had been prepared for the interpreters, but the latter were to ignore them and lie on the floor.[22]

At about 11:00 A.M., officials arrived with gifts from the plenipotentiaries to the admiral.[23] There were a lacquer writing box with a butterfly decoration, sent by Tsutsui, an *inro* (tobacco box, medicine case, pillbox, or seal case) with a picture of Mt. Fuji, contributed by Kawaji, pictures from Arao, painted candles from Koga, *netsuke* (a little carving worn above the girdle to hold the *inro* in place), *sakazuki* (sake cups), and other presents.[24] "Such lacquer things exist nowhere [else]," commented Goncharov.[25] But the most important and outstanding gift was a magnificent sword presented by Kawaji. Not only was it expensive and beautiful, but, as the plenipotentiaries later on emphasized more than once, "a gesture of friendship" and "an expression of Japan's relation to Russia."[26] Reported Putiatin: "The plenipotentiaries explained that the presentation of a sword was an expression of considerable goodwill, and implied that it was proof of the high regard with which the Japanese government beheld the Russian one."[27]

In the early afternoon, a whole flotilla of boats left shore. Some fifty or sixty sampans surrounded two large curtain-covered, coffin-like double-decked barges.[28] The plenipotentiaries travelled on the one belonging to Hosokawa Etchu-no-kami. Clad in ceremonial dress bearing the Tokugawa crest, they sat on the upper deck behind a red crepe de Chine curtain. Tsutsui's and Kawaji's weapons, as well as those of Arao and Koga and of Hosokawa's sailors, appeared "magnificent indeed." The second barge, belonging to the Nagasaki *bugyo* office, displayed the Tokugawa family crest on a red curtain. "The drums resounded. The rowers rhythmically chanted 'rokyoshi.' It was cheerful."[29]

When the Japanese boats approached the Russian vessels, they were greeted by music.[30] "The rhythm and the sound were very heavy and not clear," wrote Koga; "it was the music of barbarians. I cannot endure hearing it."[31] Gun salutes were fired, notwithstanding the recent Japanese protest. A ladder was let down, and junior officers descended to meet the plenipotentiaries. "The Russians were very happy to have us strangers come," noted Kawaji.[32] Pos'et and Goncharov met the officials as they came up; Putiatin, at the door of the cabin. The Japanese were shown about the frigate. The admiral himself pointed out items of interest. Goncharov was surprised to see that the aged Tsutsui had come also, but the old man displayed "amazing vigour," walked along deck, descended to the lowest part of the vessel, the arsenal, and showed no signs of tiredness.[33] The Russian senior officers and interpreters would take Tsutsui's arm and help him downstairs. "They treated us as kindly as if they had put the shoes before us," recalled Kawaji.[34]

The Japanese carefully inspected the vessel. "It makes a man's hair stand up," confessed Koga.[35] Kawaji was surprised to see that cannon balls were stacked up like *kuri ishi* (round stones for walls). "And they walk on them. It is very strange to see."[36] "The passages were dark," wrote Koga, "and we bumped into each other, unable to distinguish between foe and friend. Facing these strange things, we did not have time to ask what they were used for, what they were called, and of what they were made. The smell of fish came to [my] nose. It was difficult to breathe. [I wished] to be happy by only seeing heaven and sun."[37]

The plenipotentiaries were ushered into the admiral's cabin. There, seats had been prepared for them by covering a wide and low divan with colorful English carpets.[38] "It is softer than a *futon* [a Japanese mattress or blanket]."[39] Kawaji noted that the books in the cabin were arranged "especially nicely." "There are mirrors [*sic*] on the left and right," added he in his diary, "and these mirrors themselves are the portraits of the emperor, prince, and younger boy.... As for the mirror on which the portrait was, when a person stands in front of this mirror, he is reflected and apparently stays in such manner on the mirror without being extinguished.... They make them by medicine. It is too long to explain and I shall not write about it here."[40]

Having sat in the cabin for a while, the Japanese went up to the tent on deck. "The plenipotentiaries conducted themselves like refined persons who have lived a lifetime in society," Goncharov observed with amazement. "Everything must amaze them, as they have never seen a European vessel, [its] furniture and decoration. With every step there was something new for them. They confessed to that the next day, but on this occasion betrayed neither surprise nor enthusiasm through gestures or glances. They heard the music also for the first time, and only one of them swayed his head in measure as melomaniacs do in our country [when] sitting in the opera."[41]

Tea was served. Although, as already mentioned, the Japanese were not favorably impressed by its "medicine-like" taste, they praised the sugar that went with it. The lumps, or "snow white balls," were of "excellent quality." "I have not come across anything better," noted Koga.[42]

Meanwhile, the crew had been piped on deck and was put through the manual-of-arms a number of times and marched up and down. An alarm was sounded, and everyone rushed to his battle station. Very "effective." Having watched gun practice, the plenipotentiaries thanked the admiral and asked him to convey their thanks to the sailors. "*Spasibo rebiata* [Thank you, boys]!" shouted Putiatin. "*Rady starat'sia* [Glad to exert ourselves]!" answered four hundred voices. "Again [it produced] effect," noted Goncharov.[43] Even Koga conceded that their "steps [were] in rhythm, very orderly, without fault."[44] But although Kawaji agreed that "the appearance of their replying [to orders] was very skillful," he felt that the cannoneers were "simple" and "foolish."[45]

The Russians showed the Japanese "something like a curtain" on which Russian and Japanese emblems had been painted like joined crests, and said: "This curtain was made because Russia considers Japan so friendly."[46] Commented Kawaji: "It is the same as when an Edo prostitute falsely flatters a *kimban* person."[47]

As mentioned above, tables had been set for the plenipotentiaries and the master of ceremonies in the admiral's cabin. In the dining room, arrangements had been made to entertain eleven of their followers, and in the wardroom, ten more. The Japanese guard received refreshments on the gun deck.

Although the plenipotentiaries had requested a European-style dinner, "it was impossible to make them eat with forks and knives," and chopsticks had been prepared.[48] But they were of different length, each guest being served a long one and a short one so that Arao, for example, had to exchange one of his with Koga to be able to eat properly.[49] Rice was served instead of bread; teacups took the place of soup plates.

In the dining room, where the retinue ate, plates with preserves and pastry had been set on the table. The guests felt not unnaturally that food was there to be eaten, and consumed all the pastry and candy before soup was served. Dishes with fish, fowl, and meat were brought out. The Japanese ate everything with great interest, asking many questions. They particularly enjoyed lamb pilaw and ham.[50] "The fish was not cooked properly," criticized Koga, "it was bitter.... Wishing to please [the Russians had stated that they had prepared fish as the Japanese are known to be fond of it] ... to displease instead."[51] Kawaji wrote that there was oil in the salad "so that it stays in the stomach long." "So I think they use vinegar to help it," he added reflectively.[52]

"Tablecloths, napkins, salt-boxes — everything attracted their attention."[53] Recorded Kawaji: "They gave each of us something like a white *furoshiki* with a plant pattern of the same color. [We] were told that it is spread on one's lap in case food should fall down. (We may wipe hand and mouth also; I think perhaps we can wipe the nose.)"[54] Russian dishes were made of porcelain. "They treat glass more roughly than we treat chinaware in Japan," commented he.[55]

But the plenipotentiaries quickly adapted themselves to their new surroundings. "They had so observed our order," noted Goncharov, "that one could hardly notice [any] difference between them and Europeans. Only one of them, Kawaji, momentarily stuck to Japanese custom. When some liquid dessert was served, he tasted it, took out a small piece of paper, and put everything that remained on the plate into it, folded it up, and hid it in his kimono. 'Don't think that I am taking this for some beauty,' remarked Kawaji, 'no, this is for my subordinates.' "[56]

The conversation turned to women, whereupon "the Japanese became somewhat cynical."[57]

Pos'et and Goncharov kept getting up from the table, now to fill the glasses of the plenipotentiaries with champagne, now to show them how to eat some dish or to explain how it was prepared. "They were embarrassed by our politeness and did not know how to thank [us]."[58] Testified Kawaji: "They are so skillful in serving us, it is wonderful."[59]

The Japanese drank in moderation. They tasted the wine "with great curiosity," sipping a little at a time. Only Koga finished his wineglass; he, in fact, drank some four glasses full. He did full justice to the dinner.[60] But that is not surprising, for Koga was quite a *bon vivant*. As he confided to his diary: "Poetry, wine, and wandering around are also official business."[61]

Hints the Russians dropped in regard to the impending negotiations fell upon deaf ears. The plenipotentiaries stated that they were enjoying the party so much they had forgotten all about business.[62]

The Russians served mulled wine as the Japanese had served heated sake and, also in imitation, put a beautiful box of colorful candies before each of the plenipotentiaries. After the dinner, the hosts showed them colored engravings of Russian troops and of Moscow and St. Petersburg, as well as English pictures of female heads, fruits, and flowers. Some of these were given to the Japanese as gifts.[63]

"Finally, toward dusk this whole invasion of strangers disappeared from us with the request to visit them."[64] The Russian officers drew their swords, the drums rolled, and the band began to play. The sailors lined up on the mast crossbars "without any space between [them]." Noted Kawaji: "It is truly a matter of monkeys."[65]

The plenipotentiaries returned to the Western Government Office to receive the vermillion seal.[66] They congratulated each other that nothing untoward had happened.[67]

In his report Putiatin wrote, later on, that Japanese politeness, cordiality, and sincerity led him to conclude "that the Japanese had decided to give in to time and circumstances, having convinced themselves of the impossibility of resisting the ascendancy of the foreigners, and apparently only desired to postpone the time of this *rapprochement*."[68] The plenipotentiaries had accepted his invitation to visit the frigate "with apparent pleasure." "Judging from the fact that the governor had in no way dared to return my call, this visit of a foreign vessel by important dignitaries must lead to very remarkable and, as much as is known from descriptions, unprecedented events, at least in modern times."[69]

5

Getting Down to Business

On the morning of January 16, 1854, Japanese interpreters visited the *Pallada* to learn how many Russians were coming ashore for the meeting. When they heard that only a few planned to do so, they asked that more — at least all senior officers — be invited, since there would be a formal reception followed by a big dinner. And, as Goncharov commented, "How can one not go to a big dinner?"[1]

The Russians were festively received at the Western Government Office. Tsutsui and Kawaji announced that they had a state paper from the Supreme Council for transmission. They pointed at a white ironbound chest and a silk-covered box with tassels. "Who will receive the letter?" Goshkevich stepped forward. The master of ceremonies (Nakamura) opened the box and handed it to him. Holding it with difficulty, Goshkevich carried it to the lounge, while Japanese attendants followed with the big chest. The Russian officers watched with great curiosity as the chest was opened. In it was another chest, somewhat smaller, then a third one, and a fourth one, each one a little smaller. And into the fourth one fitted the silken box, the fifth in number. In it was a sixth and last box of white lacquered wood with a delicate finish and silver mounted edges. The official answer from the *Roju* to the letter from the Russian government lay in this box. Written on thick gilded paper, the document had been wrapped in several silken *furoshiki*. "What clever scoundrels!" growled Goncharov.[2]

Nakamura announced that the Shogun had sent gifts for the Russian ambassador and asked that each item be touched with both hands to indicate acceptance. The Russians were disappointed. The presents consisted primarily of silk and cotton wool.[3] Wrote Goncharov: "The material is of two colors, white and red, with web pattern, but it is so simple that in a good home one cannot make window drapes out of it."[4] But the Japanese also sent some fine porcelain cups and, for the crew, one hundred bags of rice and one thousand boxes of soy sauce (each box containing six earthen containers, the size of a bottle) and twenty pigs.[5] The admiral reciprocated with gifts for the Shogun. There were pieces of rich, golden brocade, large mirrors, bronze table clocks, flower vases, and carpets.[6]

During the festive dinner, a great variety of dishes was served. "I was particularly reconciled with this cookery by the absence of all vegetable oil," wrote Goncharov. "Their portions are so small," continued he, "that their dinner will not make a snack for a man with a good appetite.... Golovnin was right when he said that the sailors who were in captivity with him [1811-1813] received little to eat. According to their [standards] the Japanese gave enough, but for them it was [too] little."[7]

At dusk, the Russians returned to the frigate. Officials followed aboard to inquire whether they were satisfied and to bring their gifts. "*Kakoe nakazanie s etimi podarkami* [What punishment (we receive) with these presents]!" complained Goncharov. "To throw the boxes into the water is awkward, the Japanese will see them and will say that we spurn their gifts; to save them there is no room." There were boxes for fish, boxes for candy, boxes for sweetbread — "samples of patience and at the same time of paltriness." The gifts from the Shogun had also been brought aboard and piled up on deck. "One cannot get through anywhere," grumbled Goncharov.[8]

When the Russians sat down to study the long-awaited state paper, they found that they could not decipher it. They communicated, therefore, with the Japanese (January 17). As Koga testified: "The barbarian envoy says that the state letter is difficult to read. He requests that we add a Dutch translation. Yet, our interpreters also do not understand *kambun* [Chinese, in which official Japanese correspondence was written], and say that without a Japanese translation they cannot render it into Dutch. Consequently, I drafted a Japanese translation."[9] By evening, the Dutch version was ready. As a result of this incident, it was decided that in the future each note must be sent simultaneously in Japanese, Chinese, and Dutch.[10]

On January 18, 1854, the negotiations finally began. From now on, the Russians visited Nagasaki almost daily without further ceremony on either side.[11] The admiral would go ashore accompanied only by Pos'et, Goshkevich, Goncharov, and one or two other officers.[12] Japanese officials called for them each time, Russian requests not to do so to the contrary. "But they still want to show the people that foreigners cannot go ashore other than under their escort," observed Goncharov. There was little the Russians could do about it. They would tell the Japanese to leave, but the latter would only row away some distance and stop and wait for the Russian boats.[13]

Determined to sit on chairs during the conferences, the Russians had to bring their own chairs each time they went ashore. Putiatin wished to leave them in the governor's building, but the latter did not permit it. They might be lost in a fire or damaged by rats — it was just too great a responsibility. Putiatin assured him that the Russians would not sue him for recovery, that they had other chairs, but to no avail. The governor did offer, however, to send Japanese boats after them so that the Russians would not have to carry them back and forth themselves. And so it was done.[14]

A peaceful spirit predominated throughout most of the negotiations. Instances of friction were more conspicuous by their rarity than their intensity. Only once was there a serious verbal clash — and that of a temporary and inconsequential nature. Putiatin's interpretation of one of the statements in the *Rōjū's* reply had differed from that of Kawaji and Tsutsui. When the plenipotentiaries accused him of not understanding the whole letter, he flared up: "We do understand your letter, but the meaning is not clear. Such superficial sentences! How can our government respect [your government]?" "You two have come from afar in the east," he fumed. "What are you [supposed to] do? We cannot understand it." Tsutsui and Kawaji replied that their government had feared that the Russians might misunderstand the letter and therefore had sent them to clarify it. "If it had been twenty years ago," they added, "we would have rebuffed [you] and not received [you]."[15] Wrote Koga: "The [Russian] attitude was very stubborn. Below my belt, the voice of [my] sword[16] sang that matters relating to the joy and sorrow of the [Japanese] people cannot be solved satisfactorily. I felt depressed."[17]

"The barbarian envoy," Koga recorded, "still continued to impose on [us] by threats and said: 'Nagasaki harbor is your nation's important trading center. It is carefully defended, but having looked it over today, [we find] the defenses remiss. Were two ships to come and attack them, they would be shattered to powder.'"[18] "Even though we are saying this," Putiatin was quoted to have continued, "we really have no bad intentions because we are neighbors. We only hope that your honorable country's military might will exceed [that] of all [other] countries. If you need big guns and steamers we shall deliver them immediately."[19]

The setting of time and date of meetings was left to the Russians. As the plenipotentiaries pointed out: "We have come here because of you. We have no other business."[20] Once (January 22, 1854), Putiatin scheduled a conference for three days later (January 25), but to his surprise the Japanese asked to have it sooner (January 24).[21] Why? — Goncharov claims that Kawaji wanted to get back to his wife in Edo, and, therefore, pushed the negotiations. "More than once he said: '[My] body is here, but [my] soul in Edo.'"[22] Koga, on the other hand, states: "We tried to rush the time, not wishing them to accomplish [their mission]."[23]

As will be seen in Chapter X, negotiations were focussed on issues concerning Japan's northern possessions, the opening of Japanese ports as havens of refuge and coaling stations, and, last but not least, commerce.

Repeatedly, the admiral tried to demonstrate to the Japanese that they needlessly feared trade, "that trade can only diffuse abundance among the people, and that no nation had fallen into decay because of trade, but on the contrary had become richer."[24] The Japanese lacked "the first domestic necessities." Paper windows resulted in dark and cold rooms. The Russians could bring them glass, could teach them also how to make it. There was much fish off Kamchatka and other Russian possessions near Japan. But Russians lacked salt, which was obtainable in Japan. "Why use all your hands for the cultivation of rice?" argued Putiatin. "Utilize them to mine ore and let rice be brought to you from the Sunda Isles. You will be richer."[25] The Japanese did not comment, but when the admiral broached the subject again on another occasion and inquired why they took such pains to delay commercial relations with foreigners, Kawaji replied: "Trade in our place is new. It has not yet matured; one must deliberate how to trade, where and with what. . . . You give a maiden into marriage when she grows up; our trade has not yet grown up."[26] But Putiatin did not desist. The letter from the *Roju* had stated that "[one] cannot take old customs to regulate present affairs." "If you decide to discard the old customs," he remonstrated, "then to open the ports for trade is easy."[27]

On January 24, the weather was terrible. "A stormy wind howled since evening and rain poured as from a bucket." The Japanese did not expect the Russians to come; they did not call for them nor wait for them on shore. But the Russians put on raincoats, took their umbrellas, and went anyway.[28] When the Japanese inquired whether they had had trouble getting ashore in such stormy weather, the admiral replied: "The wind helped; the boat travelled very fast." Though Koga realized that "it was assuredly mockery" and that the Russians had been forced to use three additional oars, he admitted that Japanese boats could not have done it. That day no Japanese boats went out.[29] Wrote Goncharov patronizingly: "The Japanese opened their mouths [with surprise] when they saw us. They sat in their corners like flies during bad weather."[30] The boots of the Russians were covered with mud. As the mariners did not remove them before entering the Japanese building, they soiled the floor mats. "How impolite of the barbarians," noted the Confucian scholar.[31]

The negotiations began to drag. By January 26, Koga confided to his diary: "It seems that wide experience and full knowledge have been completely exhausted, and that all discussion has also been drained...."[32]

Finally, the plenipotentiaries announced that they must return to Edo. The Russian demands could not be met for the present. The new Shogun (Tokugawa Iesada) was very young and would have to show the people his respect for the old laws before starting to break them. His appanage lords must be called together for counsel. All this would take time, much time.[33] Russian objections were of no avail.

On February 1, the plenipotentiaries paid their last visit aboard the frigate *Pallada*. A conversation ensued that bears repeating:

Putiatin: "Yesterday you gave me a Chinese translation of your paper, and I have compared it with the Dutch translation. It states that Russia differs from other countries and that the relationship is different. We certify that there is no error in this."

Kawaji: "Your country is a neighboring country with boundaries adjacent [to ours]. It therefore differs from other countries and deserves special consideration."

Putiatin: "We desire then, that, excluding China and Holland,[34] if and when communication and trade be requested by countries other than China and Holland, [you] notify Russia."

Kawaji: *"Should communication and trade be permitted to foreign countries, it will of course be permitted to Russia."*[35]

Putiatin: "I want that if this permission to trade [will] be given, as [mentioned] before, all the points of agreement permitted to the foreigners [will] be permitted also to Russia."

Kawaji: *"If trade will be permitted, the things permitted to for-*
           eigners will also be permitted to Russia. We shall make
           no difficulties."

Putiatin: "As I must report in writing the two items you have just
           mentioned, could you please transmit them in an answer
           letter."

Kawaji: "I have some question as to what the ambassador is say-
           ing, because I do not know what our government is think-
           ing. What I do know is that *even when in the future we*
           open amicable relations, because your country is a great
           country with boundaries adjacent to ours, we consider you
           as a defense against other countries. But from what you
           have just said, it would seem that that purport has not
           been expressed."[36]

Putiatin: "Although your doubt is natural, *in the event that people*
           from other countries cause violent disturbances, we are
           prepared to give you any assistance. But I do not know
           yet how our government will treat your government, and
           therefore I wish to send to my government your replies
           to the two clauses."[37]

But Koga remained suspicious: "You can never tell what is in their mind," he jotted down.[38]

Before dinner, the plenipotentiaries once more witnessed gun drill.[39] The roaring of the cannons, though only percussion caps were used, startled the Japanese. "It was clear," wrote Goncharov, "that this pleasure did not fully delight our guests. The old man Tsutsui became ill with fright."[40]

The seating arrangement during dinner was European: the Japanese plenipotentiaries, the master of ceremonies, and the Russian senior officers all ate at the same table. Nishi and Moriyama, however, still lay on the floor at the feet of the two elder officials. The food was served Russian style. Goncharov assisted Kawaji; Pos'et, Tsutsui. Kawaji ate with discrimination and asked questions about every dish. The Japanese drank more and "with greater pleasure" than the first time. They had learned to toast to one's health. As Kawaji recorded: "If it were in Japan we would say '*ippai shinjo*' [drink sake, cup by cup], but there they drink, saying to a person 'to [your] health,' and drink bringing the glasses together." The Japanese persistently refilled the glasses of their hosts as well as their own. Wrote Goncharov: "We drank a little at a time, but they goodnaturedly emptied the wine glass each time."[41]

Interested in Kawaji's paper-covered fan, Goncharov took it out of his hand and examined it. When he wanted to return it, Kawaji begged him to keep it "in remembrance." Goncharov, thereupon, unfastened the gold chain from his watch and gave it to Kawaji. The latter listened to the translation of Goncharov's compliment and replied that he accepted the gift. Then he got up from the table and whispered something to Moriyama. Kawaji and Tsutsui had prepared two boxes of pipes each for Pos'et and Goncharov. Now that Kawaji had accepted the gold chain, he deemed the presents inadequate. Moriyama made the ordered changes, and as a result Pos'et received all four boxes, while on the following day three pieces of silk and four tobacco pipes were sent to Goncharov.[42]

To Tsutsui, Goncharov gave a gilded silver spoon with black enamel decoration and expressed the wish that he would get accustomed to eating with it and would teach his children "in the hope of dining more often with the Russians." Tsutsui sent Goncharov two small wooden boxes, one lacquered and inlaid with mother-of-pearl, the other covered with sharkskin. Lesser gifts were exchanged with Arao and Nakamura.[43]

Farewell presents for the admiral included beautiful porcelain vases and cups, exquisite lacquer ware, tables, cupboards, *étagères*, screens, dolls, a dagger, and others. The Japanese also sent soy sauce, one official alone sending fifteen vats full. "That is simply a punishment," groaned Goncharov. Then there were sake, dried fish, caviar, and greens.

After dinner, Putiatin gave Kawaji a gold watch "for the gold chain" he had just received. (Kawaji had an awkward old silver watch, which he had shown the Russians time and again.) Tsutsui also received a gold watch, somewhat smaller in size. In addition, both received pieces of cloth.[44]

Lantern slides were shown to the enjoyment of the Japanese. "[They are] bigger than ours," noted Koga. "When you change, you do not have to stop."[45] Later on, model trains, operated on alcohol, were displayed on a large table. They "went around and around." "Wonderful to look at," commented Koga.[46]

At eight o'clock, the Japanese left the frigate. They had not rowed away far, when suddenly the whole vessel and her surroundings were illuminated by "the phantastic redness of Bengal lights."[47] As Goncharov wrote: *Eto proizvelo effekt* [this produced an effect]."[48] Two days later (February 3), Putiatin received an important note from the plenipotentiaries. "Should our country finally permit trade," they promised, "it will be first to your country."[49] Priority of treatment had thus been promised to Russia!

There would have been little sense for the Russians to remain in Nagasaki upon the departure of the plenipotentiaries, particularly since it was obvious that the Japanese were going to take their time studying the issues posed by Russia. The squadron was therefore readied for departure and, on February 4, the farewell visit of the Japanese was repaid.

Expressions of friendship were exchanged. Peace was made even with the governors. Putiatin told them that, although their relationship had not been wholly satisfactory as regards the assignment of a place on shore, he was aware of the fact that they were only following orders. He thus had nothing personal against them, on the contrary thanked them for the various favors they had done. But he did want them to pass on to their superiors that, if Japan intended to enter upon any relations with foreigners, it was high time for them to think about revoking all these restrictions which to every honorable country will appear insulting.[50]

The governors were each sent a piece of cloth and reciprocated with gifts of their own. "So many boxes were brought," noted Goncharov, "that we got tired of even wondering what was in them."[51]

The dinner was fully enjoyed by the Russians. Now Nakamura moved about as Goncharov and Pos'et had done and kept the bowls and cups of the guests filled.[52] Wrote Koga: "Barbarians intoxicated, faces very red, two old men [Tsutsui and Kawaji] also the same."[53] After dinner, more gifts were presented to the Russian officers, this time directly from the Shogun. They consisted of various materials and of thin, almost transparent, porcelain cups.

Kawaji tried to learn when and whereto the Russians were leaving.[54] He still feared lest they sail to Edo and nullify all his pains. But Putiatin, who had decided that Aniwa Bay (Southern Sakhalin) would make a safer place than Nagasaki for resuming his negotiations, as the outbreak of war with England and France seemed imminent, suspected that disclosure of his plan might lead to new arguments and, therefore, dodged all queries until he weighed anchor; and only then, at the last minute, sent word to the plenipotentiaries to be in Aniwa Bay in spring.[55]

On February 5, 1854, the *Pallada, Olivutsa,* and *Kniaz' Menshikov* went out to sea. The schooner *Vostok* had left somewhat earlier for Shanghai to gather information about developments in Europe and China. She was to rejoin the squadron at the Liu Ch'iu Islands.[56]

When Koga climbed up to Anzen Temple and looked at the sea, the Russian vessels had disappeared.[57]

On February 15, Koga started back. On March 20, Tsutsui and Kawaji, who had had a head start, arrived in Edo. (Arao and several others had been ordered to stay behind to meet any foreign vessels that might arrive.) The following day, Koga returned also. He went to a friend's house near the seashore. He looked at the ocean and there, amidst water and smoke, faintly discerned nine "barbarian" (American) vessels a mile or so from shore. "I could not help shivering," confided he to his diary. And well he might have been disturbed. In ten days, Japan was to sign a treaty of friendship with the United States as a result of this show of force.

On March 26, 1854, Tsutsui, Kawaji and Koga were received by the *Taikun*[58] in audience and thanked for their labors. On the 28th and 29th, all Japanese who had been on the journey received special compensations.[59]

6

To the Shores of Siberia and Back

THE TIME OF THE YEAR PROHIBITED PASSAGE TO THE RUSSIAN possessions in the north. The squadron was in need of replenishing supplies, but this could not be done on the desert shores of the Straits of Tartary and the Sea of Okhotsk. Putiatin decided, therefore, to utilize the remaining two months before spring, at which time he was to go to Aniwa Bay, to proceed to Manila, to which Russian letters of credit had also been addressed.[1] The wind was favorable, the weather quiet. There was no necessity for the ships to travel as a unit. The admiral thus released them, ordering them to sail independently to the Liu Ch'iu Islands, rendezvous of the expedition.[2]

On February 13, 1854, the three vessels had anchored at their destination. Four days later, they were joined by the *Vostok* with news from Europe.[3]

At Naha (Nawa) on Great Liu Ch'iu (Okinawa) Island, the Russians met several members of Commodore Perry's expedition, which had briefly stopped at this place earlier in the month en route from China to Japan.[4] An American master's mate put before the admiral a document that stated that the Liu Ch'iu Islands were "entering the possession of the United States in reclamation for some demands that had not been satisfied by the Japanese government under whose protection these islands stand, paying tribute to her."[5]

Although the native official who boarded the frigate soon afterwards

[68]

denied Japan's influence over the islands and pointed out that tribute was paid to China, a local Protestant missionary confirmed that the whole island group was dependent on the daimyo of Satsuma.[6]

The Russians had had no opportunity to wander about in Japan, hence strolled with pleasure through the colorful dales of Great Liu Ch'iu Island. Putiatin bestowed on the native officials various gifts, as well as a document in which he requested that hospitality be extended to all Russian vessels that might come to Naha, and that trade, if needed, be not denied to them. But the governor evaded giving a clear-cut answer; a fact which, as Putiatin reported, "must be attributed, in the opinion of the missionary, to the presence of numerous Japanese spies on the island and in the empire."[7]

On February 21, 1854, the *Pallada, Olivutsa,* and *Kniaz' Menshikov* weighed anchor. A week later (February 28), they reached Manila. The schooner *Vostok* had left earlier in order to survey an island (Borodin) discovered by *Leitenant* Ponafidin. She rejoined the squadron (March 7), mission accomplished.

The French steamer *Colbert* lay in the harbor. Her captain paid his respects to the admiral. Learning of the imminence of a break with England and France, and gathering from the cold reception extended him by the new governor-general of the Philippine Islands — who had just arrived from Spain — that he was not welcome, Putiatin cut short his stay. Laden with fresh supplies, the squadron started back (March 11, 1854).[8] Additional fresh greens were taken on at Bataan.

Ever since the *Pallada* had weathered a severe storm in the China Sea, her foremast and main sails had shown signs of questionable reliability. She was in no condition to proceed further north, as strong winds could be expected in that region. Putiatin decided, therefore, to lead the *Pallada* and *Olivutsa* back south to Camiguin Island (Babuyan Islands), reputedly a suitable anchorage for repairs, while sending the *Kniaz' Menshikov* and *Vostok* ahead to Hamilton Island, via Shanghai and Liu Ch'iu Islands respectively.[9]

The frigate was repaired according to plan. On April 2, 1854, she set sail for Hamilton Island. Slowed down by calms and then unfavorable winds, she did not arrive there until April 14.

Meanwhile, the corvet *Olivutsa* had been sent to Petropavlovsk to assist in the defense of Kamchatka. The schooner *Vostok*, which had visited the Liu Ch'iu Islands in quest of news about the activities of the American squadron, awaited the frigate at Hamilton. The transport *Kniaz' Menshikov* arrived three days later. Papers and letters that she brought from Shanghai confirmed the break with England and France.[10]

The three vessels departed for Nagasaki, where they arrived less than twenty-four hours later (April 18, 1854).[11] The admiral asked the governor to transmit to the plenipotentiaries a letter in which he restated his intention of meeting with them at Aniwa. Supplies replenished, the squadron departed (April 26, 1854).[12]

The transport sailed directly to the harbor that had been selected as rendezvous for the expedition and delivered the supplies for safekeeping on shore. The schooner, on the other hand, surveyed Goto Retto (Goto Islands), and then hastened to Shanghai in time for the arrival of mail from Europe. The captain did not steer the *Vostok* into the harbor, but cautiously anchored in one of the branches of the Yangtze River, proceeding from there to Shanghai in a Chinese boat. Having received mail and diplomatic papers from the American consul[13] and having inquired about the latest developments in Russian-Anglo-French relations, he returned to the schooner and sailed to the Straits of Tartary.[14]

The frigate first went to Korea. Fearing to encounter ice in the north, Putiatin had decided to take advantage of the month that remained until spring to survey the eastern shore of that country and to fill in the "very incorrect" maps of that region. The survey did find "considerable errors" on the map of Captain Krusenstern's atlas,[15] as well as on that of the English admiralty ("The Peninsula of Korea"), the best map then available. In the extensive Broughton Bay, Putiatin discovered a new port and named it after the late Admiral Lazarev.[16]

The harmonious intercourse between members of the expedition and local inhabitants was marred by an "unpleasant" incident. As a result of "some misunderstanding," a mob of "Korean rabble" attacked one of the cutters that had landed at a little Korean settlement in Lazarev Bay and showered its crew with stones and pieces of lead. The sailors replied with rifle fire, wounding several Koreans.[17] The following day, Putiatin went ashore with an armed landing party and demanded an apology from the village elders. These "humbly asked for forgiveness," explaining that "worthless scamps" had, without cause and without knowledge on their part, incited the mob to this hostile action. To counterbalance possible misrepresentation of this incident by local officials, Putiatin left at another village for delivery to the Korean capital a document in Chinese with his version of the occurrence.[18]

With the above exception, relations were peaceful. "Although the Koreans," wrote the admiral, "most probably are subject to the same restrictions, regarding dealing with foreigners as all other Far Eastern nations, since foreigners had never appeared in the places that we visited, insufficient measures had been taken by the government to prevent our intercourse with the people. As a result of this negligence, Koreans freely visited the frigate and did not obstruct our walks along shore. . . ."[19]

Putiatin sent an official paper to the Korean government proposing the establishment of trade with Russian subjects. He promised to call for an answer in summer. Political events later on were to prevent this, "but I suppose," reported he to the admiralty, "that it would be useful to renew the negotiations at the first opportunity."[20]

Thick fogs that enveloped the frigate in May forced the discontinuance of the survey in Pos'et Bay (latitude 42°31′ N). Maneuvering out, the frigate scraped against rocks off the deepish shore. She incurred no serious damage, although the daily inflow of water increased temporarily. Continuing north through unending fog, the frigate safely reached one of the bays along the eastern shore of Siberia (June 3, 1854), where the transport *Kniaz' Menshikov* already lay at anchor. Several days before, the frigate had chanced upon the *Vostok*. The squadron had thus been reunited.[21]

The commander of the schooner brought unofficial tidings of the outbreak of the Crimean War as well as orders from the Russian government to take the vessels of the expedition to De Kastri Bay and there await further instructions from Lieutenant General Murav'ev, governor-general of Eastern Siberia. The admiral sent the *Vostok* to De Kastri Bay to receive and bring back Murav'ev's orders. But the governor-general came in person to see Putiatin (July 4, 1854). He instructed the frigate to sail into the Amur River, and there seek shelter from ice and foe. The transport was released to the local authorities of the Russo-American Company, while the schooner was given some other assignment by Murav'ev.[22]

From July on, Putiatin's undivided attention and efforts were devoted to the task of taking the *Pallada* to the Amur. Though not without difficulties, the frigate, with full load, penetrated to Cape Lazarev, some forty miles from the mouth of the river. But from there on, the little-known estuary presented obstacles that later on were to prove insurmountable "in spite of the untiring effort of officers and crew."[23]

At Cape Lazarev, the frigate was unloaded, while estuary and fairway were further examined. Operations were retarded by strong winds and currents. Meanwhile, Putiatin was informed that the frigate *Diana* had arrived in De Kastri Bay.[24] He hastened there on a gig. Three days later, he reurned aboard the *Diana*.[25] On August 16, he officially transferred to this new frigate. He took with him all the officers, except Unkovskii, and many sailors who had served on the *Pallada*. Total complement of the *Diana*: 484 men. The *Pallada* retained only a skeleton crew. The remainder of the crews was sent to Nikolaevsk.

Goncharov took advantage of this occasion to leave the expedition. As already noted, the Crimean War had brought about a change in the assignment of the vessels. The discussions with Japan were pushed into the background. Although Putiatin planned to return to Japan

on the new frigate to make arrangements for the resumption of negotiations at a later date, no one could foretell what measures the war
might necessitate. The *Diana* might have to stay at the shores of
Russia, she might have to go out to sea in search of enemy ships, or
else might have to seek refuge in some neutral harbor, such as San
Francisco. Faced with such uncertain prospects, his wanderlust stilled
by two years at sea, Goncharov wanted to get back to his circle of
friends at home. Although he had been assigned as secretary to the
admiral for the duration of the expedition, Putiatin finally released
him. "All right!" he said, "Go! I know that now it will be boring for
you here."[26]

On August 19, 1854, another attempt was made to lead the *Pallada*,
stripped of all armament and heavy equipment, into the Amur via the
western fairway. But all endeavors to lessen her eighteen feet draught
in the face of a maximum depth of fifteen feet proved futile. The frigate then crossed over to the eastern (Sakhalin, or Karafuto) fairway
to attempt entry there. She reached the so-called northern roadstead,
where the fairway flows into the Sea of Okhotsk, but here ran into
a storm (September 19), during which her ten-oar cutter was carried
away and her two longboats were considerably damaged. Two American whalers were wrecked there at the same time. The loss or damage of the main rowboats, and the discovery of a sandbank in the path
of the frigate forced the commander to turn back (September 26)
and return to Cape Lazarev.[27]

Unable to lead the frigates into the Amur and without shelter from
ice in this extensive estuary, Putiatin departed (October 6) with both
vessels to one of the ports on the east coast. At the designated bay
the frigate *Pallada* was definitively disarmed. Only ten men remained
behind as guard.

On October 15, 1854, the frigate *Diana*, now the only vessel of the
Russian Japan Expedition, set sail for the shores of Nippon.[28]

7

Shimoda

HOPING TO SAVE TIME BY SENDING AHEAD WORD OF HIS RETURN, Putiatin stopped at Hakodate (October 21, 1854) to dispatch a letter to the Supreme Council. He wrote that he was on his way to Osaka[1] and requested that the plenipotentiaries be sent there to conclude the negotiations. Several officials and an interpreter came aboard at Hakodate. They told the admiral that the Japanese government had already written the Russian government through the Dutch, suggesting that somebody be sent to conclude the negotiations he had begun. He learned also that Commodore Perry had visited Hakodate in May and that this port was one of those "opened" by the recently concluded Japanese-American treaty of amity and friendship (March 31, 1854).[2] "Supposing that the Americans during their stay in port had, of course, not denied themselves the pleasure of landing and walking about," Putiatin reported, "I decided to go ashore from the very first day on without asking the governor for permission, and to demand unhindered access to the city and its environs. To avoid creating unpleasant incidents, however, I gave advance notice of this intention to the officials who had arrived on the frigate to greet us."[3] The Japanese objected, but, realizing the determination of the intruders, modified their stand and asked only that the Russians land at a certain place and not enter the city without one of them as guide.[4]

After dinner, the Russians started ashore. A Japanese boat cut across

[74]

their path and an interpreter shouted to them that the governor had not found it possible to consider the admiral's request, but they rowed on regardless. When they landed, they were met by officials and led to the government office. Here they were seated on high, cloth-covered tabourets, while their refreshments were put before them on the floor. Once more, the Russians had to perform acrobatic feats to drink their tea.

The fact that the officials had been waiting for the Russians at the wharf and that tea and refreshments had been prepared indicates that the Japanese themselves had not believed that the Russians would heed their interdiction. Yet, the Japanese did not discontinue their effort to stop or at least hinder penetration. When the Russians stepped out of the building after tea to continue toward the city, they saw to their surprise that a large, padlocked gate had been hastily erected athwart the street. The Japanese officials, satisfied with their ingenuity, smiled and bowed happily. But Putiatin was angry. He assembled his oarsmen and announced that if the gates were not opened at once he would have them broken down. The threat was effective: one of the officials took the key from his kimono sleeve and unlocked the portals.[5]

The Russians visited some of Hakodate's Buddhist temples and gardens. The clean streets of the city were thronged with persons who would step aside and squat as the Russians passed. The people were "always modest, although apparently not embarrassed by the presence of their officials."[6] In the evening, surrounded by a multitude of paper lanterns and escorted by soldiers and officials, the Russians returned to their boats.

On October 22, the Japanese brought fish and vegetables aboard the frigate, but refused money on the ground that trade with foreigners was forbidden. The Russians accepted only what had been sent in the name of the governor, giving a gift of their own in exchange, and rejected the rest. Negotiations continued for two days. Finally, the Japanese agreed to take payment. They returned, however, the money that some of the officers had spent in town on souvenirs.[7]

On October 25, the assistant governor visited Putiatin. The governor himself refused to come aboard to accept the letter to the Supreme Council, although he readily admitted that it would not befit the admiral's position for the latter to call on him first. It was decided, therefore, that Pos'et visit the governor the next day to transmit the document.[8] Putiatin had not intended to spend more than two or three days in Hakodate, but these discussions concerning payment for supplies and acceptance of the communication detained him beyond expectation.

On the morning of October 26, Pos'et, *Leitenant* Nikolai G. Schilling II, and several other officers went to meet the governor. Schilling carried a special portfolio with the letter to the *Roju*, and Dutch and Chinese translations thereof. Orderlies accompanied the officers to dust off their boots before entering Japanese houses. Officials and a guard-of-honor met the Russian officers on the shore and guided them to the governor's office.

The Russians entered an oblong room, in the rear of which the governor of Hakodate sat on a lacquer tabouret. Pos'et was seated on a similar tabouret vis-à-vis the governor, the other officers on a bench along the wall. Japanese officials occupied a bench across the room. Their subordinates squatted behind them.

After the customary civilities, Schilling handed the letter to Pos'et, who then transmitted it to the assistant governor. The latter placed it into a lacquer box and with a low bow presented it to the governor. Having promised to forward the letter without delay, the governor withdrew leaving his aides to entertain the visitors. As the Russians were starting back, they noticed that the Japanese servants were busily wrapping up the remains of the refreshments. They had hardly returned to the frigate when these leftovers were delivered aboard.[9]

During the eight days that the Russians spent at Hakadote, they not only reconnoitered the roadstead but also made frequent trips ashore. The Japanese authorities did not object and, "thanks to the commendable conduct of the lower ranks," no untoward events occurred. Having surrendered the communication to the Supreme Council, Putiatin weighed anchor (October 28). But strong winds that persisted throughout the day blocked the *Diana's* attempts to go out to sea. Unwilling to risk a night passage through the little-explored strait, the admiral returned to the roadstead.[10]

Putiatin reports that several nights before this, a Japanese fisherman climbed aboard the frigate and declared his desire to stay, that he had been put back into his boat and led away from the vessel, but had reappeared on deck just before sailing, having this time pushed away his little boat so that he could not have been taken ashore unobserved. Realizing that to surrender him to the Japanese authorities would have meant to surrender him to almost certain death, and feeling that he was not a fugitive from justice, since "if that had been the case he certainly would have been arrested ... between his first and second arrival on the frigate," but that he had acted "only out of the desire to cross over to Russia, whose manners and customs he liked more," Putiatin decided to take him along and include him among the orderlies, "having taken all possible measures" that his presence among the Russians not be noticed. "Thanks to the good sense of the Japanese himself," reads Putiatin's report, "and the measures taken by the commander of the frigate [*Kapitan-leitenant* Stepan Stepanovich Lesovskii], the suspicious officials that surrounded us did not discover him later on, even though we spent some three months on shore, and he now is at the mouth of the Amur."[11] This Japanese must have been Tachibana Kosai, who, according to Schilling and Japanese sources at our disposal, actually joined the Russians only at Heda, where he had been living at the Renge Temple.[12]

The governor of Hakodate had made no objections to the frequent walks the Russians took on land. But, on October 29, when the frigate had already hoisted her sails and was about to depart, the governor sent a letter aboard in which he stated that although he had not prevented the Russians from going ashore, they had, nevertheless, done so in violation of the laws of the country, and that this could not serve as a precedent for going ashore in other ports. "I did not deem it necessary to postpone my departure to answer this empty objection," noted Putiatin, "the more so, since the governor had, of course, written it solely to justify himself before his government.[13]

The passage from Hakodate to Osaka took ten days. As the frigate hugged the eastern shores of Japan, sketches were made of the coast line. Weathering a storm at the longitude of Edo Bay on November 3, the frigate reached the outer gates of Osaka Bay on November 7. The following afternoon (3:00 P.M., November 8), surrounded by hundreds of Japanese boats, the *Diana* entered the roadstead and cast anchor at the foot of Mt. Tempo. The arrival of the Russians came as a complete surprise to the inhabitants and officials of Osaka and caused much consternation in their midst. The admiral knew that, upon hearing of the presence of Westerners, the governor would take measures to prevent them from landing and attempted, therefore, to get some of his officers to the city before this could happen. But the boats that were sent out penetrated only some way up the Yodo River, when they were forced ashore. The officials who faced the Russians would not permit them to proceed any further. In vain the Russians protested, presenting a note in Chinese, which stated that they had to see the governor to inform him of the purpose of their arrival. The Japanese strung a chain of large boats, a number of rows deep, athwart the river, and there was little the Russians could do but return to the frigate.[14]

The next day (November 9) a large body of Japanese troops encamped along the shore, while guard boats took up positions near the mouth of the river. In answer to these "malignant" preparations, Putiatin brought the frigate closer, to within a mile and a quarter from the mouth of the river. Japanese officials came aboard, but without interpreters. Goshkevich, however, communicated to them in written Chinese the admiral's intention of awaiting the plenipotentiaries at this roadstead. The Japanese agreed to send a special courier to Edo to inform the government of the Russians' arrival. Meanwhile, they surrounded the frigate with guard boats to prevent any communication with the shore.[15]

The Shogunate's reply was negative. It stated that Osaka was not open to foreigners and thus unsuited for negotiations, but that the previous plenipotentiaries would proceed to Shimoda and there await the Russians. It did not add, of course, that Shimoda, one of the ports open to the United States, had been selected because the harbor was poor and the town was isolated from the rest of the country by mountains. Having taken on water and spent some more time fruitlessly negotiating for supplies "which the governors probably feared to release, lest European vessels be caused to enter this port in quest of provisions," the *Diana* departed (November 22).[16]

During the expedition's stay in Osaka Bay, Russian boats had surveyed the roadsteads of Osaka, Sakai, and Amagasaki. Before continuing toward Shimoda, Putiatin had sent several boats to reconnoiter the eastern shore of Osaka Bay. When the frigate set sail, she hugged the western coast[17] until she entered the strait. There she crossed over to the eastern shore and picked up the aforementiond boats (November 23). These had carried out their mission with success. They had never been molested and had readily obtained fresh fish from the natives in exchange for trinkets. They confirmed that the coast was covered by an almost "continuous row of settlements among which [one] not infrequently comes upon cities."[18]

Evaluating his stopover in Osaka Bay, Putiatin reported: "Athough I did not succeed in winning the governors over to a friendly reception, or in remaining for the continuation of the negotiations in the most industrial city of the empire, I still dare to hope that the visit of our vessels to Osaka Harbor resulted in two contributions: firstly, it proved to the Japanese that even their innermost sea ports are accessible to large European vessels; secondly, it proved wrong [von] Siebold's belief that the roadsteads of Osaka and Sakai are extremely shallow and that the Portuguese who traded there had left because of their inconvenience."[19]

In Yura-kaikyo,[20] one of the Japanese waifs who had been returned to Japan on the *Kniaz' Menshikov* came aboard the frigate and warned Putiatin that an English detachment, consisting of a frigate, a corvet, and two steamers had been in Nagasaki waters as late as October.[21] Sir James Sterling, commander of the squadron (H.M.S. *Winchester, Encounter, Barracouta, Styx*) had signed a treaty with Japan (October, 1854) which "contains nothing about commerce, yet... opens the way, and prepares for future negotiations on this important point."[22] At the same time, he had sought Japanese permission to engage the Russian vessels in Japanese waters. "They [the Japanese] have now been told of the war between Russia and Europe, of the causes which combined to render the war inevitable, and the alliance which indicates a speedy termination of it. They understand why England, who did not intrude much upon them before, has now to perform a duty to herself, and must see that no foe shall avail himself of her forbearance to ensconce in the secluded harbours of Japan the hostile man-of-war or treacherous privateer."[23] But the Japanese turned down the English request. Commented Koga: "Most barbarians dislike [the] Russians, therefore [stories about] their cruelty must be correct. But I blame the British for anchoring at Nagasaki because they wanted to attack the Russians.[24]

The passage to Shimoda was stormy. When the place was finally reached (December 4), it was found to be unsatisfactory as anchorage; but, foreseeing the delays that would arise were he to sail to a more convenient harbor, Putiatin decided to stay.

The possible presence of an English or Anglo-French fleet in Japanese waters necessitated constant alertness. The frigate was so moored off the western, easily accessible shore as to permit her at any time to pull up closely. She would then be reasonably protected from raking fire or an attack from opposite sides. A signal post was set up at the most outlying promontory of the bay to keep a lookout for the enemy.[25] As Koga testifies, the Russians were fully prepared for an Allied attack.[26]

Meanwhile, the Shogunate ordered various officials to Shimoda, including Kawaji, Tsutsui, and Koga, all of whom had been at the Nagasaki negotiations. Three new officials, Izawa Mimasaka-no-kami, the Shogun's chief representative at Shimoda, Matsumoto Jurobee, a chief censor, and Muragaki Yosaburo,[27] a finance inspector, were sent as assistants.[28] Both Kawaji and Koga note that messengers met them on the way, urging utmost speed lest the Russians proceed to Uraga. "The Russians are importune. They will go to the capital. All you gentlemen must shorten your voyage and arrive quickly."[29] Kawaji reached Shimoda during the night of December 10 to 11; Tsutsui and Koga on the 12th.[30]

Meanwhile, the Russians had walked about town and environs without hindrance. "Lately," wrote Koga, "groups of Russians have been roving about town. Some blow bugles, others sing barbarian tunes in unison. The children of the town follow them noisily."[31]

After lengthy discussions between Japanese messengers and Russian junior officers regarding the place, type, and ceremonial of the impending negotiations, it was agreed that the first meeting was to take place on December 20. Officials carefully measured the height of the Russian chairs to prevent the construction and use of "inferior" seating platforms for the plenipotentiaries.[32]

The Russians repeatedly asked for permission to sleep on land. Commented Koga indignantly: "The barbarians request increasingly more — very much like the eating habit of a silkworm.[33]

Gales and heavy seas forced the frigate to abandon her position close to the shore, and she laid to, halfway between the coast and the high crag of Inubashiri (December 15).[34]

On December 19, gifts were sent ashore by the Russians. Most of the Japanese officials were overjoyed. That night Koga could not sleep. He kept thinking of the old saying: "The miseries of the world are begun by thieves and barbarians, but completed by degenerate officials."[35] "How painfully true this saying is!" he mused. He pulled up the wick and wrote poetry until the cock crowed. Only then did he go to sleep.[36]

On December 20, 1854, Putiatin went ashore with great ceremony. Before long, however, he sent the guard-of-honor back to the frigate and moved about somewhat less formally. The first meeting took place at the Fukusen Temple at Ryosen.[37] The admiral was accompanied by Lesovskii, Pos'et, and Goshkevich.[38] Anxious though Putiatin was to get down to business as quickly as possible, this first conference was perforce limited to the presentation of gifts from the "temporal government" of Japan to the Russian government and the introduction of the new officials who accompanied the Russians' "old acquaintances." The presents consisted of bookcases, gilded screens, and table decorations of "most exquisite workmanship."[39] "The barbarians do not have [such things]," wrote Koga, "but they like them very much."[40]

The Russians were cold. They asked permission to use the Japanese kitchen to light a fire. They were told, however, that Rezanov (?) had not done so. The Russians replied that he had come when it was hot, not cold as now, but the Japanese remained adamant in their refusal. If the Russians needed warm things, they should have more people work; then they would not worry about food being cold.[41]

The next day (December 21), the plenipotentiaries returned the admiral's visit. They had met at the Government Office before noon to deposit their vermillion seals. It had not taken them long to cross over to the frigate, as the *Diana* was only seven or eight *cho* from shore.[42] They were festively received. Once more there were colorful flags, gun salutes, nautical drill, and ship inspection. "But the boat was not as wide as before [that is, as wide as the *Pallada*]. It was 33 *ken*[43] long, 8 *ken* wide, and 7 *ken* deep. There were 54 guns and 500 barbarians."[44] Walking through the vessel, the Japanese were very much impressed by the very tall and husky figure of *Leitenant* Aleksandr Mozhaiskii. The latter liked to paint and had drawn a picture of the Russian boats entering Osaka Harbor. Kawaji, who had served at Osaka and knew the harbor well, complimented him. "The barbarian was very happy."[45] The walls of the cabins were covered with pictures. Koga was surprised to find one depicting two naked Japanese women "[the kind] that I have seen in bathhouses," as he remarked.

Inspecting the *Diana,* Koga must have come upon Father Avvakum. Noted he: "There was much hair on his face and he wore a wide long gown. I suspected that he was an evil priest. My hair stood up and I quickly passed him."[46]

The Russians told Kawaji to fire one of the cannons. He pulled the cord, but "his strength was weak and it did not fire." The Russians tried it and the cannon went off. When Kawaji tried again he succeeded, but mumbled that the guns made by Egawa Tarozaemon[47] were much better. "Russian firearms are really inferior [to those of] other foreigners," added Koga.[48]

The Japanese dined aboard ship; the higher officials in the admiral's cabin, the others in the wardroom.[49] The Russians had held up five fingers and, pointing between the fingers, had indicated the seating arrangement: one Russian, one Japanese, one Russian, one Japanese. ... The dinner was not so sumptuous as on previous occasions, as the expedition was running low in supplies. There was chicken, duck, and pork, but no beef; and "only three kinds of wine."[50] One of the officials who had "peculiar food habits" and could not eat many things was not too happy about the Western-style dinner. Goshkevich, who sat between him and Koga, paid much attention to Koga but ignored him. "Are you bored?" asked Koga. "I can still endure it," sighed his countryman.[51] Again, the Japanese would wrap up in paper samples of food, and hide them in the wide sleeves of their kimonos. One of the guests filled his wineglass with vinegar and butter, another one buried some paper with mustard in his kimono.

The sea became rough, and as the frigate was tossed about more and more, the departure of the officials was hastened. Koga fell asleep on his way back. He was drunk. Ashamed, he promised himself not to let this happen again. During the night, the winds attained the proportions of a storm. A second anchor was cast and the yards and topmast struck.[52] Thirty-three Russians went ashore with a note from Pos'et requesting permission for them to stay ashore, as the waves were high. But the Japanese replied: "The barbarian letter can come, how can you not sail on sea? ... Ryosen is for the daytime rest of the ambassador's retinue, not to provide many with [a place for] spending the night."[53]

Toward morning, the wind calmed down, but the topmast and yards were not braced, as it had been decided to repair the rigging. Preparations were made to cross over to the more quiet northeastern corner of the bay.[54] This day (December 22) the negotiations were taken up again at Fukusen Temple.[55]

8

The Last Days of the Diana

ON THE MORNING OF DECEMBER 23, 1854, A TERRIFIC TREMOR SUD-
denly shook the frigate. The admiral and many of the officers rushed
on deck. Within fifteen minutes, the water near the town of Shimoda
seemed to be boiling. The current of the river had become stronger
in the shallows and produced breakers and wash. An excessively high
tide bubbled around the island of Inubashiri and the promontories.

The water level began to rise rapidly. The junks that had lain off
Shimoda started up the river. The *Diana's* boats which were returning
with the towline were at once recalled. The water ebbed fast, and
a second anchor was cast. Before the rate of the drop began to
decrease, a new flow followed, with the result that the frigate began
to turn now to one side, now to the other, and then, when the force
of the rise reached its climax, made a complete rotation within a
few seconds. From that time on, ebb and flow interchanged rapidly,
forming a perfect whirlpool between Inubashiri Island and the shore.
Not only was the frigate being turned around and around, but was
carried now toward the island, now toward the shore, in spite of
her two anchors and good ground. Within the first thirty minutes
of this merry-go-round, the *Diana* made forty-two complete rotations.
More than once she had been in danger of being smashed to bits
against the island or one of the nearby promontories.[1] Irresistibly,

she had moved broadside toward Inubashiri. The noise of the rip, compressed between the frigate and the threatening crag, had increased steadily. Then, within a stone's throw, she had suddenly halted, and in a few minutes hauled back. "It still pleased Providence to save us," noted the admiral.[2] The receding water carried the frigate in the opposite direction.

The *Diana* continued to turn, approaching now the town, now the mouth of the bay. Junks were scattered everywhere. One of them sat on the hawsers of the *Diana* and broke her flying jib boom and main jib boom. Then the stern of the native craft itself was shattered by the chains of the frigate. Two Japanese were taken off the junk before she foundered. When the *Diana* cast a third anchor, another junk piled up on her right side. When a change of current pulled the junk away, a young man was left struggling in the water. The Russians threw him the end of a rope, but he would not take it, gesturing that he might forfeit his head for doing so. A minute later, he had disappeared.[3] As Spalding commented on the choosing of death by many Japanese in preference to accepting aid and safety from the Russians: "If it be the best government which governs least, that is not the government of Japan; like the law of gravitation it is always in action: its Briarian [*sic*] arms are everywhere, and its subjects are a community of Arguses. When storm is on the deep and its mariners are clinging to their long tillers and shuddering at the yawning sea, each lightening flash of heaven shows them an etiolating hand, that will crush them, if they dare leave their craft, until half engulfed."[4]

Ebb and flow interchanged so rapidly that the depth would differ by more than seven feet within half a minute. Lodesmen barely had time to call out the measurements. The great difference in the levels of the tide reached as much as thirty-eight and a half feet.

By the twelfth hour, the *Diana* turned more slowly. During one of the rotations, she was in danger of smashing her bowsprit against the vertical shore of the island. All guns were ordered secured, but before the crew could carry out the command, she began to career to port, and the inclination became so dangerous that "All hands on deck!" was piped. The frigate was about to keel over. The crew were clinging to the starboard nettings. Through the silence that descended upon everything, there resounded "And the will of the Lord be done" and "Don't cower, lads!" For about a minute, the vessel lay on her side and creaked in all parts. Then, with a new flow, she began to straighten up.[5]

Groans were heard aboard the *Diana*. Before the earthquake, two guns below deck had been turned along the broadside to facilitate the receiving of cablets through the portholes and make room for the coils. When those who were securing the guns were piped on deck, one of the cannons had overturned, killing Seaman Sobolev, breaking Noncommissioned Officer Terentev's leg, and tearing off Seaman Victorov's leg below the knee.[6]

Having straightened up again, the frigate dropped off into deep water. Leakage had greatly increased in her hold, and all pumps were put into operation. Part of her keel appeared on the surface of the ocean. A quarter of an hour later, the frigate tilted with a new fall, but less than the first time. With the rise, she was further pushed ashore. During the next fall, the frigate did not careen, in spite of the fact that a whole foot of the stock of her anchor was seen above water and that only six feet of water remained. On the contrary, she was carried forward with the strong current. Thrice more she tilted, but each time less and less. The *Diana* finally halted within seventy feet of the submerged rocks. In her hold, water rose at about two feet an hour. An inspection of the outside showed that sternpost and rudder had been torn off.[7] The Russians were "thunderstruck." "We forgot all about the former horrors," wrote Schilling, "forgot that God had just delivered us from certain destruction, and the question as to how such damage could be repaired, [damage] with which it would be impossible to return home, particularly during wartime, engulfed all our thoughts."[8]

The second billow of the tidal wave with its boiling-water-like white foam had been most damaging for the town of Shimoda. It had resounded as if the axis of the earth had been broken.[9] The sea had risen some twenty-one feet above the normal level and had inundated the whole settlement. For several minutes, only the roofs of the temples had been above water. The ebb that had followed had filled the bay with parts of houses, junks, whole roofs, domestic utensils, corpses, and people clinging to wreckage.[10]

A turbid stream had carried much of the debris toward the *Diana*. In spite of their own predicament, the Russians had let down ropes from all sides of the frigate in the hope that some of the victims might be able to climb aboard, but with one exception all had been carried past at too great a distance. The exception was an old woman who had been washed to the broadside of the frigate. One of the sailors had hastily tied a rope around himself and had jumped onto the straw roof on which the woman was sitting. He had hardly grabbed her, when the whole mass of wreckage had been swept away. Hanging on the rope, sailor and *baba*[11] had been pulled aboard safely.[12]

Smoke had enveloped Shimoda, and a sulphury smell had spread through the air. Four more billows and all trace of the town had been washed away.[13] Of Shimoda's 856 households, 813 had been completely demolished, 25 partially so, and only 18 had been left fully intact. About 85 persons (out of a population of 3,907) had been drowned.[14]

"Part of the buildings had been swept into the sea," reported Putiatin, "others to the foot of the mountains surrounding the valley of Shimoda. These same mountains stopped also a considerable number of junks, some of which were carried a whole mile inland. The northeast corner of the bay, opposite the settlement of Kakizaki — also partly destroyed[15] — was full of broken junks, buildings, and generally all kinds of belongings; all this, pressed together here by the current, formed a solid mass which seemed to serve as a continuation of the shore."[16] (Amidst this wreckage, there lay also part of the *Diana's* keel, the false keel and part of the deadwood, and two garboard planks. The socket of the sternpost was empty, but the calking of the false sternpost, with several chips of that wood, had remained in place.[17] The sternpost was believed to have sunk, together with the rudder and all loops.)

The harbor was filled with corpses — and people who searched among them for friends and relatives. The mountains were all rock; there was but little earth with which to bury the dead. Throughout the night, the air was filled with the stench of corpses and the howling of foxes and jackals.[18]

Thieves and hoodlums added to the distress of the townspeople. More than 800 men had been conscripted in the capital and sent to aid the suffering community.[19] But these men were "all hoodlums and bad youths, quite old hands at robbing." They took advantage of the misfortune of others to enrich themselves. Wrote Koga indignantly: "Even death penalty is not enough to punish their crime."[20] He dispatched a messenger to inform his mother that he was alive.[21]

Koga had been quartered near the shore. Aroused by commotion in the streets, he had stepped out of his house to see what was happening and had found himself face to face with the tidal wave. He had barely saved himself on Mt. Daian-ji. As he recorded later on: "Tiles were flying, people crying and calling. All of a sudden, I heard a tidal wave coming very forcefully. Alone, I ran east and west. Other than a pair of swords, not one thing was left."[22] "Today's misfortune," he noted, "is the biggest I have ever met in my life. Is it because of fault in my speech that I have encountered this? ... Not only shall I be cold and hungry on the way [back], but upon getting to my native place shall be in want for the rest of my life."[23] He had climbed the mountain "gathering all his strength." His left hand had hit against a stone and was bleeding. On the mountain, he had met other officials. Downcast, they had congratulated each other on being safe. Then they had watched the Russians down below. "Like a group of ants" they had clung to their ship. "Why does Heaven not kill the thieves, but mistreat our own people?" queried Koga.[24]

For two weeks, Russian divers conducted a thorough but fruitless search for the lost sternpost, rudder, and loops, along the route the frigate had covered on December 23.[25] As Schilling pondered: "What must have been happening in the heart of the admiral and of the captain!" On them lay the heavy responsibility for the safety of the crew in a strange place, a country into which for centuries foreigners had not been admitted.[26]

The *Diana* had to be keeled. Use of a more protected bay than that of Shimoda was essential. The admiral, who amidst all these problems and tasks had found time to resume his negotiations with the Japanese,[27] insisted, therefore, that he be shown a nearby bay suitable for such repair work. He was directed to Ajiro Bay, on the eastern shore of Izu peninsula.[28] Schilling and Aleksandr Kolokol'tsov, together with two Japanese officials, an interpreter (Tatsunosuke), and two Russian helmsmen with plummets proceeded on a Japanese boat to examine that place. They reached Ajiro in the evening (11:00 P.M.) and, at first sight, understood that the bay was utterly unsuitable for the keeling of the frigate. It was so shallow that only its southern part offered a good anchorage to the not-deep-lying Japanese junks. Lodgings had been prepared for the party in one of the temples, and the night was thus spent at Ajiro. But the next morning, the Russians announced that they had decided to inspect Atami Bay. They had learned of the latter from one of the boatmen who, having babbled out this information, got very frightened and refused to answer any further questions. The officials insisted that Atami must not be visited, but when the Russians set out alone, they hastened to follow them.

In Atami, the Russians, as Europeans, attracted much attention. But this bay also proved unsatisfactory. After a refreshing hot spring bath and dinner, the mariners gave in to the officials' pleas and retraced their steps to Ajiro and then Shimoda. As the expedition had been unsuccessful, Putiatin ordered the officers to explore the western shore of Izu peninsula.[29] They now were to proceed on a Russian cutter, so as to be independent of their Japanese guides. But bad weather set in, and the admiral succeeded in persuading the officials to let the Russians travel by land. On January 5, 1855, the procession got under way. Four officials and one interpreter accompanied the party. Each had three attendants as well as bearers. The mountains were crossed in single file, and the relatively large retinue of the Japanese strung out in a long line. Often the tail of the groups was still in the valley when the head had already reached the summit. As time passed, the officials became tired and climbed into their *norimono*. Though the Russians were offered the same convenience, they preferred walking. When the procession would approach a village, one of the attendants would blow a horn, to which another horn in the village would reply. The latter would be a round-up signal for relief bearers. Theirs was not an easy job. Almost all of them developed swollen excrescences on their shoulders. Some had deep, pus-filled wounds from which blood flowed when the end of the weighed-down *norimono* arm was lowered onto their shoulders.

Bay after bay was inspected: Nagatsuro, Mera, Matsuzaki, Tago, Arari, and Heda. Arari Bay proved acceptable, Heda Bay even more so. Heda Bay was spacious, about seven thousand feet in width, completely closed in the south and with at least three places near shore deep enough for the keeling of the frigate. The bay was separated from the sea by a headland consisting of a row of boulders piled up on top of each other.[30] Koga noted that Putiatin highly praised Heda. Inside the harbor, there were no waves at all. It was deep enough to anchor a big ship. Repeatedly, the admiral pointed at the bay and said: "How your nation can misuse this good port."[31] On January 11, the party reported back to the admiral, having returned via Shuzenji and Nashimoto.[32]

While the bay had been sought, all the artillery with gun carriages had been put ashore (December 26-28, 1854) to lighten the weakened frigate. An interlarded sail had also been brought under the stern-post. Fierce westerly winds and high seas slowed down these jobs. The leak finally decreased by half — from eighteen to nine inches an hour. A makeshift rudder, or *"potes,"*[33] had been constructed on shore and the boats had been repaired.[34]

Upon return of the exploration party, the frigate weighed anchor (January 12) to proceed to Heda — or at least Arari.[35] The day before, permission had arrived from Edo to let the Russians sail to Heda. "Russian envoy very happy."[36] The disproportion of the *Diana's* sea gauge of bow and stern, however, delayed luffing, and anchor had to be cast again. Heavy things were transferred to the stern and the bow lightened.[37]

On January 13 (New Year's Day, Russian style), Tsutsui and Kawaji sent aboard food and expressed their best wishes. The admiral thanked them and presented to them several silver-plated utensils.[38] After several other attempts, the frigate finally left Shimoda Bay on January 14 with a moderate westerly wind. Simultaneously, in accordance with a Japanese suggestion, a Japanese junk manned by a Russian crew sailed along to save the men on the frigate, should the leak greatly increase at sea.[39] Pos'et and Goshkevich stayed behind at Shimoda.

"Now that the barbarians have left the harbor," wrote Koga, "there is no need to send them things. I thus bought a whole leg [of a suckling pig] to eat by myself. I have been eating vegetables so long; now I have meat. [This is a] real extravagance."[40] There was little for the plenipotentiaries to do. As Koga recorded the next day (January 15): "[I] stay home and think about poetry, cook pig and eat it with followers. Having a wonderful time...."[41]

The frigate sailed safely around the southern promontory of Izu peninsula and then headed north. Three times, changing breezes necessitated turning around the overstay. The frigate obeyed the rudder well and in the fifth hour was within seven miles of Arari. But an unfavorable wind arose, and Putiatin decided to seek an overnight anchorage in the open bay of Matsuzaki. Close as the *Diana* approached the shore, however, none could be located. Nor did the bay offer protection against the westerly winds that blew in that region during winter. Putiatin decided, therefore, not to remain in it, and set the frigate to the starboard tack. The night did not promise to be stormy, and Putiatin planned to continue under small sails.[42] But the wind (southwest-to-west) gradually increased in intensity and raised a heavy sea, which worsened the leak of the frigate. When by ten o'clock the frigate began to boxhaul on the starboard tack, she hardly bore up under the wind; and the pressure of the tossing sea tore off the *potes's* seizing and knocked the *potes* itself out of place.[43]

Repairs were begun immediately. To strengthen the *potes* and attach it more securely to the stern, it was let into the center port-hole of the stern cabin. To cut down speed, the mizzen topsail was secured and the main topsail hoisted. When it appeared that the frigate was near shore, the main topsail was again taken in and the fore-topsail and foresail raised instead. Once more the Russians began to boxhaul, but the vessel would not work windward, as the equilib-rium between bow and stern had been upset.[44] Attempts to decrease the pressure on the cheek by turning with bellied-out fore-topsail proved fruitless. Neither could the overstay be turned. The frigate that had taken on speed — while the rudder had been placed into the wind and the staysail had been down — refused to hug the wind. All that was left for the crew to do was to proceed at minimum speed and then cast anchor at moderate depth. The proximity of land per-mitted no further maneuvers. By 2:30 A.M. (January 15), two anchors were cast at a depth of 140 feet. All sails had been taken in and the topgallant mast let into the well deck (?). Upon sliphooking the cables, the *Diana* had a 63-foot depth at stern. She remained in this position until morning.[45]

Dawn revealed that the frigate was opposite Mt. Fuji, within a cable's length from the sandy beach, along which there was heavy surf. The wind was strong, and Putiatin ordered topmasts and lower yards taken in and a third anchor cast.[46]

During the night, the sail of the Japanese junk that accompanied the *Diana* had been torn, and the Russian crew had been forced to run her aground the sandy beach north of the frigate.[47]

On January 15 and 16, the pumps were operated almost continu-ously to lighten the stern of the frigate as much as possible. But the wind did not let up, and the swell weakened the vessel more and more. Pumps kept breaking down and the leak increased steadily so that, finally, steps had to be taken for saving the crew, should the frigate founder.

Before sundown (January 16), a ten-oar cutter was lowered from the davits, crossed the surf, and was pulled ashore with the aid of Japanese men gathered there. Appreciating this help, the ship's chaplain later recorded: "A good people; truly a good and humane one! May you good people prosper for many years, may you live and remember that your good turn saved up to five hundred persons, foreigners, [who] survive indebted for their life, gratefully remembering the 4th [16th] of January, 1855."[48]

A rope's end from the frigate had been brought ashore and now a gig with six men was sent along the rope. Although the sailors reached land safely, they did so only with the greatest of difficulty; and the planned evacuation of the two men who had been injured during the earthquake had to be postponed until the following morning.[49] By evening, the pumps had begun to break down from constant tossing and continuous operation, and the crew could barely keep the water in the vessel down to the same level.

When the wind had somewhat subsided in the morning, a cutter was ordered to seek out a place suitable for the landing of the sick and the unloading of goods. Meanwhile, a raft was constructed out of the fragments of the keel. The rowboats were let down into the water. "Not expecting the frigate to remain afloat long," reported Putiatin, "and since, furthermore, the crossing of the surf at night involved great danger, I finally decided to take the crew ashore."[50]

An attempt to send personnel ashore on the raft was given up as too dangerous. The men were transferred to the longboat, which would both row and be pulled along the cable to within throwing distance from shore. There the sailors would jump off one by one. Around their waists they would have a rope, one end of which was kept on the boat, the other one on shore. This way they could be pulled out safely. The oarsmen would then row back to the frigate and pick up another load. By 4:00 P.M., the whole crew had been brought ashore.[51]

The evacuation had proceeded smoothly. "I had been ordered," reported Schilling, "to watch in the battery that nobody climb through the gun-ports into the longboat, and I must say that not one attempt was made to save oneself out of turn."[52]

The captain left the *Diana* on the longboat with the last group. The admiral pushed off at the same time on the cutter, with Schilling at the rudder. Lesovskii and Putiatin had thus left only after everybody else had been evacuated from the frigate. The nose of the admiral's cutter ran aground, while the stern was raised by a huge wave in such a way that everybody, including Putiatin, fell into the water. Fortunately, men with ends of ropes tied around their bodies rushed out and dragged cutter and former occupants ashore before they were carried out to sea.[53]

After all personnel had been taken off the *Diana,* the longboat went out once more to pick up some of the things that had been left aboard. Meanwhile, wind and breakers increased so much that the oarsmen could not get ashore and had to spend the night on the boat.[54]

Throughout, the Japanese had shown the Russians all possible assistance. They had collected a large number of straw mats and clothing in the neighboring villages, though they themselves had suffered great loss in the earthquake. By evening, almost the whole crew was protected from the piercing wind and the cold. (The temperature was 3° R, or about 39° F).[55]

The next day (January 18), the Russians took advantage of a decrease in wind and surf to bring ashore a few guns, cartridges, and some personal belongings that had not yet been inundated. The frigate subsided less than might have been expected, considering the fact that water in the hold had already reached the orlop deck. Putiatin decided, therefore, to try out another Japanese proposal, namely, to tow the *Diana* into the sheltered harbor of Heda, not more than fifteen miles away, and there run her aground, pump out the

water, and then keel her.[56] An Izu official who had brought provisions, copper kettles, and many other important items kindly offered
his services. In accordance with the admiral's request, he instructed
the neighboring villages to send their fishing boats to the frigate
the next morning. All fishermen between sixteen and fifty were
pressed into service.[57]

Meanwhile, news had reached Shimoda that the admiral had fallen
into the water, and Nakamura hastened west to inquire after his
health. Nakamura had wanted Pos'et- to come along, but the latter
insisted that his orders demanded that he stay in Shimoda.[58]

On January 19, 1855, over one hundred[59] boats of all kinds appeared and took the frigate in tow (10:00 A.M.). A reward had been
offered by the Japanese officials to the one first to drag her out.[60] The
admiral, the captain, several of the officers, and some twenty sailors
joined the flotilla of boats, but the rest of the crew remained on
shore. At first, everything proceeded rather satisfactorily. Within
three hours, the *Diana*, in which the water had risen considerably,
was towed some five miles. Success seemed close at hand. "Suddenly,"
reads Putiatin's report, "we saw, to our great surprise and for no
apparent reason whatsoever, that the Japanese boats hastened to
leave the frigate and hurried toward the places whence they had
come."[61] There was no way of stopping them, but their brusque
departure soon became understandable. Tatsunosuke had hardly had
time to explain that a white cloud had covered the summit of Mt.
Fuji, and that this was a sign of an impending storm, when a squall
from the southwest raised such big waves that the Russians barely
found shelter in Enoura Harbor, some fifteen miles east-north-east
from Miyajima. The wind turned the frigate around and drove her
back. Soon she careened, turned over, and disappeared.[62]

It is of interest to note that Koga and, presumably, the other
officials were told by the fishermen that the admiral had asked them
to leave, and not that they had deserted the frigate "to our great
surprise and for no apparent reason," as Putiatin's official report
testifies. Koga recorded that when wind and waves increased, "the

admiral said: '[Frigate] definitely cannot be saved.' Ordered all boats to cut hawsers and flee."[63]

In his diary, Koga expressed the feeling that it was good that the frigate had overturned completely, but that it would have been better had she done so during the tidal wave. Now, though they were foreigners, the Japanese must save them and give them relief. "[The] will of Heaven really cannot be understood."[64]

"During these events," Putiatin reported, "everything was carried out with the required order and subordination, and I must give credit to the capable leadership of the commander and the zeal of the officers. Neither can I leave unsaid the readiness of the Japanese to give us all assistance and to supply us with whatever [we] needed. Officials who had immediately been sent by the government sympathized with our plight, hurriedly constructed houses to shelter us from the rigorous winter season, and tried by all means to alleviate our situation. If we are to add to this that in the village of Miyashima, near which we had gone ashore, not one house was left that had not been destroyed by the earthquake, one cannot praise enough their philanthropic care for us."[65]

The day after the great earthquake, Putiatin, Pos'et, and the doctor had gone ashore to inquire whether they could help the Japanese. Moved, Tsutsui and Kawaji had said: "[We] incurred misfortune [and were] careless in managing affairs. [We had] no leisure to inquire after [your health]. [You] on the other hand asked [us] first. [We are] deeply ashamed."[66] But Koga believed that the Russians were only scheming to weaken Japanese resistance by playing on their gratitude. Pointing out in his diary that the Russians had received just as much, if not more, aid from the Japanese, he queried: "The term host and guest — what does it mean?"[67]

9

Heda

SHIMODA WAS IN A STATE OF GREAT DISTRESS. IT HAD BEEN "CLEANSED like a desert plain" by the tidal wave and was difficult to administer. Although food, labor, and gold flowed in from the capital, it would have been impossible to provide adequately for all the Russian waifs in addition to the needy Japanese. There was also the danger (from the Japanese point of view) that Americans would come — Shimoda was one of the two ports opened by the treaty of Kanagawa — and "the two barbarians would mix." The Japanese government felt, therefore, that it would be wise to invite the Russians to Shimoda only after Russian sampans had been constructed and conditions in the city had improved.[1] It decided to accommodate the waifs in Heda, whose harbor, about thirty miles farther from the sea than Shimoda's, was secure and well sheltered.[2] Appropriate instructions were dispatched and officials were sent to communicate this to the Russians, expressing at the same time the commiseration of the *Taikun* at their misfortune. Putiatin gratefully accepted the offer of shelter at Heda. But difficulties arose when he insisted on going by land. He wanted to walk along the shore to Miyajima where most of the crew had remained, picking up on the way whatever parts of the frigate and cargo had been washed ashore. The Japanese begged him not to go by land. They promised to deliver to Heda the remainder of the crew and everything saved from the frigate. But the ambassador would not listen. He considered the Japanese boats too dangerous. "At this distressful occasion, you still utter these unsympathetic and cruel words," remonstrated he. Unable to dissuade him, the officials followed (January 20, 1855), "willing to be punished."[3]

"Only during the trip itself," wrote Schilling, "did we understand why our good guides had been so persistent in demanding that we go to Heda by sea: for a long stretch, we walked along the road leading from Ieddo [Edo] to Miiakko [Miyako, or Kyoto], and the Japanese at that time ... feared nothing as much as the approach of foreigners to the large cities."[4]

The procession was led and followed by Japanese troops. But in Schilling's words: "In spite of a certain martialism in the outward appearance, our relations with the Japanese were peaceful and later on even amicable."[5] Along the road, refreshments of oranges, tea, and sweets had been prepared. By evening, the Russians were back in Miyajima.

Early the next morning (January 21), only two days after the *Diana* had sunk, the admiral was already at work at his new desk — an old door placed on top of a little barrel — drafting plans for a small vessel that could bring news of the shipwreck to Russia, and making preparations for the moving of his men to Heda. At the same time, he renewed his negotiations with the Japanese.[6] The latter were now much more cooperative, and before long Putiatin's efforts were to be crowned with success.[7]

On January 23, Putiatin and approximately half his officers and men left for Heda. The remainder followed the next day. Once more they walked part of the way along the wide, even road that led from Kyoto to Edo. Heda had also been severely damaged by the earthquake. Nevertheless, barracks had been erected for the crew, and a large shrine with subsidiary buildings cleared for the officers. "Our quarters," narrated Schilling, "were in the temple itself, where the idols had been placed facing the wall, probably so that they would not be embarrassed by the sight of Christians in their holy places."⁸

The Japanese authorities informed Putiatin that the Japanese government considered the Russians its guests and hoped that throughout their stay they would live at its expense. The admiral insisted that the Russian government would reimburse the Japanese for everything he and his men received. "Your nation's relief expenditures must be very great," he said time and again. "The gold and silver we have left is not enough to repay you. I beg that we settle this at a later date." Kawaji replied: "Your country is a big nation. Repayment at a later date is all right. But [your] boat is going to cross the sea. You must have money in case of taking shelter from wind in other foreign ports. Better keep what you have left for an emergency."⁹ It was finally agreed that accounts were to be kept from the date of the definitive stay in Heda, while everything that had been delivered before that was to be regarded as a gift.¹⁰ Said "the long big barbarian" (Mozhaiskii): "The behavior of other countries towards [us] is not as generous as that of your nation." But as Koga noted in his diary, it had not been difficult for Japan to treat the Russian waifs well, "pouring whole strength of nation to entertain one ship." But what would happen, pondered he, if thousands of vessels were to frequent the shores of Japan? Would one ship in distress still be able to get "the generous treatment of today"?¹¹

On January 26, 1855, the United States steam frigate *Powhatan* entered Shimoda Harbor. The Japanese plenipotentiaries gathered at Rendai Temple, "looked at each other, put out their tongues in regret," and lamented this unexpected development. "Hitherto," commented Koga, "they all had wished to play the Russians against the Americans. [This was] now difficult to conceal. Would it be of profit or harm to invite the Russian ambassador [to Shimoda]?" The Japanese had tried to hide from the Russians the presence of Commodore Perry's squadron. Now that the *Powhatan* had arrived at Shimoda, they were worried. "If the Russian ambassador knows that the Americans have come and we have not informed [him], it will appear [that we have] clandestine desires. [He (they?) will] certainly [become] hateful and obstinate...."[12]

Kawaji finally decided to have the negotiations continue at Shimoda and sent a note to Heda to inquire whether Putiatin, though tired, would come down. Nakamura was ordered to accompany him.[13] "Now is the end of your nation's year," the admiral replied, "and Tsutsui-*kun* has reached a high age. We must not let him wait too long. I really wish to confer [with you]." When the interpreter stated that the Americans had come and that there were many things going on at Shimoda so that the official notice authorizing the journey might be delayed somewhat, the ambassador had voiced no objection. "His attitude was very calm, his face showed neither gladness nor anger."[14] He did add: "I am old and my feet are soft. I wish to travel only six or seven miles a day."[15]

On January 29, Putiatin left for Shimoda, accompanied by Peshchurov and Kolokol'tsov. En route, he received word from Pos'et about the arrival of the *Powhatan* with the ratified Japanese-American treaty of amity and friendship and, later on, near Matsuzaki another message, informing him that a French whaler had entered port. He immediately sent Kolokol'tsov back to Heda with orders to arm and dispatch at once two boats to Shimoda and there board the enemy vessel in a night assault.[16] The Japanese were very much upset. "At this time, all confusedly barked at shadows," recorded Koga. "I was like a wall amidst water, standing alone without assistance."[17] But when Putiatin reached Shimoda, the whaler had already left. "It seems," wrote Schilling, "that the Americans having accidentally learned of our intentions, had been afraid to permit the violation of the neutrality of a Japanese harbor in their presence, and had advised the French to withdraw."[18] When the *Diana*, upon arrival at Shimoda, had been placed into a strategically defensive position, Schilling had explained: "Our enemies would hardly have respected the neutrality of a Japanese port."[19] The Russian attempt to capture the whaler shows that the English and French would not have been the only ones to violate international law. Be that as it may, with *Napoleon*

III — the excellent French three-master — had sailed away the hope of the Russians for a speedy return to their country. The Russian boats (a longboat commanded by Petr Iolkin and Kolokol'tsov and a cutter commanded by Schilling and Pavel A. Zelenyi), manned by eighty sailors armed with bayonets, cutlasses, and hatchets saved from the frigate — firearms were not used, as the little ammunition that had been gotten ashore had been drenched — arrived in Shimoda by dawn.[20] Theirs had been "a very successful but useless passage."[21] Koga sighed with relief: "Two barbarians fighting [off] our shores truly [would] involve [us]. One day [has] mistakenly passed [and] kindness and hatred both [have been] forgotten. It seems that Heaven has helped."[22] Kawaji had been impressed by the Russian venture. He noted down with admiration: *"Puchyachin wa ikanimo goketsu nari"* (Putiatin is indeed an excellent leader).[23]

While negotiating at Shimoda, the Russians lived at the Fukusen (Gyokusen) Temple, about one mile east of the city, along the harbor road.[24] Putiatin thanked the Japanese officials for their generous treatment: "I have been to four continents, [yet] have not received treatment like [that from] your country. The generosity of your govenment can never be forgotten. When our sovereign will hear of this, he too will certainly be thankful and happy." Koga recorded skeptically: "Old attitude of offering flattery just the same." The admiral continued: "The year is at its end and your families must be waiting. Let us finish the matter quickly so that you can all go home to welcome the new year."[25]

The Japanese did not relish the possibility of Russo-American cooperation. "There still is faithful and polite intercourse between ourselves and the Russians," wrote Koga. "Had the Americans not come, the treaty might have been completed soon. Now things have changed. Settlement seems uncertain. It makes people sigh." Kawaji did not want the Russians to go aboard the *Powhatan*. Koga pointed out that Western custom required assistance to ships in distress: "[If] we relax this, [and] prevent [it], [I] fear [they will] not listen." Kawaji replied: "No, [if they do] not listen to the opposition, they are in the wrong."[26] The Japanese went so far as to conceal their own boats, but the Russians had already signalled the Americans, and a cutter was sent ashore. When an interpreter attempted to stop the Russians, the latter pushed him, jumped into the boat, and said: "Why utter stupid words?" They shook hands with the Americans and patted them on the back. There was nothing the Japanese officials could do.[27] American officers had come ashore to invite the Russians for dinner. The admiral had declined, but all the other officers had gone — all, that is, except Iolkin, who spoke only Russian. When the American officers noted his absence, they concluded that he was ashamed of his worn-out uniform. A party was sent ashore and, almost by force, put an American uniform on Iolkin, who could not protest in English. During dinner, Iolkin's neighbor persistently tried to engage him into a conversation in French. Only once did Iolkin respond. When he grasped that the officer was talking about the earthquake and the foundering of the *Diana*, he emphatically exclaimed: *"Oui, occasion très terrible!"* and from that time on Iolkin was known as *"Occasion très terrible."*[28]

When a Japanese official tried to hinder Russo-American dealings on another occasion, Putiatin scolded him: "You do not understand things, stupid man. I am going aboard the steamer. Send somebody and stop me. [If] foreigners see foreigners, what concern is it of yours? Why do you try to prevent it?"[29]

On February 2, 1855, Commander Adams paid his respects to Putiatin. On the 4th, the admiral returned the visit. Gun salutes were fired.[30] The Americans offered assistance. As Putiatin reported: "The captain [McCluney] and all his officers showed us the most obliging attention. The steamer supplied us with a certain amount of sea-provisions which could not be obtained in Japan, with nautical clothing and boots which the crew needed most. I personally thanked McCluney, the commander of the vessel, and Commander Adams for all these services and at the same time reported it to the Ministry of Foreign Affairs."[31] Putiatin further wrote that Captain McCluney had offered to take the men of the *Diana* to Shanghai, but that he had refused, lest they be captured by the English or French. He did request, however, that the captain notify the commander of the American squadron in the Pacific that, should he deem it possible to assist the Russians by taking them back to their fatherland, he send a steamer for them in April to transport them to Petropavlovsk.[32]

Upon his return to Miyajima (January 21, 1855) from Enoura, Putiatin had found a detailed description of the *Opyt,* the yacht of the commandant of Kronstadt Harbor, in an issue of the *Morskoi Sbornik,* saved from the frigate.[33] Using these data, the admiral had drawn up plans for a schooner. Informed of the Russian intention of building a vessel, the Japanese not only had not objected but had pledged their help. As one of the Russians put it: "The Japanese appraised very well this fortunate circumstance that gave them the opportunity to learn by experience our shipbuilding, which they would not have achieved for a long time with their own means."[34]

Construction of the schooner was begun in one of the recesses of Heda Bay. At first, the work progressed very slowly because the Russians had no instruments, and there were but very few Japanese blacksmiths at Heda and these, unaccustomed to their new work, tried to reproduce every item from samples given them with pedantic exactitude. Many parts were made in Numazu, where there were more and better artisans.[35] The absence of the admiral during his negotiations in Shimoda and of part of the crew during their attempt to capture the French whaler further slowed down the construction. And yet, by the time of Putiatin's return (February 14), considerable progress had been made and — what was most important — instruments, building materials, and artisans had been brought to Heda. A Russian blacksmith's shop had been constructed, making the Russians thus somewhat independent of the Japanese smith, who worked "in general rather unskillfully and quietly."[36]

The Japanese helped with great zeal, "a [fact] to which the novelty of their work, which extremely interested them, contributed considerably."[37] Officials and artisans proved eager students. Throughout the building of the schooner, Japanese officials supervised all work.

They wrote down in detail what was done each day, making drawings of each item and recording its Russian name. The artisans did likewise. Every one had a booklet into which he sketched his work.[38] For different jobs, different artisans and officials were attached to the Russians. They would continue doing the same work, so as to become proficient in it. As many as sixty artisans assisted the Russians at one time.[39] At the same time, as the body of the schooner was being built, her equipment had to be made as well. Hard and fast as the Russians worked,[40] they probably would not have been able to prepare enough ropes had they not bought some from an American vessel.[41]

While the construction of the vessel was proceeding according to plan and a request for Japanese junks had been filed, the American schooner *Caroline E. Foote,* chartered by William C. Reed and T. T. Dougherty at Honolulu, arrived at Shimoda on March 15, 1855, a fortnight before United States treaty rights could be invoked at that port. The vessel arrived with a cargo of ship's chandlery to supply forty American whalers, whose captains expected to outfit at Hakodate in the following season. Aboard were also three American families, of which two intended to settle in Japan.[42] Putiatin hastened to Shimoda (March 18) to hire the schooner. He succeeded in this, but first had to persuade the Japanese governor to let the American families ashore. Permission was finally granted.[43] The self-styled "American pioneers in Japan" landed and were housed in two temples in Kakizaki; the cargo, which, according to Schilling, was of "very dubious quality," was purchased by the Russians and unloaded and stored at Fukusen Temple.[44] On March 22, the Americans united with the Russian officers in the temple to celebrate by music and dancing the birthday anniversary of one of their number.[45]

On March 26, Putiatin returned to Heda aboard the American schooner he had hired to transport the crew to Petropavlovsk. He had learned from the Americans that Petropavlovsk was threatened by a strong enemy squadron and hoped to get there in time to assist his countrymen.[46] The schooner was of about the same size as that the

Russians were building. Her arrival greatly facilitated further construction, as the Japanese artisans could go aboard ship to see what remained to be done on the Russian vessel.

While the *Caroline E. Foote* was being loaded with Japanese rice and weapons that had been saved from the *Diana,* Kawaji and Mizuno arrived with a group of other officials to protest in the name of the Japanese government the landing of the Americans, as well as to clear up certain clauses of the Russo-Japanese treaty that had meanwhile (February 7) been signed. "I evaded these new explanations," reported Putiatin, "and after several meetings with me, the noted persons returned to Edo."[47]

The departure of the *Caroline E. Foote* was further delayed, as Putiatin feared that ice outside of Petropavlovsk Harbor might slow her down — a fact which in view of her limited supply of fresh water might entail disaster. On April 11, 1855, the second day of Russian Easter, however, the American schooner finally went out to sea under the command of her old skipper (Captain A. J. Worth), carrying back to Russia Lesovskii, eight officers, and one hundred and fifty men.[48]

As the schooner was nearing completion, the giant American clipper *Young America* arrived in Shimoda (April 16). The admiral ordered Schilling to hurry to Shimoda and charter the clipper. It was night, and the Japanese were unwilling to provide boat transportation before morning. Without hesitation, Schilling departed on foot. He became completely lost and thus was forced to sit down in an unfamiliar spot and there await dawn. When it became light, he went down to the sea, where a fisherman consented to take him to Matsuzaki. From there, he proceeded across the peninsula (Izu) to Shimoda. He arrived at 4:00 P.M., having been on the way for fourteen hours, twelve of which he had spent walking.

At Shimoda, Schilling met Mr. Babcock, the captain of the clipper, and urged him to sail to Heda and there negotiate directly with the admiral. Babcock would not hear of it at first, as he had no maps of the locality, but finally agreed with the understanding that Schilling would act as pilot. The clipper took aboard the sailors that had remained in Shimoda to look out for vessels and proceeded to Heda, where she arrived the following day.

The admiral immediately opened negotiations concerning the chartering of the clipper. But "the crafty Yankee" had already decided some time before, that "a good piece of money" could be made on this deal. He had learned at Shanghai about the predicament of the Russians from officers aboard the *Powhatan* and had sailed to Shimoda to offer his services. He demanded $50,000. The admiral offered him $18,000. Going down in price by $5,000 at a time, Babcock reached $30,000. But the admiral would not go a penny above his original offer and the Yankee went out to sea.[49]

On April 21, the *Young America* returned. Babcock informed the admiral that he had met the French corvette *Constantin,* and that the French had started back for China when told by the Americans that the Russians were no longer in Japan. Babcock said that he had assured himself that there was no danger of meeting Allied men-of-war at sea, and that he would therefore carry all the remaining Russians and their property to Petropavlovsk for the $18,000 offered by the admiral.[50] No sooner had a contract been signed than Babcock tried to change several paragraphs. The admiral was highly displeased.

The crew of the clipper confirmed Babcock's story as regards meeting the *Constantin,* but they warned that the corvette had not returned to China. They said that Babcock had visited the French captain and that after a prolonged meeting, the *Young America* and the *Constantin* had sailed to Japan together. Putiatin would not let this report deter him in the least.

On April 23, toward evening, the Russians "with the help of almost all the inhabitants of Heda" transferred their belongings and provisions aboard the clipper. Grigorii Semenov and two of the sailors who had been sent to Shimoda after Babcock's original refusal to come down in price, and Nikolai Kovalevskii, who had been dispatched to recall them, were to be left behind if they did not return by sailing time. Putiatin was all set to depart at dawn (April 24).

Then the unexpected happened. The crew of the American clipper mutinied. Unwilling to sail with the Russians lest they be captured by the French or English, most of the men jumped overboard and swam ashore. Some did not make it. Though the Russians could have manned the clipper themselves, a crew was needed for her voyage back. Putiatin, therefore, requested the Japanese authorities to round up the fugitives. The Russians spent the night aboard the clipper. Kovalevskii, Semenov, and the sailors rejoined their comrades.

In the morning, when everything was ready for the departure — the escaped crew had been returned aboard the vessel — Babcock appeared with the contract. He had torn it to pieces. He announced that he could not transport the Russians, as not only his crew, but also his officers had refused him obedience. Angered, the admiral ordered his men ashore. Later on, Babcock revisited the admiral and informed him that by means of special financial compensation he had persuaded his men to agree to the voyage after all, and that he was thus prepared to sign a new contract. By this time, however, Putiatin would have nothing to do with Babcock and the latter sailed away cursing (April 25).

Once more, Russian hopes centered on the *Caroline E. Foote*, which was to return to Heda and pick up the remaining *Diana* complement.[51]

Meanwhile, a certain amount of excitement had been created by the surreptitious addition of a new member to the Russian crew: a Japanese of the Kakegawa clan (Shizuoka), by the name of Tachibana Kosai (Kumezo). This fabulous character, whose past as a military man and Nichiren priest had been overshadowed by a record of gambling, swindling, imprisonment, murder, and woman trouble — and who, in later years, as Vladimir Iosifovich Yamatov was to play an intriguing role as head of a Russian household, official of the Russian Ministry of Foreign Affairs, professor of Japanese at the University of St. Petersburg, and interpreter on Russian men-of-war, before repatriation to Japan and retirement in Buddhist meditation — joined the Russians in Heda. He had been in contact with

Goshkevich, whom he taught some Japanese and to whom he sold some Japanese books and a map of Japan. His activities apparently became known and he had to flee for his life. To hide him from his countrymen, the Russians clad him in a Russian sailor suit and a black hemp wig, and when Japanese officials inspected Russian quarters in search of him, surrounded him by a throng of sailors and marched him from room to room. When the suspicious officials posted a guard at the well-illuminated wharf and brought a lantern to the face of every person that approached the gangplank, the Russians sent Tachibana aboard ship in a box, where he arrived, incidentally, upside down.[52]

The Japanese, accustomed to flat-bottomed junks, were greatly interested in the keel of the schooner that was being built. They were particularly curious about how such a vessel could be launched. They refused to believe that it would slide safely down the ways and laughed off Russian explanations.

April 26 was the big day. All officials who were in Heda gathered aboard the schooner. As the Japanese were skeptical about the possibility of launching the schooner the Russian way, they refused to take the responsibility of cutting away the slip blocks and simply watched the proceedings as spectators.[53] "It is easy to guess the feelings with which we made all the preparations for the letting down of the schooner," wrote A. K. (Aleksandr Kolokol'tsov?). "The Japaenese saw this for the first time and expected some wonder; should it have happened to our misfortune that the schooner would not slide down the ways, we would have lost in their eyes all confidence in ourselves as shipbuilders."[54] But the vessel was launched without mishap. She was christened *Heda,* in honor of the place where she had been built. A threefold hurrah accompanied her as she slid into the water.[55] Two flags, one of the Russian Empire and one of the ambassador, fluttered from the ensign staff.[56] The Japanese — officials, artisans, and spectators — watched the schooner float on the waters, then hastened over to the ambassador to extend their congratulations, "bowing deeply in gratitude for the lesson they had been given."[57]

A celebration followed. The workers were dined on the stocks; the officials, in the temple in which the Russians stayed. Many toasts were offered, among them one to the founding of a Japanese navy. "The Japanese were delighted, and this time did not hide their feelings."[58]

10

The Treaty of Shimoda

RUSSO-JAPANESE NEGOTIATIONS FELL INTO THREE DISTINCT PHASES: ONE of Japanese hostility and disdain, one of increasing Japanese respect, and one of expressions of mutual admiration and friendship. The first phase (August to November, 1853) lasted as long as the Japanese government ignored — or at least appeared to ignore — the Russians. The second phase (January to December, 1854) followed, when dignitaries were dispatched from Edo to receive the admiral and his retinue with much ceremony. The third phase (December, 1854 to July, 1855) began with the shipwreck of the *Diana*. As masters of the situation, the Japanese could afford to be friendly.[1]

The avowed demands of the Russians are clear. They were communicated to the Japanese in Nesselrode's letter to the *Roju*. They were concerned with two major points: the clarification of boundaries and the opening of Japanese ports to trade. Nesselrode insisted that "the important [matter] of the daily boundary problems between the two countries" could be postponed no longer. He asked that a joint conference, conducted "for the benefit of both countries," determine which islands constituted the northern and southern boundaries of Japan and Russia respectively and decide also to whom the southern coast of Sakhalin (Karafuto) belonged. Nesselrode noted that Russia had been vast in territory since ancient times. He assured the *Roju* that the Tsar had no further territorial ambitions; he only wanted to safeguard the just profits belonging to the inhabitants and, therefore, considered the determination of the boundaries "the basis of mutual peace."[2] Nesselrode continued that the Tsar wished to see Japanese ports opened to Russian subjects for trade and to Russian men-of-war en route to North America for taking on supplies in case of an emergency. It was not Russia's intention, Nesselrode insisted, to deprive the Japanese of profit. He pointed out that Russia and Japan were neighboring countries, and that it was "natural" for them to have friendly intercourse; that this differed from having relations with distant countries, and that such a request was not "contrary to propriety." Nesselrode expressed confidence that the Japanese government would receive the Russian plenipotentiary with respect and due ceremony, and that all points at issue could be worked out to the mutual interest of Japan and Russia.[3]

The desires of the Japanese government are no less clear than those of the Russian one. It wanted to have nothing to do with any and all Westerners — except the Dutch, whom it suffered to stay on Deshima Island under narrow restrictions. When it became evident that Japan's seclusion could not be maintained forever, the governmen strove to delay the inevitable as long as possible.

The tactics of the Japanese government can be summarized in one word: procrastination. The Japanese naively hoped to tire out the Russians by noncooperation and passive resistance. "They reckoned," Putiatin wrote, "that, upon wearing out our patience, they would succeed in forcing us to abandon completely our intention of establishing trade with them, or at least to postpone the latter for an undetermined time."[4]

Not all procrastination was deliberate. Part of the delay was inherent in the Tokugawa administration. As Tokutomi Iichiro has put it: "The Bakufu's chronic disease lay in procrastination. Nothing could be settled speedily."[5] Part of the delay was incidental to the unexpectedness of the Russian arrival, the Shogun's death, panic, and bad communications. Reporting the slow-down tactics of the governor of

Nagasaki, Putiatin explained: "Without doubt, he acted this way on the basis of old rules ... from which he did not presume to deviate, lest he be subject to the strictest accountability before his government. But the government itself had not expected the appearance of a number of men-of-war off the shores of Japan ... and had of course not had time to supply the governor with new directions...."[6]

Exactly one month passed between Putiatin's first arrival at Nagasaki (August 21, 1853) and the acceptance of the Russian state letter he had brought (September 21, 1853). Almost four more months went by before he received a reply (January 16, 1854). Only then did the negotiations commence, and were continued off and on for another thirteen months (until February 7, 1855).

Secreting of all intelligence from the enemy was part of the Japanese scheme. A curtain of silence or evasion concealed much. All that Goncharov had received an answer to the query, how many inhabitants were in Nagasaki, had been: "Sometimes there are less, and sometimes more."[7] Asked the name of the Shogun, the Japanese had replied: "We do not know."[8] "What a people!" Goncharov had complained, "what a system of guarding against contraband of all kind. What hope does it seem there could be for trade, for the introduction of Christianity, for enlightenment, when the building is so securely locked and the key has been lost? How and when will all this come? But come it will, there is no doubt, although not soon."[9]

Putiatin's way of dealing with the shilly-shally tactics of the Shogunate and its representatives has been described by him as follows: "Taking into consideration the Imperial wish of our late Sovereign, the Emperor, and the instructions given me by the Ministry of Foreign Affairs, I mapped out for myself a line of action [to be followed] in dealings with this nation.... I adopted a kind of friendly approach towards it, the indulgent compliance with those laws and customs of the country which are not contrary to the dignity of our nation and my calling, and a firm, quiet insistence in negotiating concerning my mission."[10] Reporting about his first visit to Nagasaki, he noted: "I tried to maintain friendly relations with the governor and his officials ... and instill into them as much more confidence as possible in the intentions of our government."[11] But Putiatin was not above resorting to threats. "Although I knew from the history of all preceding embassies to Japan how slowly all official business is transacted in this state," he reported, "I considered it necessary, however, to show at times a certain persistence so that the Japanese on their part would exert greater speed in their relations with us.... My entreaties alone could not have led to the desired success had they not been backed up by my frequently expressed readiness to sail to Edo in order to attain there as quickly as possible the purposes of my coming, through direct dealing with the highest authorities.

"Their fear of seeing near the capital some more men-of-war in addition to the American ones, which were already there, was so great that on that occasion and on many others they hastened to satisfy our just solicitations.

"I consider it my duty to add," he concluded, "that expressing my readiness to go to Edo, I intended to decide on it only in case of extreme necessity, such as if the Japanese refused to deal with me or named too distant a date for a reply to the letter I had brought."[12]

Putiatin's approach extended to seemingly insignificant items of discussion. "All these were such trifles about which it would have been strange to argue," Goncharov pointed out, "had they not entailed rather important consequences. Giving in to their demands concerning trifles might cause them to demand concessions in important matters as well, and might conceivably lead to a certain amount of presumption in their relations with us. For that reason, the admiral followed always the method he had adopted in his dealings with them; that is, gentleness, politeness, and firmness in insignificant as well as important matters. It was up to the Japanese to form an opinion about us from those trifles with which our relations began, and up to us [to use these trifles] to fix the tone which was to prevail in future negotiations."[13]

The first phase of Russo-Japanese negotiations was merely a prelude, since the officials with whom the Russians met had no authority to determine anything the Russians demanded. The transmittal of the Russian state paper was the outstanding event.

It was during the second phase that the groundwork was laid for the Treaty of Amity and Friendship. The plenipotentiaries brought with them the *Roju's* reply to Nesselrode's letter. Its tone is significant, for it was devoid of all the arrogance that had permeated similar communications in the past. "Your country has come with good intentions," it stated, "how could our country not answer with good intentions?" The *Roju* reviewed the Russian demands one by one. It agreed to a clarification of the boundaries of the outlying territories, in view of the fact that the Russians insisted that they were "exceedingly unclear." Border fiefs had already been ordered to make a careful investigation, and envoys would be sent to confer with Russian officials. "But since a sound investigation of boundary fiefs involves the use of maps and documents and, for the sake of reliability, calls for the most scrupulous analysis of the problem, such an investigation cannot be done today."[14] The Japanese pointed out that their ancestors had left laws strictly prohibiting trade. They had never disobeyed these laws. In the past, Russia had requested the establishment of trade relations; and Japan had decidedly refused. "We felt that your officials must have understood the beginning and end of this matter."

"But today the world situation is changing rapidly," the *Roju* admitted, "and trade is developing daily; merchant ships have sailed around the five continents. We definitely cannot take [the] old tradition and laws to regulate present day affairs."[15] The reply noted that the Americans had just requested trade, and many other countries would soon follow suit. Were Japan to have a treaty with Russia when all these nations would come to demand trade, difficulties would arise. "If we trade, we shall trade with all [countries]," explained the Japanese, "if we refuse, we shall refuse all. If we sign a treaty with your country, we cannot but sign treaties with all nations. Considering that we have only the strength of one nation to supply the demands of ten thousand nations scattered like stars, we do not know whether our resources will suffice." If Japan needed things from other countries, they did not know what. A study of potential exports and imports must be made. "There are numerous and complicated problems that cannot be decided in a day or a night." Moreover, the Sovereign had just taken office and everything was new to him. Such an important matter must be reported to Kyoto,[16] and notices must be sent to all feudal lords. Discussions would follow. "From the looks of things, it will take at least three to five years," the Japanese wrote. "Although this may seem like postponement and delay, you should follow our words with even temper and wait."[17]

The *Roju* promised to inform the Russians of its decision promptly, and warned that they would be wasting their time were they to return again and again in the hope of speeding matters up. "What advantage would you gain from this endless running around?" Meanwhile, the Russians could obtain firewood, food, and water at Nagasaki. "We are ashamed that it has to be this way," concluded the members of the *Roju*, "but we cannot keep quiet, therefore, answer you like this." Signed: Abe Ise-no-kami Masahiro, Makino Bizen-no-kami Tadamasa, Matsudaira Izumi-no-kami Noriyasu, Matsudaira Iga-no-kami Tadayoshi, Kuze Yamato-no-kami Hiroshika, Naito Kii-no-kami Nobuchika.[18]

Putiatin did not rest satisfied with this reply. "Such superficial sentences!" he complained to the plenipotentiaries. "How can our government respect [your government]?"[19] And yet the letter shows how the Japanese government was beginning to yield. The *Roju* did not refuse to discuss boundary problems, nor did it object to trade. It admitted that "present day affairs" could not be regulated by "old tradition and laws." All the Japanese asked for was time to study all the matters involved — a not too unreasonable request for a nation that had lived in seclusion for over two centuries. As Putiatin demanded more concrete commitments, the plenipotentiaries tried to reassure him that "should communication be permitted to foreign countries, it will of course be permitted to Russia,"[20] a recapitulation of the *Roju's* declaration that "if we trade, we shall trade with all [countries]." On February 13, 1854, they actually went so far as to promise Russia preferential treatment. A note to Putiatin stated that "should our country finally permit trade, it will be first to your country."[21] The plenipotentiaries declared that they considered Russia "a defense against other countries" and extracted from Putiatin the promise that "in the event that people from other countries cause violent disturbances, we [the Russians] are prepared to give you [the Japanese] any assistance."[22]

One month later, the treaty of Kanagawa was signed. It did not establish trade relations between the United States and Japan, but it did provide for the care of American waifs, and opened two ports to American vessels. The promise of preferential treatment for Russia had not been kept. Why? Because the plenipotentiaries in Edo knew nothing of the promise made in Nagasaki. Liaison was inadequate and communications too slow. Kawaji and Tsutsui learned of the conclusion of the Japanese-American treaty only on their way back to the capital. They were very much upset. So were other officials. Abe Masahiro, head of the *Roju,* almost resigned. To appease Kawaji and Tsutsui, the Shogunate reappointed them plenipotentiaries with authority to grant the Russians — should they return (they had left in February) — the same concessions as had been made the Americans.[23]

When Putiatin arrived at Shimoda to take up again the negotiations that had been interrupted ten months before, he found Japanese resistance lessened. Having learned before his return to Japan of Commodore Perry's success, he came confident not only of his ability to obtain a similar treaty but also that, now that several harbors had been opened to the Americans, the seclusion of Japan as a whole must come to an end, treaties or no treaties. American whalers would not pass by the opportunity to enter the harbors, particularly since the Japanese, unwilling to permit anything resembling trade — at least for the time being — would not accept payment for firewood, provisions, and water. What could be better for the whalers? But the ports had been opened only for taking on fresh supplies. The Japanese would restrict the movements of the whalers. There would be quarrels, then brawls — at first in isolated circumstances, then more frequently. "It is known to what all this leads," Goncharov commented.[24]

As the plenipotentiaries had come prepared to grant the Russians whatever concessions Perry had received, Putiatin could have concluded a similar shipwreck convention in no time. But he wanted more. He wished to settle boundary questions and substitute other ports for those opened by the Americans.

Putiatin asserted that only the southernmost Kuril Islands belonged to Japan, but Kawaji objected that, "quite contrary to what you have said," the Japanese knew the northern islands "like the palm of our hand." "There is no reason why we should discuss the boundary with you," he added.[25] Putiatin insisted that one of the islands was Russian. "A hundred years ago it belonged to us," he argued. "A thousand years ago it belonged to us," Nakamura rejoined. Concerning the boundary of another island, the Russians were "cunningly quiet." Write Koga: "If they can win a big island with a three-inch tongue, it is really smart beyond description and the accomplishment is worth recording."[26]

There was division in the Japanese camp as to the tactics to be followed. Koga, who disliked Kawaji even more than the "barbarians," disagreed wherever possible. He believed that the border people would work with the Russians and objected to Kawaji's brazen statements. When the latter replied that orders from Edo stated that all Kuril Islands wholly belonged to Japan, he insisted that " 'wholly belong' to us cannot be uttered." There was no proof. "Going back to ancient days," he wrote, "our countrymen have never been east and north of 50°." It was dishonest to claim possession of all the islands. The instructions from Edo might have been misread or copied down incorrectly, "but I have other understanding in my heart," he added reflectively.[27] Anti-Russian or antiforeign as Koga was, he insisted that propriety be observed. "Elder brother's treatment of the barbarians should be like the clear blue sky and the white sun," he had remonstrated when Kawaji had tried to secrete the conclusion of the Japanese-American treaty from Putiatin. Koga warned that if they were not frank with the Russians, the latter would not only become suspicious, but further increase their demands. He pointed out that to assume that the Russians did not know yet about the treaty was dangerous, and to think that the Americans might modify their position, unrealistic.[28] The Russians actually obtained a copy of the Japanese-American treaty by bribing the interpreter Tatsunosuke. Once Kawaji realized that the Russians were familiar with the provisions of the treaty, he became more yielding.[29]

The ports opened to the Americans were unsatisfactory. Perry had forced the Japanese at gun point to name two harbors, and the Japanese had quite understandably chosen two of the least value. Shimoda was isolated from the rest of Honshu by mountains; Hakodate was removed from the political and commercial centers of the main island. The Japanese offered to add Nagasaki to the list; but it, too, was undesirable — far out of the way of Russian merchant vessels. When Putiatin had first declared: "At Shimoda, wind and waves are dangerous. We do not ask you to open it. We wish you could open another port for the Russians," Kawaji had argued (on December 22, 1854, the day before the fatal earthquake), "Shimoda has never had the danger of a sinking ship. It is a lucky port. Why do you want to avoid it?"[30] When Putiatin had persisted in demanding "another harbor and Hakodate, as stated in the [American] treaty," Kawaji had asked him to suggest a port. He chose Osaka. Kawaji refused. "You will not agree to Uraga near Edo," continued Putiatin, "how about Hamamatsu?" Again Kawaji refused. Neither did he approve of Hyogo or any other of the Russian choices.[31]

The loss of the *Diana* off Shimoda did not make the Russians like that port any more. But they did not use the tidal wave as an argument for changing harbors, agreeing with Kawaji that such a disaster was neither common nor confined to Shimoda. The real threat lay in the lack of cover from waves and wind. "The Americans, the Dutch, and the Chinese have gladly agreed;" said Kawaji, "why are you so stubborn and do not agree?" The Russians answered that neither the

Dutch nor the Chinese had anchored at Shimoda, hence did not know the real situation. The Americans had not encountered heavy wind and waves. Besides, they had received most of what they had wanted and hence had had no wish to discuss further whether or not the harbor was good and had happily agreed to what the Japanese had proposed. When Kawaji maintained that "there is really no new port that can be opened," Putiatin pointed out that the rebuilding of Shimoda would involve countless expense. He argued that when the Americans would see the destruction wrought by the earthquake, they too would object to Shimoda, and the Japanese would have to open another port. "Isn't it a waste of money and time then?" he asked. "If you use the money [intended] for recovery of this harbor to open a new port, there should be no difficulties."[32] And so the discussion continued.

Russian arguments for trade were backed up by gifts, selected to arouse interest in Russian goods. Wary of the potential persuasiveness of the latter, the Japanese government tried to prevent any distribution of things Russian among its subjects. Moriyama Einosuke informed Pos'et one day that a Russian sailor had given an empty bottle to a Japanese. "So what?" Pos'et had asked. "Permit [us] to send it back," Moriyama pleaded, "otherwise it will be bad: the one who accepted the gift will be punished." "Throw it into the water," Pos'et replied. "[That] cannot [be done]," insisted Moriyama; "we shall bring it and then you throw it out yourself."[33]

The third phase of the negotiations, following the shipwrecking of the Russian expedition, saw the successful completion of the negotiations. Tokutomi Iichiro notes that the disaster was really a blessing in disguise. "The good will and kindness of Japan toward the Russians greatly moved their [Russian] hearts and thus all the negotiations proceeded smoothly."[34]

The Russians had time and again threatened to go to Edo,[35] but now their tone had changed. Noted Koga: "I hear the barbarians are in extreme distress; it seems it will be easier to talk [to them]."[36] Wrote Kawaji: "The Russians were repeatedly humble in speech...."

Their words tamed us greatly."³⁷ The loss of the *Diana* had put the Russians completely at the mercy of the Japanese. The latter had been anxious to hide the weakness of their government from the Japanese people. Concessions to an armed foreign force involved much loss of face. But now that the Russians were in distress, the Japanese government could afford to be generous. As Koga noted in his diary, the country of the "barbarians" was at war and might be destroyed. They had had to flee and hide from a strong enemy. Shipwrecked in a tidal wave, they had barely escaped death. Even though "they deserve being killed for their plans and schemes," their suffering seemed to arouse pity.³⁸ The fact that the Russians were shipwrecked off Shimoda after Kawaji had refused to let them seek shelter in a more protected bay, assuring them that this was a "lucky" port, may have also aroused in Kawaji pangs of conscience, for he always thought of himself as a *gishi*, "a man of rectitude," and to such a man "nothing is more loathsome . . . than underhand dealings and crooked undertakings."³⁹

Russian assistance to Japanese victims at the time of their own distress, and Japanese concern for Russian safety, as well as the cooperative building of the schooner *Heda*, helped create an atmosphere of greater trust and respect, if not friendship. The Japanese complied with Putiatin's request to hide the guns of the foundered *Diana*. "Protecting our interests in such a way against any attempts on the part of the English and French," the admiral reported later on, "the Japanese clearly showed how much they troubled themselves concerning our circumstances." Certainly they showed that they no longer feared Russian encroachment and aggression. "I dare hope," concluded the admiral, "that the proposal, sent to the Japanese government in accordance with the wish of His Imperial Highness, to accept the frigate's guns, which have remained with them, as a gift, will be for them the fairest and dearest reward."⁴⁰

By February 1, the "original items" of the discussion had been settled. "I drank alone and celebrated," recorded Koga in his diary.⁴¹

By February 7, the final drafts of the treaty were ready for signature.[42] The Japanese and Russian delegates met at the Choraku Temple and, after checking the Japanese, Chinese, and Dutch copies for accuracy,[43] signed them, attached their seals, and exchanged copies.[44]

The treaty reads:

In order to establish peace and friendship between Russia and Japan and to affirm them by treaty, His Highness the Emperor, Autocrat of all Russia, has appointed as Plenipotentiary His Adjutant-General Vice-Admiral Evfimii Putiatin,[45] and His Highness the Great Sovereign of all Japan has appointed as Plenipotentiaries His eminent subjects: Tsutsui Khizenno-Kami [Tsutsui Hizen-no-kami] and Kavadzi-Saiemonno-Dzio [Kawaji Saemon-no-jo].

The [above-]mentioned Plenipotentiaries have laid down the following articles:

ARTICLE I

Henceforth let there be continuous peace and sincere friendship between Russia and Japan. In the possession of both Empires, Russians and Japanese enjoy protection and defense in regards to their personal safety as well as to the inviolability of their property.

ARTICLE II

Henceforth the boundaries between Russia and Japan will pass between the islands Iturup [Etorofu] and Urup [Uruppu]. The whole island of Iturup belongs to Japan and the whole island Urup and the other Kuril Islands to the north constitute possessions of Russia. As regards the island Krafto [Karafuto] (Sakhalin), it remains unpartitioned between Russia and Japan, as has been [the case] to this time.

ARTICLE III

The Japanese Government opens for Russian vessels three ports: Simoda [Shimoda] in the principality Idzu [Izu], Khakodate [Hakodate] in the district Khakodate, and Nagasaki in the principality Khizen [Hizen]. In these three ports, Russian vessels can henceforth repair their damages, supply themselves with water, firewood, victuals, and other necessities, even coal, where it can be obtained, and pay for all this with gold or silver specie, and in case of lack of money substitute for it goods from their store.

With the exception of the [above-]mentioned harbors, Russian vessels will not visit other ports, except in cases when because of extreme exigency the vessel will not be able to continue the voyage. Outlays made in such cases will be reimbursed in one of the open[ed] ports.

ARTICLE IV

Shipwrecked vessels and people in both Empires will be shown all kinds of assistance and all survivors will be delivered to open ports. Throughout all of their stay in the foreign land they [shall] enjoy freedom, but submit to the just laws of the country.

ARTICLE V

In the first two of the opened ports, the Russians are allowed to exchange desired goods and property for goods, property, and money brought.

ARTICLE VI

The Russian Government will, when it finds it indispensable, appoint a consul to one of the two first mentioned ports.

ARTICLE VII

If some question or matter demanding consideration or decision should arise, it will be considered in detail and set in order by the Japanese Government.

ARTICLE VIII

A Russian in Japan, as well as a Japanese in Russia, are always free and are not subject to any constraints. [A person who] has committed a crime can be arrested, but is tried in no other way than according to the laws of his [own] country.

ARTICLE IX

In consideration of the proximity of both Empires, all rights and privileges which Japan has granted at present or will give in the future to other nations extend at the same time also to Russian subjects.

This treaty will be ratified by His Highness the Emperor and Autocrat of all Russia and His Highness the Great Sovereign of all Japan, or as stated in the attached special agreement, and the ratifications will be exchanged in Simoda not sooner than in nine months or as circumstances will permit. As for the present, copies of the treaty bearing the signatures and seals of the Plenipotentiaries of both Empires are exchanged, and all its articles come into force from the day of signature and will be observed by both negotiating parties faithfully and inviolably.

Concluded and signed in the city [of] Simoda in the 1855th year from the birth of Christ, on the 26th day of January (7th day of February), or in the first year of Ansei on the 21st day of the twelfth month.

Signed:

Evfimii Putiatin

Tsutsui-Khizenno-Kami [Tsutsui Hizen-no-kami]

Kavadzi-Saemonno-Dzio[46] [Kawaji Saemon-no-jo][47]

EXPLANATORY ARTICLES OF THE TREATY BETWEEN RUSSIA AND JAPAN

Corroborated by the Russian Plenipotentiary Adjutant-General Vice-Admiral Evfimii Putiatin and the Japanese Plenipotentiaries Tsutsui-Khizenno-Kami and Kavadzi-Saiemonno-Dzio.

TO ARTICLE III

A. In the first two of the designated ports, the Russians can go [about] freely; in the city of Simoda and its environs for a distance of seven miles counting from Inubashiri Island, and in Khakodate for a distance of five Japanese miles. They can also visit shops, shrines, and, until the arrangement of inns [hotels], designated houses for resting. As for private houses, they must not enter them,[48] except by invitation. In Nagasaki — as will be determined later on for the others.

B. For the burial of the deceased, a place will be set aside in each port and these cemeteries must be inviolable.

TO ARTICLE V

The release of goods will take place in a specially designated government building,[49] whither the goods and gold and silver specie brought will also be delivered. The Russians, having selected in the shops goods or property and having agreed with the vendor on the price, pay for them or exchange them for the goods brought on the vessel in the designated house through the mediation of Japanese officials.

TO ARTICLE VI

A. Russian consuls will be appointed, from the year 1856.

B. Places and houses for the consulate will be determined by the Japanese Government and the Russians [will] live in them according to their own customs and laws.

TO ARTICLE IX

The rights and privileges mentioned in Article IX, of whatever sort they might be, given to other nations, are similarly extended to Russia without further negotiations.

These explanatory articles have all the force of the treaty and are equally binding on both negotiating parties, in proof of which they are countersigned by the signature and seals of the Plenipotentiaries of both Empires.

Concluded and signed in the city of Simoda in the 1855th year from the birth of Christ, on the 26th day of January (7th day of February), or [in] the first year of Ansei on the 21st day of the 12th month.

Signed:

Evfimii Putiatin
Tsutsui-Khizenno-Kami [Tsutsui Hizen-no-kami]
Kavadzi-Safmonno-Dzio [Kawaji Saemon-no-jo][50]

The Russians kept their copy of the treaty in an impressive case with a golden two-headed eagle; the Japanese, in a plain box wrapped in a *furoshiki,* "because all felt that this is personal property, not official property." "Kawaji repeatedly said things that put shame on country," wrote Koga, and with a sigh concluded: "You would not expect him not to put shame on the document."[51]

The copies of the treaty having been exchanged, Putiatin addressed Tsutsui and Kawaji: "I have bothered you two gentlemen during this whole year. Today I have finally gotten what I wished. How fortunate!" Promising to make special mention of his indebtedness to the Japanese, he asked: "Can we be of service to your country?"[52]

Celebrations followed. Both Russians and Japanese had lost most of their supplies in the recent disaster and thus could not entertain as lavishly as on previous occasions. Some wine had been saved, but no glasses, and tea cups had to be used. "Should this meeting get into the newspapers at [some] other time," said Kawaji with concern, "[I] hope our stinginess will be hidden."[53]

Upon giving Commander Adams copies of the treaty and various reports for transmittal to St. Petersburg, via Vienna and Washington, Putiatin started back to Heda. Pos'et and seven men were left behind at Shimoda to maintain continuous communication between the two ports and to keep a lookout for Western vessels.[54] Before his departure, Putiatin had sent a note to Tsutsui and Kawaji, in which he wrote that he was sorry that the prolonged stay of the expedition had kept them away from home so long. He realized their concern over a possible clash between Russian and Allied forces and reassured them that "now [that] the treaty has been completed, we definitely shall not involve and bother your honorable nation." Should an armed conflict prove "really necessary," the Russians would go out to sea and fight there. "We are now leaving for Heda," the admiral concluded; "you two gentlemen feel at ease."[55]

11

The United States and Russia

THE UNITED STATES AND RUSSIA HAD APPROACHED JAPAN FOR SIMILAR reasons. There were minor variations, such as American emphasis on the protection of seamen and the taking on of supplies, and Russian interest in the settling of boundary questions; but, essentially, each wished to establish relations with Japan before the other — or any other power — obtained exclusive privileges.

Western expansion in China had led Russia to seek to safeguard her position in the Far East by establishing friendly relations with Japan. As Francis L. Hawks noted correctly, "If she [Russia] aims at being a commercial nation, the possession of Japan would make her eminently so."[1]

The United States was alarmed. It felt that "there is no power in the other hemisphere to which the possession of Japan, or the control of its affairs, is as important as it is to Russia. She is on one side of the islands, the United States on the other. The Pacific Ocean is destined to be the theater of immense commercial undertakings. Russia is, in a great degree, shut out by her local position from easy access to the Atlantic; but with such harbors on the Pacific as Japan could give her, she might hope to become the controlling maritime power of the world."[2] "If she possessed Japan," Hawks wrote, "she would have an abundance of harbors, unrivalled in the world for excellency, and with her resources would control

[127]

the commerce of the Pacific." "It is not, therefore, the interest of any part of the commercial world," he concluded, "that Russia should ever own Japan."[3]

And yet there is no evidence that Russia had at that time considered taking possession of Japan, nor that she had even sought exclusive commercial privileges. Americans feared that "if Commodore Perry unfortunately should fail in his peaceful attempts, and be brought into hostile collision with the Japanese, Russia was on the spot, not to mediate, but to tender to Japan her aid as an ally in the conflict, and if successful, to avail herself of the moment of confidence to get a foothold in some port of the Kingdom, with the intention, at the proper time of absorbing all."[4] Putiatin did promise the Japanese assistance in case of foreign aggression, but this seems to have been more of a pro-Japanese than anti-American move. There are no comments hostile toward the United States in any of the Russian diaries or reports at our disposal[5]; except, perhaps, for the somewhat condescending attitude toward merchants and particularly "crafty Yankee traders." Putiatin actually offered to join his forces to the American squadron. Perry, however, suspicious and jealous of Russian activities, "civilly, but decidedly" declined the proposal.[6]

Perry had instituted strict censorship aboard the American expedition "to keep intelligence about the mission from the eyes and ears of the Russians and of any other people who might be planning a similar project."[7] He had refused to employ the well-known Japanologist, Philipp Franz von Siebold, because he suspected him of being a Russian agent.[8] Perry's anti-Russian disposition was not to be shared by Commander Adams and Captain McCluney, who were to offer assistance repeatedly to the shipwrecked Russians, nor by the lonely Townsend Harris, America's first consul in Japan (1856-1859), who welcomed and enjoyed the company of Russian officers. We cannot find anything in our sources to justify Perry's mistrust, but admit that a century later his words appear prophetic:

It seems to me [Perry had predicted] that the people of America will, in some form or other, extend their dominion and their power, until they shall have ... placed the Saxon race upon the eastern shores of Asia. And I think too that eastward and southward will her great rival in future aggrandizement [Russia] stretch forth her power to the coasts of China and Siam: and thus the Saxon and the Cossack will meet.... Will it be friendship? I fear not! The antagonistic exponents of freedom and absolutism must meet at last, and then will be fought the mighty battle on which the world will look with breathless interest; for on its issue will depend the freedom or the slavery of the world.... I think I see in the distance the giants that are growing up for that fierce and final encounter; in the progress of events that battle must sooner or later be fought.[9]

In China, Americans and Russians worked hand in hand. They would let British and French gunboats obtain concessions, then demand identical privileges for themselves. Thus the United States and Russia shared in the profits, but not, to the same extent, in the stigma of Anglo-French imperialism. But in Japan, there were no English or French men-of-war to follow. Either the Americans or the Russians or both now had to play the role of the British. As united action was unacceptable to Perry, and the possibility of a Russo-Japanese agreement prior to the conclusion of a Japanese-American treaty a grave threat in his eyes, Perry stepped into British footsteps.[10] The Russians, on the other hand, continued their old policy of sharing in the profits arising from the aggression of others. And theirs was the better part of the bargain, for not only did they receive all the concessions threats had bought, but also the good will of all the people threats had alienated.

Perry considered the Japanese "the common enemy of mankind." His official instructions from the State Department, dated November 5, 1852, and written by himself, stated:

Every nation has undoubtedly the right to determine for itself the extent to which it will hold intercourse with other nations. The same law of nations, however, which protects a nation in the exercises of this right imposes upon her certain duties which she cannot justly disregard. Among these duties none is more imperative than that which requires her to succor and relieve those persons who are cast by the perils of the ocean upon her shores. This duty is, it is true, among those that are denominated by writers on public law imperfect, and which confer no right on other nations to exact their performance; nevertheless, if a nation not only habitually and systematically disregards it, but treats such unfortunate persons as if they were the most atrocious criminals, such nations may justly be considered as the common enemy of mankind.[11]

Perry regarded the Japanese as weak and semibarbarous. The orders noted:

That the civilized nations of the world should for ages have submitted to such treatment by a weak and semi-barbarous people, can only be accounted for on the supposition that, from the remoteness of the country, instances of such treatment were of rare occurrence, and the difficulty of chastising it very great. It can hardly be doubted that if Japan were situated as near the continent of Europe or of America as it is to that of Asia, its government would long since have been either treated as barbarians, or been compelled to respect these usages of civilized states of which it receives the protection...."[12]

Thinking that none of the Japanese understood English idioms, the Commodore and his officers often sounded off, "calling the whole race savages, liars, a pack of fools, poor devils; cursing them and then denying practically all of it by supposing them worth making a treaty with."[13]

The Russians were more tolerant, in a condescending sort of a way. They found much in the Japanese that they admired. Their manners were proper, their bearing polite. "In a word," Goncharov summed up, "in everything they would be pretty good people, except that one cannot have anything to do with them: they delay, deceive, and then refuse. To beat them, one feels pity. They have set up such an order at their place that even if they wished not to refuse, or in general do something that has not existed before, even if good, they cannot do so, at least not voluntarily."[14]

"They see," Goncharov wrote later on, "that their system of locking [themselves] in and alienation in which alone they sought safety has taught them nothing and only stopped their growth. Like a school plot, it has collapsed instantly with the appearance of the teacher. They are alone, without help. There is nothing for them [to do] but break out in tears and say: 'we are guilty, we are children,' and like children put themselves under the guidance of elders.

"But who will these elders be? Here are the crafty indefatigable manufacturers, the Americans, and here a handful of Russians: the Russian bayonet, although still peaceful and inoffensive, still a guest, has already sparkled in the rays of the Japanese sun, and on the Japanese shore [the command] '*vpered* [forward]!' has been heard. *Avis au Japon!*

"If not we, then the Americans, if not the Americans, then those who follow them — whoever it might be, is soon fated to pour into the veins of Japan those healthy juices which she has suicidally excreted from her body together with her own blood [so that she] has grown decrepit in weakness and the gloom of a pitiful childhood."[15]

Japanese sources credit Putiatin and his men with conduct that won the respect of the inhabitants. Putiatin was always considerate of the population. When he walked on the road, he would keep to one side to let other people pass. Once, he learned that a Russian sailor had cut down some wood. He went over and scolded him publicly. "Not an inch of grass or a foot of wood has been disturbed," Koga recorded appreciatively.[16]

American sailors, on the other hand, were responsible for a number of incidents. One day, for example, several sailors stopped three Japanese and demanded to see their swords. When the latter refused, one of the Americans hit one of the Japanese. These became very angry and wanted to chop his head off. One of the sailors, "who looked as if he had been drinking," interceded, gesticulating that his comrades were drunk. The Japenese reported this incident to Koga: "The American barbarians are very despicable," they complained. There were no walls to protect them from the Americans, and, as Shimoda was surrounded by "wilderness" on four sides, there was no place to ask for help. "We better move to escape from the barbarians," they concluded. "I agreed with what they said," Koga recorded, "but it was night and we could not do anything."[17]

As time went by, attitudes changed. Koga noted that previously the Americans had been very much disliked for all the incidents they created. "But now," he continued, "[the Japanese] are praising the Americans more than the Russians, because the Russians are stingy and the Americans extravagant, the Russians dirty and the Americans rich and clean."[18] Be that as it may, Koga continued to appreciate Russian adherence to Japanese custom. "The American drinking habit is very much like that of the Russians," he observed, "but the Russians like to follow our custom while the Americans want to boast of their own." Describing an American reception aboard the *Powhatan,* he noted: "Before the drinking ended they and we both stood up, both raised our drinks and finished them in one gulp, no drop left, to toast the health of the President. . . . It is one good laugh."[19]

Hawks, Heine, and Goncharov, the troubadours of the American and Russian expeditions, have thrown little light on the character of Perry and Putiatin. This is hardly surprising, for they were in the employ of the commanders, and could not have freely criticized them. As Heine noted when praising Perry: *"Als meinem Befehlshaber muszt ich ihm schon Liebe und Achtung zollen, jetzt nöhtigt er mir Bewunderung ab* [As my commander, I already owed him love and respect, now he demands my admiration]."[20] Before long, Perry and Putiatin became legendary figures. Half a century ago (1905), Basil Hall Chamberlain pointed to the process of immortalization of Perry. "Perry being . . . a hero," he had written, "fancy and myth have already begun to gather round his name. Patriotic writers have discoursed on 'the moral grandeur of his peaceful triumph,' and have even gone so far as to try to get people to believe that the Japanese actually enjoyed knuckling under him."[21] Chamberlain predicted that a memorial, constructed on the spot where Perry had landed, would assist the "mythopoeic process, if memory lets slip the circumstance that this memorial was proposed, not by the Japanese, but by an American survivor of Perry's expedition, and that the Japanese government's share in the matter was but a courteous following of American official lead."[22]

But the perusal of diaries and accounts published since the deaths of Perry and Putiatin shows that both commanders were overbearing, and not on the best of terms with their subordinates. The editor of the abridged edition of *Fregat Pallada,* for example, specifically points out that Goncharov said almost nothing of Putiatin's "*samodurstvo* [conceited stupidity or stubbornness]," his continuous clashes with Unkovskii, the commander of the *Pallada* — so severe that they almost ended in a duel[23] — and the highly tense atmosphere that reigned on the frigate "because of the abnormal relationships among the commanding officers."[24]

Both Perry and Putiatin were nevertheless skillful diplomats. Their theatrical bearing commanded the respect of the Japanese. Their combined efforts, notwithstanding Perry's rejection of the idea of Russo-Japanese cooperation, brought about the reopening of Japan to intercourse with the West. Hawks insisted that "we are not indebted in the slightest degree to Russia by any direct act of hers to that end."[25] Von Siebold, on the other hand, wrote that "the honor of the peaceful winning over of the Japanese Government to the measure, so rich in consequence, is ascribed unanimously and justly to the Russian expedition under the command of Admiral Putiatin."[26] Neither Hawks nor von Siebold was right. It was the triple threat constituted by the presence of an American squadron and a Russian squadron and the expected arrival of men-of-war from other countries that persuaded the Japanese that resistance was useless, at least for the time being.[27] They had been kept *au courant* of international developments by the Dutch, and the specter of the Sino-British war (1839-1842) and the treaty of Nanking (1842) was haunting them.

Hawks' contention that the Russo-Japanese treaty was "copied from ours, with no change but that of the substitution of the port of Nagasaki for Napha in Lew Chew"[28] is not correct, as a comparison of the text of the two treaties will readily show.[29] Both did contain similar provisions for the protection of shipwrecked persons and vessels in distress, the opening of certain ports to their ships and permission to purchase supplies, the appointment of consuls and most-favored-nation treatment; but the Russian treaty was more elaborate. Not only did it open three ports (Shimoda, Hakodate, and Nagasaki) instead of two (Shimoda and Hakodate) and provide for consuls at Hakodate as well as Shimoda, but it delineated the Russo-Japanese boundary, dwelled upon other territorial differences, and, most important of all, provided for extraterritoriality.[30]

12

The Long Voyage Home

ON MAY 1, 1855, THE NEWLY CONSTRUCTED *Heda* WAS LOADED WITH provisions and water. On the evening of the 2d, the officers and crew went aboard. The next morning, the schooner went out to the roadstead. The Japanese officials were invited aboard for a farewell dinner. Putiatin thanked them once more for all their assistance and informed them that *Leitenant* Musin-Pushkin had been put in command of the remaining Russians. He expressed the confidence that the Japanese government would continue treating the remaining Russians with kind attention. At 1:00 P.M., the *Heda* weighed anchor for a trial run. The Japanese aboard rightfully shared in the pleasure of the Russians at the good performance of the vessel, for it was their vessel too. Having let the Japanese off, the Russians started out to sea, but a fresh wind and several newly discovered imperfections forced the *Heda* back into port.[1]

On the evening of the 4th, the schooner weighed anchor again but was detained by calms throughout the night near Mt. Fuji. There were no pumps aboard ship; and water had to be poured out in buckets. As this proved unsatisfactory it was decided to go back to port to build pumps there and to put ashore some of the crew for whom accommodations were inadequate. Various parts of the pumps had been prepared beforehand and so everything was ready by May 8. At 3:30 P.M., the *Heda* weighed anchor for the third time, with Putiatin and forty men (less than one-eleventh of the complement of the *Diana*) aboard.[2] All the remaining officers accompanied the schooner on the cutter to the mouth of the bay.

The *Heda* passed Shimoda and Edo Bay (May 9) and, going out to sea (May 12), headed north. The Russians were in constant danger of capture. Just ten days before their departure, the French steamer *Colbert* had been at Shimoda. As A. K. wrote: "It was apparent from everything that our enemies sought us and were on guard."[3]

The *Heda* sneaked into Petropavlovsk on May 22, when the Allied vessels were already gathering at the mouth of the bay, only to learn that all ships had been ordered to evacuate the port and to proceed to De Kastri Bay. Lesovskii and the other Russians who had been brought to Petropavlovsk from Japan on the *Caroline E. Foote* had already departed there on the American merchantman *William Penn*.[4] Putiatin thus went out to sea again in the early morning hours (May 23), and under cover of darkness slipped past the English squadron. On June 20, the *Heda* cast anchor in the mouth of the Amur after forty days at sea. Thrice, Putiatin and his staff had been near capture by the enemy. At Nikolaevsk, they transferred onto the cutter *Nadezhda*, instructing that the *Heda* be returned to Hakodate or Shimoda at the first opportunity. Putiatin reached Moscow on November 10, 1855, after a long and tedious trip.[5]

In Japan, there had remained after the departure of the *Heda*: Musin-Pushkin, Schilling, Zelenyi, Kovalevskii, Urusov, Mikhailov, Iolkin, the doctor, the priest, and two hundred and seventy-five men of lower rank. They were to proceed in two parties to Petropavlovsk or De Kastri, depending on the news that they would receive with the arrival of the *Caroline E. Foote* from Petropavlovsk. Musin-Pushkin had permission to hire another American vessel, should the schooner for some reason be unable to complete the remaining runs.[6]

The American government had not considered it possible to send a man-of-war to transport the Russians back to their country, as Putiatin had requested through Commander Adams, but had assured the Russian agent in Washington that, except for this, it would take

all steps to ensure the well-being of the Russians at Shimoda, adding
that Captain John Rodgers' United States Surveying Expedition was
on its way to Shimoda.[7] The 700-ton sloop-of-war *Vincennes* and the
bark-rigged tender *John Hancock* entered Shimoda on May 13, 1855.
The governors refused to grant the Americans permission to proceed
to Heda to visit the Russians.[8] The following unsigned memorandum
was sent to Commander Rodgers through an interpreter:

The proposition to go to Hedi [*sic*] and visit the Russians has
been made at the convention the day before yesterday but since it
was communicated that this proposition cannot be permitted, so it
speaks for itself, that the passage cannot take place.

Afterwards it was again asked, and explained, that the visit to the
Russians was founded upon friendship, that the arrival of American
vessels must have been expected from the notification of Commdre.
Perry of last year, and that the necessity of a survey of all coasts
had been stated in the letter lately handed over, and read, so there
should be no objection to the trip to Hedi.

But of American ships has been nothing heard, and besides it
the acquiescence of the government to the just mentioned written
petition is very uncertain. So the trip to Hedi, and the survey of
its harbor, cannot take place.

Should it have become necessary to communicate with the Russians,
they shall be called there to this place.

This word is communicated in writing that no misunderstanding
might take place.

The 4th Sigreato [Fourth Month].[9]

The Americans refused to listen to Japanese objections, and the
John Hancock proceeded to Heda. In Commander Rodgers' reply to
the above note, it was stated, among other things:

Now the Russians are in distress. The Russian Emperor is the
friend of our President, and our President is his friend. The two
countries are at peace, and in friendship. Were the Japanese wrecked
in Russia, and far from their country, if the Americans were coming
to Japan they would go to see the Japanese that they might tell their

countrymen they were well, that they had been seen, and that they were in a comfortable situation.

Now it is not expedient to talk about the Treaty. That must be discussed in Jeddo, but the treaty does not talk about the duties of friendship, and we can discuss that.

The American Commodore has power to ask permission to survey where he wishes, but has the Governor of Simoda power to refuse him permission, or to grant it to him for other parts of the Empire of Japan? Therefore the American Commodore would rather talk about his friendship for the Russians. Both countries permit friendship, and admire heroic examples of it.

Besides how can anyone refuse permission under the treaty without knowing that his government wishes him to do so. It is a very small matter. The port is known. It has been surveyed. Vessels have been into it.

To so great a government a small steamer going into a known port is of little moment, and whether the Hancock goes or does not go, is not worthy of any long discussion.

If after the Hancock is in Heda, and she has seen the Russians, should it be agreed to carry them away, then it will be done.[10]

The *Caroline E. Foote* returned to Shimoda in the third week of May. Although her skipper had signed a contract in which he had obligated himself to transport the Russians to Petropavlovsk in three trips, he refused to do so, afraid lest he be captured by a British man-of-war.[11]

On July 7, 1855, a messenger arrived from Shimoda to report that a German brig had cast anchor. Musin-Pushkin and Schilling hastened there and succeeded in coming to terms with Captain Thaulow, skipper of the *Greta*.[12]

On July 14, the Russians bade farewell to the Japanese officials, "who have left us the most pleasant memories." "Whatever we had needed," wrote Schilling, "they had always brought us without delay, and on credit to boot as we had only the most insignificant amount of crown-money left. . . ." The accounts were closed and duly signed, and the Russians boarded the brig. "Here Pushkin and I decided to go ashore once more," reminisced Schilling, "and pay a farewell visit to Nakamora Tamea [Nakamura Tameya], whom we respected, and his assistant Uekava Danitsero [Uekawa Danichiro]. Our expressed gratitude noticeably touched the old man Nakamora and he accompanied us at the head of a whole flotilla of Japanese boats to the exit from the bay."[13]

The *Greta* was crowded. Space was so limited that part of the Russian crew had to take turns sleeping on deck. Strong winds plagued the brig, and she was almost wrecked during a storm weathered off the southern shore of Honshu. Rain and fog enveloped her throughout her voyage, so that she proceeded with great caution. The Russians crossed the Kuril Archipelago between Uruppu and Etorofu. On August 1, 1855, near the northern extremity of Sakhalin, the fog suddenly lifted and the Russians found themselves, to their horror, near an English man-of-war, who immediately turned toward them and with a shot ordered the brig to stop. So as not to arouse English suspicion with the size of the crew, the Russians hid in the hold of the ship while the captain raised the American flag. But the British sent an armed party aboard just the same. Captain Thaulow told them he was carrying provisions to American whalers, hence flew an American flag, though his ship papers were from Bremen. "This fable," wrote Schilling, "was of course not believed, particularly since several Chinese who were among the crew gave us away out of cowardliness."[14] Arguments that the Russians, as unarmed persons not participating in military operations, could not, according to international law, be considered prisoners of war, fell on deaf ears. Four days later (August 5), Musin-Pushkin sent the following report to the agent of the Russo-American Company:

Dear Sir:

Left behind in Japan with part of the crew of the lost frigate *Diana*, I chartered the Bremen brig *Gretto* [*Greta*] for transporting myself with the officers and crew, entrusted me, to Port Aian; but unfortunately captured on July 20 (August 1) in the Sea of Okhotsk in latitude 52° by the English man-of-war *Barracouta*[15] and brought by her yesterday (July 22-August 3) to this roadstead, I and the other officers and crew have been proclaimed prisoners of war. As for the brig that was carrying us, she was declared a prize. The whole crew has been put on English vessels and will be sent to Hong Kong. Not having received permission to report myself personally to the authorities of my capture and only making use of the permission to notify you of it, I ask you to report the disaster that has befallen us to the Governor General of Eastern Siberia as well as to Adjutant General Putiatin and the commander of the former frigate *Diana, Kapitant Leitenant* Lesovskii. If there are any letters addressed to the officers, a list of whom I am attaching, be so kind, please send these letters through the bearer of this letter.

Senior officer of the perished frigate *Diana*

[Signed] A. Musin-Pushkin.

P. S. Upon my request [the following] of the prisoners received freedom and discharge on shore: the priest, the doctor, and the sick sailors, twenty-one men in number. As for myself I am departing at once on the steamer *Barracouta*, with *Leitenant* Schilling, *Nadvornyi Sovetnik* Goshkevich and 95 men of lower rank.

If [you] have any newspapers, send them.

July 24, 1855 (August 5, 1855)[16]

As prisoners of war aboard British vessels, the Russians visited Hakodate and then Nagasaki, where they remained from August 28 to September 29. The Japanese authorities did not permit the British to enter the inner roadstead and even forbade them to communicate with a Dutch corvet. No contact with the shore was permitted and later on even riding about on sloops was prohibited. The Russians were finally taken to England and only after the end of the war (1856) returned to Russia. Theirs had been a long voyage home.

In St. Petersburg, they were well received by the authorities. The officers were decorated and, as they had received no pay for over a year and a half, the sums of government money that they had divided among themselves when about to be taken prisoner were not deducted from their salary. Moreover, it was ordered that every

officer of the *Diana* be paid two years' salary, one to compensate for
his loss of property during the shipwreck, one for travelling.[17] A
circular of the Inspector's department provided that the service of
the men of lower rank aboard the frigates *Pallada*, *Diana*, and *Avrora*
and the schooner *Vostok* be counted double in recognition of their
"service beyond the line of duty."[18] Putiatin had been made a count.
An Imperial ukase of December 18, 1855, had stated:

In reward for services shown by him to Our Empire, while carrying out in the Japanese State an important mission, with which he
had been charged by the late Emperor Nikolai [Nicholas] I, in spite
of many obstacles, and considering it just to preserve the memory
of such services in his descent, We most graciously confer on our
Adjutant General Vice-Admiral Putiatin and his posterity the dignity
of a count. We command the Ruling Senate, to make out a patent
of the dignity of a count for Adjutant-General Count Putiatin and
present it for Our signature.[19]

The Japanese government was duly repaid in accordance with the
accounts kept, the *Heda* was returned, and, as gesture of friendship,
all cannons taken off the *Diana* at Shimoda were presented to the
Shogunate as a gift.[20]

13

Point and Counterpoint

THE AMERICANS AND RUSSIANS, WITH THEIR NEWLY INVENTED STEAM-ships and big guns, appeared terribly important and advanced to themselves. They talked of the "nobler principles" and the "better life" of a "higher civilization" which they were bringing to Japan.[1] They scoffed at differences in custom and physical appearance. Yet if one considers, as Martin Ramming points out, that in 1852, the year of Perry's departure for Japan, the novel *Uncle Tom's Cabin* could appear in the United States and that serfdom was not abolished in Russia until 1861, one cannot help but be reminded of Mencius' parable about the soldiers who, having fled fifty paces from the enemy, laughed at those who had fled a hundred.[2]

Goncharov's writings are saturated with mockery. The Japanese are portrayed as largely "self-content, comically proud, naive, bored, full of apathy."[3] Their physiognomies are classified into "clever, lively, completely stupid or only dulled by lack of intellectual activity."[4] Goncharov relates that during official conferences the Japanese squatted motionlessly. "They stared at the floor and apparently wagered who could make a more stupid face. All of them more or less succeeded in this, many, of course, unintentionally."[5] "It is a custom of theirs, I believe, to appear as stupid as possible in the presence of an elder," he explained, "and therefore, there were many faces stupid from respect."[6] The Japanese military did not escape his ridicule. "Soldiers!" he exclaimed. "One can think of nothing more diametrically opposed to what we call soldiers. They could barely stand up from old age and had poor eyesight. Their grey little topknot could not lie on their head and stuck up. Through the sparse topknot shone the bald pate, red copper in color."[7] Goncharov admitted that they had excellent swords, "but what [can they] do with these toys?" he queried.[8] Recalling a Japanese on a "trashy light bay jade" that had been frightened by the brass band, he remarked tersely: "He must have been the representative of the Japanese cavalry."[9] In sum, he felt that "it was difficult to look without laughter at these skirt-clad figures with their little topknots and their bare little knees."[10]

Tsutsui had charmed all the Russians. "Such old men exist everywhere, in all nations," Goncharov felt. "Wrinkles surrounded his lips in rays. In his eyes, voice, in all features shone aged, intelligent, and affable goodness — the fruit of long life and of practical wisdom. Everybody who will see this little old man would want to select him as grandfather."[11] And Kawaji, Goncharov wrote, "was very intelligent, and one cannot help admiring this in spite of the fact that he displayed his cleverness in skillful dialectics against ourselves." Kawaji's speech and conduct "revealed sound mind, sharp-wittedness, astuteness, and experience." "Intelligence is everywhere the same," Goncharov commented. "Intelligent people have the same symptoms, so do all fools, regardless of difference in nation, clothing, language, religion, even outlook on life."[12] But although the Russians had been impressed favorably by the appearance of Tsutsui and Kawaji, and although they exclaimed again and again *"Nagasaki onna yoka yoka!* [Nagasaki women good! good!],"[13] physically the Japanese as a whole did not seem to attract them. In Goncharov's eyes, the Japanese were "small, largely ugly, and naked."[14] Their little topknots resembled "the tail of a rat."[15] Japanese women seemed "of swarthy complexion" and "how ugly."[16] As they tried to remain in concealment, Russians noted: "And they do well that they hide themselves [these] black-teethed ones."[17] Describing a colorful Nagasaki sunset, Goncharov wrote: "Small bays, cottages, batteries, bushes growing thickly along the edges of the cliffs like giant bouquets, suddenly were illuminated — everything was a picture, poetry, everything except the batteries and the Japanese. No rays could do anything with these."[18] "I would have been indulgent, would not have demanded much," Goncharov assures us, "but there was nothing according to our concepts resembling to human beauty in the whole gathering [of Japanese]."[19]

Not only did the Japanese appear to the Russians as generally stupid, ludicrous, and ugly, but also as feminine — hardly a characteristic Russian mariners admired in military men or officials. Baba talked "like a woman,"[20] Sadagora "resembled an old maid, only the glasses and a stocking in the hands were missing."[21] Another official was like "some unquestionably good aunt, nurse maid or other woman fondler from whom one [must] not expect intellect and schooling, but in its stead preserves, candy and indulgence — as much as one wishes."[22] "In general one can hardly see a single masculine, energetic face," wrote Goncharov, "although there are many clever and cunning ones." "And if there are any," he added, "then the queue combed up from the back and the smoothly shaven face make them look unlike men."[23]

Essentially, Goncharov understood the desire of the Japanese to be left alone. "Are they not to a certain extent right?" he pondered. "From Europe they have seen so far little good, but much evil: therefore, their very estrangement is logical. The Portuguese missionaries brought them a religion which many Japanese trustingly adopted and professed. But the students of Loyola brought thither also their passions: pride, love of power, gold, silver, and even of the excellent Japanese copper which they shipped out in incredible quantities, and in general any kind of love except Christian one. You know what the result of this was: Bartholomew's nights and alienation from the world. But if one remembers what happened during the infanthood of our old [sic] states, how novelty and discovery that were not understood were received, how physicians were burned and physicists and astronomers persecuted, the Japanese deserve more indulgence than their enlighteners in their stubborn desire to get rid of the foreigners. Is it surprising then that ... fear of a repetition of the old evils has turned them away from us?"[24] " 'God damn you!' he [Osawa] probably thinks," Goncharov realized, "and the officials think of course the same."[25] But Goncharov's understanding was overshadowed by his mockery.

Not only did Japanese official dress appear absurd — "one cannot help thinking that some rogue once posed himself the problem of dressing man as uncomfortable as possible so that he not only could not walk and run but even move"[26] — but the whole governmental structure seemed ridiculous. "The governor does not dare to make a decision. He will send an inquiry to the Supreme Council, the Supreme Council will make a report to the Shogun, the Shogun to the Mikado. The latter, the direct and immediate relative of Heaven, the brother, son or nephew of the moon [sic] could, it would seem, make the decision, but he sits with his twelve wives and several hundreds of their assistants, composes poems, plays the lute and eats every day from new dishes. The governor is ordered in any case to chase away and wipe out the foreigners or at least under no circumstances to let them to Edo."[27] And how did the governors plan to drive away the intruders? By wearing them out with subterfuge and procrastination. There were so many detailed formalities that Goncharov was led to comment surlily that "the study of ceremony forms in their [country] an important science in the absence as yet of others."[28] "And so in everything there is one unchangeable order," he noted. "To break this, to turn them to healthy sense, can be done in no other [way] than only by force." Neither slyness nor persuasion would save them from hostilities. "The only hope [lies] in their cowardliness," Goncharov concluded. "The threats on the part of the Europeans and the desire for peace on the part of the Japanese will help to obtain from them by bargain the abolishment of several constrictions."[29] (As a peaceful settlement was reached, we suppose "proof" was given of Japanese "cowardliness.")

Goncharov's *Fregat Pallada* has been widely read in Russia. Is it surprising then, that in the absence of enough other material, Russian readers at the turn of the century failed to take the Japanese seriously? Is it surprising that they believed they could "*shapkami zakidat'* " ([sink by] throwing hats on top of) the Japanese navy?

A century has passed since the voyages of the Russian Japan Expedition, but Goncharov's narrative is still popular, as a new (1949) edition attests. The fact that Mikhail Ivanovich Kalinin, onetime president of the U.S.S.R., specifically recommended the reading of *Fregat Pallada* to beginning writers has ensured its continued popularity.[30]

Goncharov and his companions failed to realize that the Japanese fully reciprocated their feelings of cultural, mental, and physical superiority. The Japanese considered themselves as superior to the Russians, as the Russians considered themselves superior to the Japanese. Goncharov portrayed Kawaji as a man who mused about personal affairs to the neglect of his official duties, who wished to get the negotiations over with, so that he could return to his wife in the capital, and meanwhile complained that "[the] body is here but [the] soul in Edo." Goncharov did not know that Kawaji had spoken about his wife to humor Putiatin, never realized that Kawaji had "condescended" to talk the kind of language "barbarians" understood. "The Russians cry with joy when they speak about their wives," Kawaji had noted in his diary. "Therefore I said: 'My wife is so beautiful she ranks first or second in Edo. When I came here I left her in Edo. I think of her often. Is there any way to forget her?' " "When I had told this," Kawaji observed, "they were very glad and laughed."[31] Apologetically, he added: "My wife is so kind to me, I would like to let the foreign people know about it. We cannot criticize these things with the feelings of Japanese."[32]

The Japanese did not consider the Russians paragons of physical perfection. "As for their faces, their noses are high and their complexion too white," wrote Kawaji, adding magnanimously, "but only that point is not so good." "All of them are good-looking men;" he continued, "if they were in Edo they would be [considered] refined."[33] "The young persons we saw were so pretty they looked like women."[34] But most Russians appeared too old. "In their country, there must be few people of long life," recorded Kawaji. "Thirty-one year old persons look like about sixty. The person who was behind the interpreter was said to be thirteen years old, but according to Japanese standards he looked as if he must have been around twenty."[35] The Russian crew seemed "foolish." "They may not be used for more than carrying powder," Kawaji commented derisively.[36] Noticing that the Russians inhaled snuff, Kawaji recorded: "They never smoke. Perhaps they are afraid of fire."[37] Russian customs appeared ludicrous. That men should shake hands or kiss each other was incomprehensible. Noting that he had heard that "the Russian ambassador met Pos'et, shook hands and kissed a long time," Koga recorded: "The accompanying [Japanese] officers laughed secretly."[38]

Japanese, familiar with only Japanese accounts of the Russians, thus had no more adequate sources for appraising their neighbors than the readers in Russia.

Beneath the cultural crust of supercilious diary entries, however, the appreciation of the necessity for better understanding seemed to mature. As the weeks went by and the novelty of unfamiliar physiognomies and customs wore off, common characteristics and feelings, similarities rather than differences, came to the fore. Soon Kawaji could write: "Although we do not understand their language ...we can almost understand them, feeling no difference."[39] And Goncharov could look at Kawaji, query, "In what is he not a European?" and answer: "In that he once during dinner hid a piece of pastry in paper and at another time licked from the plate the anchovy sauce that he liked very much: these are local customs — nothing more."[40] And on second thought, even the customs appeared not so strange. Moriyama sat like a poodle at the feet of Kawaji and ate whatever the latter would leave him, but then favorite servants in Russia, jesters, had also sat at the feet of ancient noblemen and eaten the morsels of food (*podachka* — presents) thrown to them.

And in Russia, too, sweets and *gostintsy* (gifts) were brought back from visits. "Has it been long since Griboedov in his comedy laughed at the *podachka?*" Goncharov asked himself.[41]

Putiatin could sympathize with Kawaji's loneliness, for he too had not seen his wife in a long time. Nor did Tsutsui feel differently: "Don't think that I am an old man," he noted. "If I shall have a baby hereafter, I shall let you know next time." The Russians observed: "There is a proverb in Russia: It is rare to have a baby at fifty, and one does not have one at sixty and never at seventy and many at eighty." "I want to be like that proverb," Tsutsui replied.[42]

Japanese cleanliness impressed the Russians. As Goncharov wrote: "They [the Japanese] all distinguish themselves in cleanliness and neatness of body and dress. How can there be no different odors in that bushy topknot, how can there be no spots on those gowns? There is nothing. I no longer talk about the officials: they are dressed neatly and with taste; but if you look also at the poor, you will see nakedness or a torn dress, but there are no spots and no dirt. While among the Chinese, what you will not have to suffer standing in a crowd! What the smell of sandalwood alone costs! It seems that from the garlic-saturated breath a fly will drop dead. No odor emanates from the Japanese. You look at their head: through the topknot penetrates the shaven but clean skull; the naked arms that are greatly exposed in the wide sleeve are swarthy, it is true, but clean."[43]

Western methods and technological advancement impressed the Japanese. Kawaji found that Russian lanterns "cost more to build, but less to use." "This is the Western way," he observed with admiration.[44] Learning that European wine was made with grapes, he noted, "They do not spend a thing as useful as rice supply for luxury."[45] Once, Koga surpassed Kawaji in appreciation of things Western. Kawaji had spoken disparagingly of an official: "His sampans have green sword racks and round toilet holes — all pure foreign made. This is his hobby — what a pity." Commented Koga in his diary: "Kawaji pities copying foreigners, but I pity not copying foreigners. Green and round is not enough to say that it is copying."[46]

Whereas the feelings and attitude of the Russians toward the Japanese remained uniformly friendly and tolerant, though condescending, the feelings of the Japanese toward the Russians were neither uniform nor constant. There was a greater diversity of opinion and change of heart in the Japanese camp. Koga's xenophobia persisted throughout, though he emphasized that propriety must be observed in dealing with the ambassador. "We cannot treat the Russian ambassador like a shipwrecked barbarian," he insisted.[47] No matter what the Russians would say or do, Koga would find fault. The Japanese had built plain chairs for the Russians, borrowing two red chairs from a temple for the ambassador and captain. When Putiatin used a plain chair and persistently picked bad glasses and plates for himself, Koga criticized that he was "rich in small numbers," that is to say, paid attention to little things.[48] Finding Putiatin "friendly," Koga decided "this must be the nature of a sneaky person."[49] Nakamura had given the Russians a medicine case. When they promised to wear it all the time in memory of Japanese goodwill, Koga growled: "These rascals are hard to stomach."[50] Upon hearing accounts of the Crimean War, he recorded in his diary: "I felt that [because of] the greediness of the Russians, within ten years the danger that happened to Turkey would happen to us."[51]

Kawaji's feelings, on the other hand, were thoroughly transformed. When he had first met Putiatin, he had seen in him only an uncouth barbarian. By the time his diary came to a close, however, he thought of him as a great hero. Kawaji recorded that the admiral had spent the past eleven years at sea, thousands of miles away from home and had enriched his country extending her territories. He had repeatedly come to the shores of Japan to discuss boundary questions. He had just fought against the English and French and, "having lost the vessels seen at Nagasaki," had returned with only one man-of-war. Caught in a tidal wave and "defeated by the breath of the gods," the vessel had sunk to the fathomless bottom of the sea. But Putiatin had been "not in the least downhearted" and had built another vessel. He had sent to China for a large warship, continuing meanwhile his negotiations with the plenipotentiaries. "Although we referred to him abusively as *Futeiyatsu*,"[52] wrote Kawaji, "if we think well, he has accomplished ten times, [no], one hundred times the labors of Saemon-no-jo [i.e. Kawaji himself] and others whom the Japanese *Bakufu* [Shogunate] has selected from the whole country[53] and is thus using. Truly, if we compare him with Saemon-no-jo and others he is a genuine hero."[54]

14

Conclusion

THE HISTORY OF EARLY RUSSO-JAPANESE RELATIONS IS INADEQUATELY known in this country. Since Aston's article on "Russian Descents into Saghalin and Itorup,"[1] little has been written on the subject in English. Such scattered references as do exist in several histories of Japan fail to grasp its importance. The volume of literature concerning the Russo-Japanese War, the Siberian Intervention, fishery disputes, and pre-Pearl Harbor border incidents has been mounting; partly, perhaps, because acts of war and aggression are more spectacular to record, partly because they are better documented. It very well may be that this trend of dealing with differences has furthered the fallacy that Russia and Japan are "historical enemies."[2] Part of the blame must fall on Russian historians who have almost completely ignored eighteenth- and nineteenth-century Russo-Japanese contacts in their general surveys of Russian history. Only several specialized articles have appeared. To this author's knowledge, there does not exist one over-all history of Russo-Japanese relations in Russian or any other Western language. The closest to that is Kurt Krupinski's book, *Japan und Russland, Ihre Beziehungen bis zum Frieden von Portsmouth* (Japan and Russia, Their Relations till the Peace of Portsmouth).[3]

Chauvinistic writings in Russia and Japan during the past generation or so have obscured the at times rather amicable relations

[151]

between the two countries. The long and bitter struggle between the United States and Japan during the Second World War, as compared with Russia's entry into the conflict when Japan was about to surrender,[4] has left the psychological impression that the United States has had to deal with Japan for a longer time than Russia.

Renewed interest has been shown in the origin of Japanese-American relations, and new material on the Perry expedition has been published. Again there is little or no mention of Russian activities at that time. Yet the history of Russo-Japanese relations is important if for no other reason than that the Japanese consider it so. Most Japanese histories that deal with eighteenth- or nineteenth-century foreign contacts devote considerable space to it.

The proper understanding of Japanese-American relations presupposes a certain familiarity with Russo-Japanese intercourse. Pre-Putiatin Russian attempts to establish commercial relations with Japan had been primarily economic in motive. Merchants and provincial governors had been the prime movers. It is true the central government had granted financial assistance and had even appointed an official envoy. But all in all, threatening though Russian activities had seemed to the Japanese, the Russian government in those years had not displayed any particularly vivid interest in Japan. Only when England, the United States, and other Western Powers had begun to establish themselves in China, had Russia begun to view Japan from a political and military angle. The Russian Japan Expedition of 1852 to 1855 was the product of this new attitude. It was conceived, planned, and executed by the Russian government and its forces, not by private individuals. It thus is a landmark in the course of Russo-Japanese relations, the basis of a new period. As such it merits our study. The fact that a century after the arrival of the American and Russian naval forces, militarily weak Japan is once more caught between the same two powers in a position of utter defenselessness and must thus rely again on diplomacy rather than on the sword — at least for the time being — gives added significance to our survey. It has not been our purpose to detract from the well-deserved renown of Commodore Perry, but simply to call attention to the almost forgotten achievements of Vice-Admiral Putiatin who, together with Commodore Perry, opened up Japan.

The following conclusions emanate from our study:

(1) The Russian expedition contributed to the peaceful opening of Japan by adding to the military pressure already exerted by American men-of-war.

(2) Japanese defenses at Nagasaki were weak. Advocates of coastal defense in Japan had argued that it was not enough to fortify only that harbor; they had not realized that Nagasaki itself was wide open to attack. Studies made by officers of the Russian expedition proved how limited Japanese understanding of gunnery was at that time.

(3) Japanese officials with whom the Russians dealt were aware of the inevitability of reopening Japan. Some actually confided that the sooner this would happen, the better they would like it.

(4) Putiatin's relatively friendly conduct[5] prompted to seek Russian protection. "... Because your country is a great country with boundaries adjacent to ours, we consider you as a defense against other countries," Kawaji declared. Putiatin replied: "In the event that people from other countries cause violent disturbance we are prepared to give you any assistance."[6]

(5) Preferential treatment was promised Russia by the Japanese plenipotentiaries. "Should our country finally permit trade," a Japanese note stated, "it will be first to your country."[7] A renewed American display of force and inadequate communications prevented the realization of this pledge.[8]

(6) Japanese officials were more afraid of their own government than of the foreigners. They were less concerned about making concessions than about arousing the suspicion of their government that these concessions had been made voluntarily. Hence the number of statements that were made "for the record," to protect themselves from their own superiors.

(7) The Japanese government itself was less afraid of trade and diplomatic relations with foreign countries than of showing to its people that it no longer had the power to prevent them. The spectacle of military impotence would deprive the "Barbarian-Sub-duing-Generalissimo" of any excuse for existence and invite open opposition on the part of dissident elements. Hence the insistence of the Shogunate officials that the Russians come ashore under Japanese escort, an escort not designed to control Russian actions in fact but in appearance. Once the *Diana* had been shipwrecked and the Russians were completely at the mercy of the Japanese, concessions could no longer be construed as signs of weakness. Still, although Kawaji agreed with Putiatin that "to exchange goods for goods" really was trade, "trade" could not be inserted in the treaty.

(8) Putiatin obtained more concessions than Perry. The treaty of Shimoda went beyond the treaty of Kanagawa in that it clarified the boundary line between the empires of Russia and Japan, opened another harbor in Japan, and provided for extraterritoriality.

(9) There was much misunderstanding, misinformation, and false pride on the part of both the Japanese and the Russians. The writings of Kawaji and Koga, on one hand, and of Goncharov, on the other, did little to alleviate this; on the contrary, they perpetuated mutual concepts of superiority.

The treaty of Shimoda is the most obvious accomplishment of the Russian expedition. But we must not overlook the scientific investigations conducted by the mariners during their long stay in Japanese waters. The Russians proved that Japan's innermost ports were accessible to large Western ships. They made many surveys of Japanese bays and harbors, as well as the coast line in general, not to mention explorations in other parts of the world.[9]

Putiatin's own evaluation of the mission was that he had had "the good fortune of obtaining the desired end" without ever disrupting the harmonious relationship that existed between himself and the Japanese authorities, and that, on the contrary, unison had been placed on "solid foundations" and "for a long time to come."[10]

The records of the Russian Japan Expedition are filled with adventure, disaster, friendship, and heroism. But as Vice-Admiral Putiatin concluded in his official report to the Admiralty: "In spite of all the vicissitudes of the events, political and natural, that overtook us, one cannot help acknowledge the special protection of Divine Providence accorded us, always most apparent during moments of weighty trials. The very success in attaining the main goal, at a time when we were already deprived of means to act freely and insistently, cannot be attributed to the calculations of normal actions; in this case, more than any other, honor and thanks must be given to the Sole Distributor of all things, Who displayed such manifest designs of His strength and benevolence."[11]

Appendix 1

List of Officers Aboard the Schooner *Vostok*, the Frigate *Pallada*, and the Frigate *Diana* in 1852*

OFFICERS ABOARD THE SCHOONER *VOSTOK*:

Leitenant [Lieutenant] Voin Andreevich Rimskii-Korsakov (commanding)
Leitenant Baron Aleksandr Shlipenbakh [Schlippenbach?]
Michman [Midshipman or Warrant Officer] Petr Anzhu
Podporuchik [Sub-Lieutenant] Ivan Moiseev III
Podporuchik Ivan Zarubin
Doctor Genrikh Veirikh

OFFICERS ABOARD THE FRIGATE *PALLADA*:

Fligel'-adiutant [Aid-de-camp] *Kapitan-leitenant* [Second Captain or First Lieutenant] Ivan Semenovich Unkovskii (commanding)
Kapitan-leitenant Konstantin Nikolaevich Pos'et
Shtab-kapitan [Junior Captain] Aleksandr Khalizov
Shtab-kapitan Lev Popov
Kapitan [Captain] Konstantin Losev
Leitenant Ivan Butakov
Leitenant Petr Tikhmenev
Leitenant Baron Nikolai Kriudner
Leitenant Nikanor Savich
Leitenant Ivan Belavenets
Leitenant Sergei Shvarts [Schwarz?]
Michman Aleksandr Boltin
Michman Pavel Zelenyi
Michman Aleksandr Kolokol'tsov
Podporuchik Iakob Istomin
Shtab-lekar [Regimental Surgeon] Aleksandr Aref'ev
Kollezhskii assessor [Collegiate Assessor] Ivan Aleksandrovich Goncharov
Kollezhskii assessor Osip [Iosif Antonovich] Goshkevich
Tseikhvakhter [Storekeeper] Vasilii Pliushkin
Iunker [Cadet] M. M. Lazarev
Gardemarin [Midshipman] Peshchurov
Gardemarin Gamov
Gardemarin Linden
Gardemarin Kniaz' [Prince] Urusov
Konduktor [Conductor] Kazakov
Archimandrite Avvakum

OFFICERS ABOARD THE FRIGATE *DIANA*:

Kapitan-leitenant Stepan Stepanovich Lesovskii (commanding)
Leitenant Aleksandr Musin-Pushkin

[157]

Leitenant Aleksandr Mozhaiskii
Leitenant Adolf Enkvist
Leitenant Mikhail Beriulev
Leitenant Nikolai G. Schilling II
Leitenant Kniaz' Aleksandr Obolenskii
Michman Timofei Mozhaiskii
Michman David Ivanov
Michman Nikolai Kovalevskii
Michman Maksim Gening
Poruchik [Military Lieutenant] Aleksandr Antipenko
Podporuchik Petr Iolkin
Praporshchik [Ensign] Dmitrii Kuznetsov
Praporshchik Vasilii Karandashev
Praporshchik Grigorii Semenov
Doctor Franz Krolevetskii
Kollezhskii registrar [Collegiate Registrar] Dmitrii Gubarev
Father Vasilii Makhov
Five midshipmen

Appendix 2

TABLE OF STRENGTH OF THE RUSSIAN JAPAN EXPEDITION[1]

Ranks	Pallada	Diana	Avrora	Vostok	Kniaz' Menshikov[2]
Field officers and subaltern officers	27	21	19	6	?
Cadets, midshipmen, conductors, and pupils	6	5	6	0	
Lower ranks	438	378	317	31	
Total	471	404	342	37	
Guns	44	52	44	4	

Appendix 3

The Treaty of Kanagawa[1]

The United States of America and the Empire of Japan, desiring to establish firm, lasting, and sincere friendship between the two nations, have resolved to fix, in a manner clear and positive, by means of a treaty or general convention of peace and amity, the rules which shall in future be mutually observed in

Appendices   159

the intercourse of their respective countries; for which most desirable object the President of the United States has conferred full powers on his Commissioner, Matthew Calbraith Perry, Special Ambassador of the United States to Japan; and the August Sovereign of Japan has given similar full powers to his Commissioners, Hayashi Daigaku-nokami; Ido, Prince of Tsus-Sima; Izawa, Prince of Mima-saki; and Udono, Member of the Board of Revenue. And the said commissioners, after having exchanged their said full powers, and duly considered the premises, have agreed to the following articles:

ARTICLE I

There shall be a perfect, permanent, and universal peace, and a sincere and cordial amity, between the United States of America on the one part, and the Empire of Japan on the other, and between their people, respectively, without exception of persons or places.

ARTICLE II

The port of Simoda, in the principality of Idzu, and the port of Hakodade, in the principality of Matsmai, are granted by the Japanese as ports for the reception of American ships, where they can be supplied with wood, water, provisions, and coal, and other articles their necessities may require, as far as the Japanese have them. The time for opening the first named port is immediately on signing this treaty; the last named port is to be opened immediately after the same day in the ensuing Japanese year.

. Note. — A tariff of prices shall be given by the Japanese officers of the things which they can furnish, payment for which shall be made in gold and silver coin.

ARTICLE III

Whenever ships of the United States are thrown or wrecked on the coast of Japan, the Japanese vessels will assist them, and carry their crews to Simoda or Hakodade, and hand them over to their countrymen appointed to receive them; whatever articles the shipwrecked men may have preserved shall likewise be restored, and the expenses incurred in the rescue and support of American and Japanese, who may thus be thrown upon the shores of either nation, are not to be refunded.

ARTICLE IV

Those shipwrecked persons and other citizens of the United States shall be free as in other countries, and not subject to confinement, but shall be amenable to just laws.

ARTICLE V

Shipwrecked men, and other citizens of the United States, temporarily living at Simoda and Hakodade, shall not be subject to such restrictions and confinement as the Dutch and Chinese are at Nagasaki, but shall be free at Simoda to go where they please within the limits of seven Japanese miles (or ri) from a small island in the harbor of Simoda, marked on the accompanying chart, hereto appended; and shall in like manner be free to go where they please at Hakodade, within limits to be defined after the visit of the United States squadron to that place.

ARTICLE VI

If there be any other sort of goods wanted, or any business which shall require to be arranged, there shall be careful deliberation between the parties in order to settle such matters.

ARTICLE VII

It is agreed that ships of the United States resorting to the ports open to them, shall be permitted to exchange gold and silver coin, and articles of goods, for other articles of goods, under such regulations as shall be temporarily established by the Japanese government for that purpose. It is stipulated, however, that the ships of the United States shall be permitted to carry away whatever articles they are unwilling to exchange.

ARTICLE VIII

Wood, water, provisions, coal, and goods required, shall only be procured through the agency of Japanese officers appointed for that purpose, and in no other manner.

ARTICLE IX

It is agreed that if at any future day the government of Japan shall grant to any other nation or nations privileges and advantages which are not herein granted to the United States and the citizens thereof, that the same privileges and advantages shall be granted likewise to the United States and to the citizens thereof, without any consultation or delay.

ARTICLE X

Ships of the United States shall be permitted to resort to no other ports in Japan but Simoda and Hakodade, unless in distress or forced by stress of weather.

ARTICLE XI

There shall be appointed by the government of the United States Consuls or Agents to reside in Simoda at any time after the expiration of eighteen months from the date of the signing of this treaty; provided that either of the two governments deem such arrangement necessary.

ARTICLE XII

The present convention, having been concluded and duly signed, shall be obligatory, and faithfully observed by the United States of America and Japan, and by the citizens and subjects of each respective power; and it is to be ratified and approved by the President of the United States, by and with the advice and consent of the Senate thereof, and by the August Sovereign of Japan, and the ratification shall be exchanged within eighteen months from the date of the signature thereof, or sooner if practicable.

In faith whereof, we, the respective Plenipotentiaries of the United States of America and the Empire of Japan aforesaid, have signed and sealed these presents.

Done at Kanagawa, this thirty-first day of March, in the year of our Lord Jesus Christ one thousand eight hundred and fifty-four, and of Kayei the seventh year, third month, and third day.[2]

Notes

Preface

1. Some of the more recent studies are: Harold Allison Mattice, *Perry and Japan, An Account of the Empire and an Unpublished Record of the Perry Expedition* (New York, 1942); Allan B. Cole (ed.), *With Perry in Japan, The Diary of Edward Yorke McCauley* (Princeton, 1942); Arthur Walworth, *Black Ships off Japan* (New York, 1946); Allan B. Cole (ed.), *A Scientist with Perry in Japan, The Journal of Dr. James Morrow* (Chapel Hill, 1947); Earl Swisher, "Commodore Perry's Imperialism in Relation to America's Present-Day Position in the Pacific," *Pacific Historical Review*, XVI, No. 1 (February, 1947), 30-40; Henry F. Graff (ed.), *Bluejackets with Perry in Japan; A Day to Day Account Kept by Master's Mate John R. C. Lewis and Cabin Boy William B. Allen* (New York, 1952); Sidney Wallach (ed.), abridged edition of Francis L. Hawks (ed.), *Narrative of the Expedition of an American Squadron to the China Seas and Japan under the Command of Commodore M. C. Perry, United States Navy* (New York, 1952).

2. Chitoshi Yanaga, *Japan since Perry* (New York, 1949); Edwin A. Falk, *From Perry to Pearl Harbor* (Garden City, 1943).

3. Evfimii Vasil'evich Putiatin (1803-1883): Adjutant-General and Vice-Admiral, later Count (1856) and Admiral (1858). Participated in the around-the-world voyage of Captain (later Admiral) M. P. Lazarev in 1822-1825, the battle of Navarino (1827) and other campaigns, as well as diplomatic and commercial negotiations with Persia. Advocated the sending of an expedition to China and Japan in 1843.

4. Martin Ramming, "Über den Anteil der Russen an der Eröffnung Japans für den Verkehr mit den Westlichen Mächten" (Concerning the Role of the Russians in the Opening of Japan to Intercourse with the Western Powers), *Mitteilungen der Deutschen Gesellschaft für Natur- und Völkerkunde Ostasiens,* XXI, Part B (1926), 3.

5. Baron F. R. Osten-Saken, "Pamiati grafa Evfimiia Vasil'evicha Putiatina pochetnago chlena Imperatorskago russkago geograficheskago obshchestva" (Remembrances of Count Evfimii Vasil'evich Putiatin, Honorary Member of the Imperial Russian Geographical Society), *Izvestiia Imperatorskago russkago geograficheskago obshchestva* (News of the Imperial Russian Geographical Society), XIX (1883), 388.

6. Ramming, "Über den Anteil der Russen," 12-13.

7. Evfimii Vasil'evich Putiatin, "Vsepoddaneishii otchet general-adiutanta grafa Putiatina, o plavanii otriada voennykh sudov nashikh v Iaponiiu i Kitai, 1852-1855 god" (Most Devoted Report of Adjutant General Count Putiatin about the Sailing of a Detachment of Our Warships to Japan and China, 1852-1855), Russia, Morskoe Ministerstvo (Ministry of the Navy), Morskoi Uchenyi Komitet (Naval Scientific Section), Technical Committee, *Morskoi Sbornik* (Nautical Collection), XXIV, No. 10, Part 1 (August, 1856), 43; and Ivan Aleksandrovich Goncharov, *Fregat Pallada* (The Frigate Pallada [Pallas]), Vol. VII of *Polnoe Sobranie Sochinenii* (Complete Works) (St. Petersburg: Glazunov, 1884), 228.

8. S. D. Muraveiskii, editor of a recent Soviet edition of *Fregat Pallada*, specifically states in the introduction that notes which Goncharov may have kept about the negotiations have not been handed down. (I. A. Goncharov, *Fregat Pallada*, abridged ed. [Moscow, 1949], p. 40.)

9. According to B. Engel'gardt, the archives of the Russian Ministry of the Navy contain some material about the instructions (Voen.-pokhodn. kants. sekret. po sdatochn. opisi, No. 3) and possibly about the negotiations (Kantsel. Morskogo m-va, No. 14835). (B. Engel'gardt [ed.], "Putevye pis'ma I. A. Goncharova iz krugosvetnago plavaniia" [Travel Letters of I. A. Goncharov from (the) Around-the-World Expedition], *Literaturnoe Nasledstvo* [Literary Heritage], XXII-XXIV [1935], 342.) Unfortunately Engel'gardt neither describes nor summarizes the material.

10. Chapter X summarizes Russian demands and Japanese concessions. It gives the text of the treaty concluded between Putiatin and the Japanese plenipotentiaries. Chapter XI compares Russian and American attitudes and accomplishments.

11. Koga Kinichiro (Masaru), "Roshia osetsu-kakari Koga Kinichiro (Masaru) seishi nikki" (Diaries of the Western Mission of Koga Kinichiro [Masaru], Charged with the Reception of [the] Russia[ns]), Tokyo teikoku daigaku (Tokyo Imperial University) (ed.), *Bakumatsu gaikoku kankei monjo* (Documents [Pertaining to] Foreign Relations [during] the Last Days of the Shogunate) [hereafter cited as *Bakumatsu*], Series C of *Dai-Nihon ko-monjo* (Ancient Documents of Japan), Suppl. 1 (1913), 247.

12. Goncharov, *Fregat Pallada*, p. 106.

13. Nikolai G. Schilling II, "Iz vospominanii starago moriaka" (Memoirs of an Old Mariner), *Russkii Arkhiv* (Russian Archives) (1892), pp. 274-275.

On an earlier occasion, the Russians had refused to cooperate. Japanese interrogators at Nagasaki had been very concerned to hear that the frigate *Pallada* and the corvet *Olivutsa* had not departed from Russia on the same date and had asked the Russians to say that the corvet had left Kamchatka at the same time that the frigate had sailed from St. Petersburg. They added that it would be best to state also that they had completed their voyages in the same period of time. But the Russians spread out a map and explained that one could come from Kamchatka Peninsula "in a week or two," while a voyage from St. Petersburg took about half a year (Goncharov, *Fregat Pallada*, p. 20). The Japanese did not pursue the subject any further, but the fact remains that they had attempted to juggle figures to balance their accounts.

14. All dates, Russian and Japanese, have been converted into the Gregorian calendar, the calendar now in general use. Russian names have been transliterated in accordance with the system of the Library of Congress, Japanese names in accordance with the system of Dr. J. C. Hepburn.

15. Brief biographical comments will appear in footnotes.

16. The Soviet edition of *Fregat Pallada* has been abridged in such a way as to emphasize capitalistic Anglo-American exploitation of colonial peoples and hide all traces of Russian aggression or pugnacious thoughts. To illustrate: Goncharov, describing the arrival of the Russian expedition at Nagasaki, wrote how the mariners had speculated about the future of Japanese seclusion. "Will it remain so long?" they had queried, caressing their sixty-pounders. The Soviet edition renders the query, but leaves out the part of the sentence dealing with possible reliance on force. (Compare Goncharov, *Fregat Pallada*, pp. 2-3 with

Goncharov, *Fregat Pallada* [abridged], p. 318. For other examples, see Goncharov, *Fregat Pallada*, pp. 53 ff., and Goncharov, *Fregat Pallada* [abridged], p. 347; also Goncharov, *Fregat Pallada*, pp. 186 ff., and Goncharov, *Fregat Pallada* [abridged], p. 429.) Really important paragraphs have been omitted from the Soviet version. Arguments in favor of free intercourse with all countries have been excluded and Goncharov is criticized in the introduction for not having devoted enough time and space to the class struggle in England.

One of the by-products of our study is the establishment of the fact that the original *Fregat Pallada* is a legitimate historical source. Goncharov (1812-1891) was not only a public servant but also a distinguished writer and perhaps for this reason there has been the tendency to regard his account as semifictional. Although Japanese names have been misspelled and the author's beliefs are subject to question, nevertheless his narrative is factual. He himself insisted that he was writing nothing but the truth. A careful check has revealed that what we had supposed to be embellishment had actually occurred and is recorded in Japanese sources. The only criticism that we can make is that Goncharov failed to report the great hardships and dangers encountered by the crew of the frigate.

The chapters in *Fregat Pallada* dealing with the activities of the Russian expedition in Japan appeared in the *Morskoi Sbornik* under the title "Russkie v Iaponii v kontse 1853 i v nachale 1854 goda" (Russians in Japan at the End of 1853 and Beginning of 1854) (*Morskoi Sbornik*, XVIII, No. 9, Part 1, Sect. 4 [September, 1855], 14-84; and Part 2, Sect. 4, 127-162; No. 10, Part 1, Sect. 4 [October, 1855], 299-327; and Part 2, Sect. 4, 417-453; No. 11, Sect. 4 [November, 1855], 63-128.) Our account is based on the Glazunov edition, as the latter was readily available through interlibrary loan. For a chronological listing of Goncharov's articles about the expedition and a discussion of their reception by literary critics and the public, see Dmitrii Iazykov, "Literaturnaia deiatel'nost I. A. Goncharova" (Literary Activity of I. A. Goncharov), *Istoricheskii Vestnik* (Historical Messenger), XVIII (1884), 139-140.

Introduction

1. For an account of the various restrictive measures taken by the Japanese government prior to 1639, see Yoshi S. Kuno, *Japanese Expansion on the Asiatic Continent* (Berkeley and Los Angeles, 1940), II, 45-83.

2. Sir George B. Sansom, *The Western World and Japan* (New York, 1950), pp. 178-179.

3. Kuno, 90-91.

4. *Ibid.*, 93.

5. James Murdoch, *A History of Japan* (London, 1926), III, 509.

6. Yanaga, p. 11.

7. Murdoch, 510.

8. For further detail, see Shunzo Sakamaki, "Japan and the United States, 1790-1853," *The Transactions of the Asiatic Society of Japan* [hereafter abbreviated as TASJ], Second Series, XVIII (1939).

9. Tyler Dennett, *Americans in Eastern Asia* (New York, 1941), p. 242.

10. "The application of Manifest Destiny to Asia was voiced by United States Senator Thomas Hart Benton of Missouri, father-in-law of John C. Fremont, who, in May, 1846, eloquently expressed his belief that 'the arrival of the van of the Caucasian race upon the border of the sea which washes the shore of Eastern Asia' promised a greater and more beneficent change upon the earth than any human event past or present 'since the dispersion of man upon the earth.' The Caucasian race 'must wake up and reanimate the torpid body of Asia.... The moral and intellectual superiority of the White race will do the rest: and thus the youngest people, and the newest land, will become the reviver and the regenerator of the oldest.' " (Yanaga, p. 17.)

11. Dennett, p. 253.

12. *Ibid.*, p. 250. "A year later, a shipwrecked American sailor chanced to threaten his Japanese guards with vengeance from some American ships of war; they told him they had no fears of that, as the year before a common soldier had knocked down an American Commander at Uraga, and no notice had been taken of the matter." (Murdoch, 571.)

13. For a more detailed account of early Russo-Japanese relations with reference to Russian studies about Japan and Japanese thoughts about Russia, see George Alexander Lensen, "Early Russo-Japanese Relations," *The Far Eastern Quarterly*, X, No. 1 (November, 1950), 2-37. The article is based primarily on the following sources: K. E. Baer, *Die Verdienste Peter des Grossen um die Ertweiterung der geographischen Kenntnisse* (Peter the Great's Part in the Widening of Geographical Knowledge), Vol. XVI of *Beiträge zur Kenntnis des russischen Reiches* (St. Petersburg, 1872); W. Barthold, *Die geographische und historische Erforschung des Orientes mit besonderer Berücksichtigung der russischen Arbeiten* (The Geographical and Historical Investigation of the Orient with Special Reference to Russian Works), Vol. VIII of *Quellen und Forschungen zur Erd- und Kulturkunde* (Leipzig, 1913); L. S. Berg, *Ocherki po istorii russkikh geograficheskikh otkrytii* (Essays Concerning the History of Russian Geographic Discoveries) (Moscow, 1946); Captain Golownin (V. M. Golovnin), *Narrative of My Captivity in Japan During the Years 1811, 1812, and 1813* (London, 1818); Inobe Shigeo, *Ishin zenshi no kenkyu* (Historical Study of the Pre-Restoration Period) (Tokyo, 1935); N. N. Ogloblin, "Pervyi Iaponets v Rossii" (The First Japanese in Russia), *Russkaia Starina* (Russian Antiquity) (St. Petersburg, October, 1891); Okamoto Ryunosuke, *Nichiro kosho Hokkaido shiko* (Hokkaido Historical Documents Concerning Russo-Japanese Relations) (Tokyo, 1898); D. M. Pozdneev, *Materialy po istorii severnoi Iaponii i eia otnoshenii k materiku Azii i Rossii* (Material Concerning the History of Northern Japan and Her Relations to the Asiatic Mainland and Russia) (Tokyo, 1909); Riumin, *Zapiski kantseliarista Riumina po prikliucheniakh ego s Beniovskim* (Memoirs of the Chancery Clerk Riumin Concerning His Adventures with Benyovszky) (St. Petersburg, 1822); A. Sgibnev, "Popytki Russkikh k zavedeniiu torgovykh snoshenii s Iaponieiu (v XVIII i nachale XIX stoletii)" (Attempts of the Russians to Establish Trade Relations with Japan [in the Eighteenth and in the Beginning of the Nineteenth Centuries]), *Morskoi Sbornik* (January-February, 1869); A. Sgibnev, "Istoricheskii ocherk glavneishikh sobytii v Kamchatke v 1772-1816 g." (Historical Sketch of the Most Important Events in Kamchatka from 1772 to 1816), *Morskoi Sbornik* (July-August, 1869); Tabohashi Kiyoshi, *Kindai Nihon gaikoku kankei-shi* (History

of Japan's Foreign Relations in Recent Times) (Tokyo, 1930); Tokutomi Iichiro, *Kinsei Nihon kokumin-shi* (History of the Japanese People in Modern Times) (Tokyo, 1925-1936), Vols. XXXI-XXXIII.

14. In spite of various reports from Kamchatka about the nearness and wealth of Japan, contemporary reports about the location of Japan were obscure and misleading, particularly since European geographers were spreading the false viewpoint that Kamchatka and Matsumae were one and the same. Equally limited was familiarity with the shore lines of eastern Siberia and the bordering seas and countries. (Lensen, "Early Russo-Japanese Relations," 25.)

15. Four hundred and fifty Japanese footmen accompanied Laxman from Hakodate, six hundred more from Osamarusa.

16. Lensen, "Early Russo-Japanese Relations," 17-22.

17. Rezanov's final instructions were contradictory. As he died before the Admiralty interrogated Khvostov and Davydov about the expedition, we have no clarification on this point.

18. During their captivity, Golovnin and companions gave instruction in Russian language, history, geography, and other subjects. For a discussion of this and for reproductions of Japanese drawings of the prisoners, see George Alexander Lensen, *Report from Hokkaido: The Remains of Russian Culture in Northern Japan* (Hakodate, 1954), pp. 28-45.

19. Kurt Krupinski, *Japan und Russland, Ihre Beziehungen bis zum Frieden von Portsmouth* (Japan and Russia, Their Relations till the Peace of Portsmouth) (Königsberg and Berlin, 1940), p. 21.

20. As noted in the Preface, this expedition had been scheduled to start out as early as 1843. It had been postponed for financial and diplomatic reasons until news of the imminence of an American Japan Expedition persuaded Tsar Nicholas I to delay no further. Shortly before the departure of the Russian expedition, the Russo-American Company vessel *Kniaz' Menshikov* had cast anchor in Shimoda Bay to return some Japanese waifs. Local officials reiterated that Japan wished to have nothing to do with Russia.

21. A. A. Polovtsov (ed.), *Russkii biograficheskii slovar'* (Russian Biographical Dictionary) (St. Petersburg, 1910), XV, 162-164.

22. Tokutomi, XXXI, 354.

23. Sansom, p. 245.

24. George Alexander Lensen, "A History of Russo-Japanese Relations, 1700-1860" (unpublished manuscript [Master's Essay, Department of Chinese and Japanese, Faculty of Philosophy, Columbia University, 1947]), p. 76. Hereinafter cited as Lensen, "History."

25. *Ibid.*, p. 79.

26. Sansom, p. 246.

27. *Ibid.*, p. 246.

28. For a discussion of pre-Perry Japanese opinions concerning the opening of Japan, see Kuno, II, 227-238; Sansom, pp. 247-274; and Lensen, "Early Russo-Japanese Relations," 22-24.

29. Lensen, "History," pp. 164-170.

30. Ernest Mason Satow (trans.), *Japan 1853-1864 (Genji yume monogatari)* (Tokyo, 1905), pp. 5-6.

31. *Ibid.*, pp. 7-8.

32. K. K. Kawakami, *Japan in World Politics* (New York, 1917), pp. 282-283.

Chapter 1

1. The schooner was purchased for 3375 pounds sterling. Total cost upon conversion: 5380 pounds.

2. Russian ranks are given when it would be difficult or inaccurate to substitute American terminology. *Fligel'-adiutant* is commonly translated as "Aid-de-camp [of Sovereign]," *Kapitan-leitenant* as "Second Captain" or "First Lieutenant [of a ship]." V. K. Istomin refers to the commander of the *Pallada* as "Unkovskoi" (V. K. Istomin, "Admiral I. S. Unkovskoi. Razskazy iz ego zhizni" [Admiral I. S. Unkovskoi. Stories Out of His Life], *Russkii Arkhiv*, Parts 1, 2, and 5 [1887]), but all official sources at our disposal list him as "Unkovskii." Ivan Semenovich Unkovskii (1822-1886) was considered one of Russia's most able navigators.

3. For a detailed listing of the personnel aboard the *Pallada*, see Russia, Morskoe Ministerstvo, Morskoi Uchenyi Komitet, Technical Committee, "Otchet o plavanii fregata *Pallada*, shkuny *Vostok*, korveta *Olivutsa* i transporta *Kniaz' Menshikov*, pod komandoiu General-Adiutanta Putiatina, v 1852, 53 i 54 godakh, s prilozheniem otcheta o plavanii fregata *Diana*, v. 1853, 54 i 55 godakh" (Account of the Sailing of the Frigate *Pallada*, the Schooner *Vostok*, the Corvet *Olivutsa*, and the Transport *Kniaz' Menshikov*, under the Command of Adjutant-General Putiatin, in the Years 1852, 1853, and 1854, with a Supplementary Account of the Sailing of the Frigate *Diana*, in the Years 1853, 1854, and 1855) (hereinafter cited as Russia, "Otchet"], *Morskoi Sbornik*, XX, No. 1, Part 3 (January, 1856), 132-173. Consult also the table of strength of the *Pallada*, *Diana*, and *Vostok* in Appendix II. As the original crew of the *Pallada* had been composed of members of the Guard, it could not as a whole be spared for a long voyage, and had to be replaced at the expense of other vessels of the Baltic Fleet. So little notice was given that several parties of men came aboard the frigate almost on the eve of sailing. They did not know each other, or their officers. The *Pallada* set out on the long and hazardous voyage before her crew had become a smoothly working team. (Engel'gardt, 311.)

4. Putiatin, "Vsepoddaneishii otchet," 23. Six officers and twenty-eight men is the figure given in Russia, "Otchet." The officers are identified as *Leitenant* Voin Andreevich Rimskii-Korsakov (newly appointed commander of the schooner), *Leitenant Baron* Aleksandr Shlipenbakh [Schlippenbach?], *Michman* (Midshipman or Warrant Officer) Petr Anzhu, *Shturmanskii Podporuchik* (Pilot Sub-lieutenant) Ivan Moiseev III, *Inzhener Podporuchik* (Engineer Sub-lieutenant) Ivan Zarubin, and Doctor (of Medicine) Genrikh Veirikh. (Russia, "Otchet," 138.)

5. Goshkevich later served as Russia's first consul in Japan, and did much to acquaint the people of Hakodate with things Russian. (Lensen, *Report from Hokkaido: The Remains of Russian Culture in Northern Japan* [Hakodate, 1954], pp. 65 ff.) When he objected to the Russian occupation of Tsushima Island, however, his countrymen accused him of having become "completely Japanized." (Konstantin Pavlovich Pilkin, "Zaniatie v 1862 g. russkimi sudami ostrova Tsusima" [The Occupation of Tsushima Island by Russian Vessels in 1862], extract from the journal of *Kapitan 2-go ranga* Konstantin Pavlovich Pilkin, commander of the clipper *Abrek*, *Morskiia Zapiski* [Naval Records], VIII, No. 1 [March, 1950], 2-7; and V. Mainov, "Uspekhi geograficheskikh znanii v Rossii [1855-1880]" [Progress of Geographical Knowledge in Russia (1855-1880)], *Istoricheskii Vestnik*, III [1880], 74.)

6. Putiatin, "Vsepoddaneishii otchet," 22-23; Russia, "Otchet," 132-138.

7. Putiatin, "Vsepoddaneishii otchet," 24; Russia, "Otchet," 133-134.

8. Putiatin, "Vsepoddaneishii otchet," 24. As regards the water condensing machine, the admiral reported "splendid results": "In addition to the river water, with which we supplied ourselves wherever possible, we condensed by means of the machine daily up to one hundred and twenty buckets of water that exceeded river water in purity and taste."

9. *Ibid.*, 24-25. The *Pallada* had been built in 1831-1832 and refitted in 1841. (Engel'gardt, 311.)

10. Strong unfavorable winds blew from November 15, 1852, to January 16, 1853. They delayed not only the *Pallada*, but also some one hundred and thirty merchantmen that spent about two months waiting for a change in the course of the wind. (Putiatin, "Vsepoddaneishii otchet," 25; Russia, "Otchet," 137.)

11. Putiatin, "Vsepoddaneishii otchet," 25; Russia, "Otchet," 137-138. Neither source mentions how word was sent.

12. Konstantin Nikolaevich Pos'et, "O plavanii iz Anglii na mys Dobroi Nadezhdy i v Zondskii proliv v 1853 godu" (Concerning the Sailing from England to the Cape of Good Hope and Sunda Strait in the Year 1853), *Morskoi Sbornik*, X, No. 9 (1853); Putiatin, "Vsepoddaneishii otchet," 25-26; Russia, "Otchet," 138-140.

13. Putiatin, "Vsepoddaneishii otchet," 26; Russia, "Otchet," 141.

14. Putiatin, "Vsepoddaneishii otchet," 27.

15. *Ibid.*, 27-28.

16. *Ibid.*, 28.

17. *Ibid.*, 29; Russia, "Otchet," 141.

18. Putiatin, "Vsepoddaneishii otchet," 30.

19. *Ibid.*

20. *Ibid.*, 31-32.

21. *Ibid.*, 32.

22. *Ibid.*, 33-34; Russia, "Otchet," 144.

23. Putiatin, "Vsepoddaneishii otchet," 35; Russia, "Otchet," 145.

24. Putiatin, "Vsepoddaneishii otchet," 35-37; Russia, "Otchet," 145-146; Engel'gardt, 389.

25. Perry first visited Japan with only four vessels: the steam-frigates *Susquehanna* and *Mississippi* and the sloops-of-war *Plymouth* and *Saratoga*. (J. W. Spalding, *Japan and Around the World* [New York, 1855], p. 129.)

26. Putiatin, "Vsepoddaneishii otchet," 38; Russia, "Otchet," 146.

27. Aleksandr Boltin, "Shtorm v vostochnom okeane vyderzhennyi fr. *Pallada*" (The Storm in the Pacific Ocean Weathered by the Frigate *Pallada*), *Morskoi Sbornik*, XVII, No. 7, Part 5 (July, 1855), 7-10. For further comments, including atmospherical data, see "Zamechaniia o shtorme, vyderzhannom fregatom *Pallada* v 1853 godu" (Observations about the Storm Weathered by the Frigate *Pallada* in the Year 1853), *Morskoi Sbornik*, XX, No. 2, Part 3 (February, 1856), 459-468.

28. Putiatin, "Vsepoddaneishii otchet," 39.

29. *Ibid.*, 40; Russia, *"Otchet,"* 148-149. According to Engel'gardt, Putiatin received instructions from the Ministry of Foreign Affairs to open negotiations in Nagasaki and if at all possible to refrain from visiting Edo so as not to antagonize the Japanese. (Engel'gardt, 317.)

30. Francis L. Hawks (comp.), *Narrative of the Expedition of an American*

Squadron to the China Seas and Japan, Performed in the Years 1852, 1853, and 1854 under the Command of Commodore M. C. Perry, United States Navy, by Order of the Government of the United States (New York, 1856), pp. 226-244.

31. Putiatin, "Vsepoddaneishii otchet," 40; Russia, "Otchet," 149.
32. Putiatin, "Vsepoddaneishii otchet," 40; Russia, "Otchet," 149.

Chapter 2

1. Goncharov, *Fregat Pallada*, pp. 2-3; Koga, 197.
2. Goncharov, *Fregat Pallada*, pp. 2-3.
3. Russia, "Otchet," 150.
4. *Bakumatsu*, I, 539. The reports stated that five [*sic*] white sails had been seen at sea.
5. *Ibid.*, 539-540; Russia, "Otchet," 150.
6. Goncharov, *Fregat Pallada*, p. 3.
7. *Bakumatsu*, I, 539-540; Goncharov, *Fregat Pallada*, pp. 4-5. Goshkevich, the Chinese language expert of the expedition, had written the inscription. (Koga, 381.)
8. Goncharov, *Fregat Pallada*, pp. 4-5; Putiatin, "Vsepoddaneishii otchet," 41; Tokutomi, XXXI, 324-325.
9. Putiatin, "Vsepoddaneishii otchet," 41.
10. Ramming, "Über den Anteil der Russen," 20.
11. Putiatin, "Vsepoddaneishii otchet," 41.
12. As will be seen later on, several interpreters knew some English also.
13. Goncharov, *Fregat Pallada*, pp. 6-7.
14. *Ibid.*, p. 7.
15. Spalding, p. 152.
16. Goncharov, *Fregat Pallada*, p. 8.
17. *Ibid.*
18. *Ibid.*, pp. 9-14.
19. *Ibid.*, p. 15.
20. *Ibid.*, pp. 17-18.
21. *Ibid.*, pp. 19-20.
22. Putiatin, "Vsepoddaneishii otchet," 45. For a discussion of the Russian demands as stated in these letters, see Chapter X.
23. Goncharov, *Fregat Pallada*, pp. 19-20.
24. Russia, "Otchet," 151.
25. Koga, 238; Putiatin, "Vsepoddaneishii otchet," 44.
26. Goncharov, *Fregat Pallada*, p. 35.
27. *Bakumatsu*, I, 541; Tokutomi, XXXI, 325; Ramming, "Über den Anteil der Russen," 18. Anne, daughter of Paul (Pavel), sister of Nicholas I (in whose reign the Russian Japan Expedition was sent out), married William II, king of the Netherlands.
28. *Bakumatsu*, I, 541; Tokutomi, XXXI, 325-326; Ramming, "Über den Anteil der Russen," 18.
29. Tokutomi, XXXI, 327.
30. Goncharov, *Fregat Pallada*, p. 20.
31. Konstantin Nikolaevich Pos'et (1819-1899), later on admiral and Minister of Communications. (Engel'gardt, 361.)

32. Putiatin, "Vsepoddaneishii otchet," 45; Goncharov, *Fregat Pallada*, p. 22; Russia, "Otchet," 151; *Bakumatsu*, I, 539-541.
33. Goncharov, *Fregat Pallada*, pp. 22-24.
34. *Ibid.*, p. 25.
35. *Ibid.*, p. 32.
36. *Ibid.*, p. 31.
37. *Ibid.*, p. 33.
38. Putiatin, "Vsepoddaneishii otchet," 42-44. Two couriers had arrived on August 24. One of them, *Kollezhskii Sekretar'* Bodisko, was sent to Shanghai on the *Kniaz' Menshikov;* the other one, *Leitenant* Kroun, assigned to temporary duty with the squadron.
39. Putiatin, "Vsepoddaneishii otchet," 42-44.
40. Goncharov, *Fregat Pallada*, p. 35.
41. *Ibid.*, p. 33.
42. *Ibid.*, p. 37.
43. Putiatin, "Vsepoddaneishii otchet," 47.
44. Goncharov, *Fregat Pallada*, p. 38.
45. Putiatin, "Vsepoddaneishii otchet," 48.
46. *Ibid.*
47. Goncharov, *Fregat Pallada*, p. 40.
48. Goncharov speculates that the Japanese might have been trying to imitate the actions of the admiral. As will be recalled, he had not joined the Japanese officials for breakfast on the occasion of their first visit, but had retired to his cabin while Goncharov and others had played host.
49. Goncharov, *Fregat Pallada*, p. 43.
50. *Ibid.*, p. 42.
51. *Ibid.*, p. 43.
52. Putiatin, "Vsepoddaneishii otchet," 48-49; Goncharov, *Fregat Pallada*, pp. 43-46.
53. Goncharov, *Fregat Pallada*, p. 48; Putiatin, "Vsepoddaneishii otchet," 49.
54. Putiatin, "Vsepoddaneishii otchet," 49.
55. Konstantin Losev, "O Nagasakskikh ukrepleniiakh" (Concerning the Nagasaki Fortifications), *Morskoi Sbornik*, XXIII, No. 8, Part 3 (June, 1856), 300-306; Russia, "Otchet," 154.
56. Koga, 241.
57. Goncharov, *Fregat Pallada*, p. 49.
58. *Sei-yakusho* and *hsi-yamen*, respectively, in the Japanese and Chinese records.
59. *Bakumatsu*, I, 543; Tokutomi, XXXI, 330-349; Goncharov, *Fregat Pallada*, p. 50.
60. Koga, 344. *Norimono* were not only means of transportation of doubtful convenience but also symbols of rank; hence Western insistence on use of these palanquins in China and Japan in the face of Chinese and Japanese reluctance to grant this privilege.
61. Goncharov, *Fregat Pallada*, pp. 51, 61, 64.
62. *Ibid.*, pp. 61-62.
63. *Ibid.*, pp. 62-63; Putiatin, "Vsepoddaneishii otchet," 49. As the fable goes, the Fox invited the Stork for dinner. He served the food on a plate and lapped it up with his tongue, while his guest with her long bill could not eat anything.

The Stork, in turn, asked the Fox to dine with her, and served the meal in a long-necked jar from which she could easily help herself while the Fox went hungry.

64. Goncharov, *Fregat Pallada*, p. 66.

65. Koga refers to the room as *"tz'u-shih."* It was an adjoining room of lesser importance. As it was used primarily for resting and relaxation, we shall refer to it as the "lounge."

66. Putiatin, "Vsepoddaneishii otchet," 49; Goncharov, *Fregat Pallada*, p. 67. For a discussion of the Russian letter, see Chapter X.

67. Goncharov, *Fregat Pallada*, p. 67.

68. Putiatin, "Vsepoddaneishii otchet," 50.

69. Goncharov, *Fregat Pallada*, pp. 71-72.

70. Putiatin, "Vsepoddaneishii otchet," 50.

71. Mizuno Tadanori (Chikugo-no-kami) (1810-1868) soon joined Osawa Bungo-no-kami in his duties as Nagasaki *bugyo.* Although decisions were undertaken jointly, Osawa at times dealt with the Russians alone.

72. Goncharov, *Fregat Pallada*, p. 72.

73. Putiatin, "Vsepoddaneishii otchet," 50; Goncharov, *Fregat Pallada*, pp. 73-74.

74. Putiatin, "Vsepoddaneishii otchet," 50-51; Goncharov, *Fregat Pallada*, p. 75.

75. Tokutomi, XXXI, 349. Goncharov records that he came on the 28th. (Goncharov, *Fregat Pallada*, p. 75.)

76. Moriyama Einosuke (1829-1887), later known as Moriyama Takichiro. Born into the family of a Nagasaki Dutch interpreter, he became versed in Dutch and English. He interpreted during the Russo-Japanese, as well as the American-Japanese, negotiations. In 1862-1863, he visited England and Russia as a member of a Japanese mission to Europe. (Tokutomi, XXXIII, Appendix, 21-22; Heibonsha [publ.], *Shinsen dai-jimmei jiten* [Revised Large Biographical Encyclopedia], VI, 268.) According to Samuel Wells Williams (1812-1884), the American missionary and lexicographer who served as interpreter for the American Japan Expedition, Moriyama spoke English "well enough to render any other interpreter unnecessary." He had been taught English by Ranald McDonald during his stay in Nagasaki in 1848-1849. (Samuel Wells Williams, "A Journal of the Perry Expedition to Japan [1853-1854]," TASJ, First Series, XXXVII, Part 2, 120; Murdoch, 601, n.1.)

77. Goncharov, *Fregat Pallada*, pp. 75-76.

78. *Ibid.*, p. 76.

79. *Ibid.*, pp. 76-77.

80. *Ibid.*, pp. 77-78.

81. *Ibid.*, p. 78. Reference is made here to the reception the officials received when the Russians called them aboard to protest interference with Russian boat trips. The admiral had refused to receive the Japanese and had expressed his dissatisfaction through his officers. The edition of *Fregat Pallada* here cited gives the date as September 14 (Russian style), but as this diary entry is between entries dated September 21 (Russian style) and September 25 (Russian style), it must of course be September 24 (Russian style), or October 6 (Gregorian style). The abridged Soviet edition gives it as such.

82. *Ibid.*, p. 79.

83. *Ibid.*, pp. 80-81.

84. *Ibid.,* p. 82.
85. *Ibid.,* pp. 82-85.
86. *Ibid.,* pp. 86-87.
87. Tokutomi, XXXI, 356; Goncharov, *Fregat Pallada,* pp. 88-91.
88. Goncharov, *Fregat Pallada,* pp. 90-91.
89. Tokugawa Ieyoshi had actually died on July 27, 1853. His demise was officially announced exactly one lunar month later (August 26). He received the posthumous name Shindokuin. On September 6, 1853, he was interred within the confines of Zojo-ji, a great Jodo-shu temple at Shiba in Edo. (Tokutomi, XXXII, Appendix, 2.)
90. Putiatin, "Vsepoddaneishii otchet," 51; Goncharov, *Fregat Pallada,* pp. 91-92.
91. Goncharov, *Fregat Pallada,* p. 93.
92. *Ibid.,* p. 94.
93. *Ibid.,* p. 95.
94. *Ibid.,* pp. 97-103.
95. Putiatin, "Vsepoddaneishii otchet," 52; Goncharov, *Fregat Pallada,* p. 103. Goncharov dates the return of the schooner as November 16.
96. Goncharov, *Fregat Pallada,* p. 104.
97. *Ibid.,* p. 105. Tokutomi states that Putiatin threatened to proceed to Edo: "Our officials were very much frightened and tried to detain him." (Tokutomi, XXXI, 358.)
98. Goncharov, *Fregat Pallada,* pp. 105-106.
99. *Ibid.,* p. 108; Putiatin, "Vsepoddaneishii otchet," 52; Tokutomi, XXXI, 358.
100. Goncharov, *Fregat Pallada,* pp. 108-109; Lensen, "Early Russo-Japanese Relations," 27.
101. Putiatin, "Vsepoddaneishii otchet," 52.
102. *Ibid.*
103. Goncharov, *Fregat Pallada,* pp. 109-110; Tokutomi, XXXI, 358; Putiatin, "Vsepoddaneishii otchet," 52.

Chapter 3

1. Putiatin, "Vsepoddaneishii otchet," 52-53.
2. Putiatin identified the rebels as T'ai-p'ing. According to Hosea Ballou Morse, "these 'Small Swords' claimed that they were affiliated with the Taipings at Nanking, from whom they expected support, but the Tien Wang [Hung Hsiu-ch'üan], in November sent a commissioner to investigate their claims, and, on receiving his report, issued a proclamation denouncing their 'immoral habits, and vicious propensities,' and refusing them as his adherents." (Hosea Ballou Morse, *The International Relations of the Chinese Empire* [London, 1910], I, 458.)
3. Putiatin, "Vsepoddaneishii otchet," 52-53.
4. *Ibid.,* 54.
5. *Ibid.,* 56. Arthur Walworth, in his study of the American Japan Expedition, states that Commodore Perry had attempted to restrict the movements of the Russians, collecting "all the coal on which he could lay hands" and placing it in the United States Naval Stores at Shanghai with orders to allow *no one* to take any coal without written permission from himself. But as at that time the

American vice-consul in Shanghai was also the official agent of the Russian government, Putiatin's request for a loan of twenty tons of coal was granted and the Russian vessels reached Nagasaki in spite of Perry. Unable to obtain any concessions from the Japanese, the Russians returned to Shanghai "after trying to persuade the Dutch to join them in using violence to enforce their demands." There they requested another eighty tons of coal, a plea "promptly denied by Perry." (Walworth, pp. 127-129.) It is doubtful, however, that Perry's plan, even if carried out, could have prevented the Russians from reaching Japan, firstly, because coal was obtainable outside of Shanghai and, secondly, because the Russian vessels were not wholly dependent on steam power. What does interest us considerably is the fact that the Russians were not aware of Perry's jealous and hostile attitude. Putiatin reported that he had received "a certain amount of coal" upon his return from Nagasaki — which shows that Perry's refusal must have been circumvented again — "due to the obligingness of Commodore Perry." Careful perusal of the Russian sources at our disposal has produced no evidence to the effect that Putiatin ever intended to further his mission by force, either through unilateral action or in conjunction with the Dutch.

6. According to Engel'gardt, Putiatin had learned of the declaration of war between Russia and Turkey on the evening of December 20. He had immediately ordered the schooner to rejoin the frigate (she went out to sea at dawn, December 21) to avoid capture upon the expected outbreak of hostilities with England. He himself secretly remained in Shanghai and awaited the mail from Hong Kong. He returned to the frigate incognito, aboard a private yacht, several days later, and, ". . . having ascertained that no official break had as yet occurred with France and England, hastened to Nagasaki to meet the plenipotentiaries." (Engel'gardt, 319.)

7. Putiatin, "Vsepoddaneishii otchet," 56; Russia, "Otchet," 160; Mitsukuri Gempo (Kenju), "Roshia osetsu-kakari tsuke Tsuyama hanshi Mitsukuri Gempo (Kenju) seisei kiko" (Journal of the Western Travel of the Tsuyama Clansman Mitsukuri Gempo [Kenju], Attached [to Those Charged with the] Russian Reception), *Bakumatsu*, Suppl. 1, 410.

8. Goncharov, *Fregat Pallada*, pp. 185-186.

9. Russia, Morskoe Ministerstvo, Morskoi Uchenyi Komitet, Technical Committee, "Izvlechenie iz pisem morskikh ofitserov: Zarubina, Peshchurova i Boltina, nakhodiashchikhsia na eskadre Vitse-Admirala Putiatina" (Extracts from Letters of the Naval Officers Zarubin, Peshchurov, and Boltin, Serving with the Squadron of Vice-Admiral Putiatin) [hereafter cited as Russia, "Izvlechenie"], *Morskoi Sbornik*, XII, No. 7, Part 3 (July, 1854), 324-325.

10. Goncharov, *Fregat Pallada*, p. 179.

11. *Ibid.*, p. 180. The admiral's account differs somewhat, quite possibly because of brevity: "Having informed myself that the plenipotentiaries were not yet there, I gave orders to prepare for departure, and only when the rowboats had already been raised and there was no doubt left [in the minds of] the Japanese concerning the actuality of my intentions, did they announce that the plenipotentiaries had arrived. (Putiatin, "Vsepoddaneishii otchet," 56.)

12. Russia, "Izvlechenie," 325; Goncharov, *Fregat Pallada*, pp. 180-181.

13. Goncharov, *Fregat Pallada*, pp. 181-182.

14. *Ibid.*, p. 182.

15. Russia, "Izvlechenie," 325.

16. Russia, "Otchet," 160; Goncharov, *Fregat Pallada*, p. 182.

17. Russia, "Izvlechenie," 325.

18. Goncharov, *Fregat Pallada*, p. 185.

19. *Ibid.*, p. 182.

20. Koga, 238; Goncharov, *Fregat Pallada*, p. 183.

21. Goncharov, *Fregat Pallada*, p. 186.

22. Koga, 236.

23. Goncharov, *Fregat Pallada*, pp. 187-188.

24. There were but three horses at the disposal of the four plenipotentiaries. But even if there had been four, they would not have been able to progress much faster, as their retinue travelled on foot.

25. Koga, 198.

26. Voin Andreevich Rimskii-Korsakov (1822-1871), commander of the *Vostok*, later on admiral, well known for his humanitarian treatment of sailors; excellent scholar, teacher, and writer. (Engel'gardt, 365.)

27. Goncharov, *Fregat Pallada*, p. 188.

28. *Ibid.*, p. 228.

29. Kawaji Saemon-no-jo (Toshiakira), "Roshia osetsu-kakari Kawaji Saemon-no-jo (Toshiakira) nikki" (Diaries of Kawaji Saemon-no-jo [Toshiakira], Charged with the Reception of [the] Russia[ns]), *Bakumatsu*, Suppl. 1, 134; Goncharov, *Fregat Pallada*, p. 189.

30. Koga, 239-240.

31. Goncharov, *Fregat Pallada*, p. 189.

32. *Ibid.*, p. 190.

33. *Ibid.*, p. 191.

34. Koga, 240; Goncharov, *Fregat Pallada*, p. 191.

35. Goncharov, *Fregat Pallada*, p. 192.

36. Koga, 240.

37. Goncharov, *Fregat Pallada*, p. 192.

38. *Ibid.*

39. Putiatin, "Vsepoddaneishii otchet," 56.

40. Goncharov, *Fregat Pallada*, p. 192.

41. Koga, 241.

42. Goncharov, *Fregat Pallada*, p. 194; Koga, 240.

43. Kawaji, 36. Takashima Shuhan (1798-1866) was a Japanese authority on European military science. He conducted Western-style drill. (Heibonsha [publ.], *Dai-hyakka jiten* [Great Encyclopedia] [Tokyo, 1931-1935], XVI, 300-301.)

44. Goncharov, *Fregat Pallada*, p. 194.

45. Koga, 240.

46. *Ibid.*

47. Tsutsui Masanori (1778-1859), Hizen-no-kami. Other given names Shiko, Samasuke, Sajiuemon, and others. Son of Kuse Hirokage, heir of Tsutsui Sazen. Diplomat of the Bakumatsu period. Entering the service of the Shogunate as a *shoin hanshi*, he was promoted to the position of Edo *machi-bugyo* (1821). He had a good reputation, distinguished for uprightness. He resigned after twenty-one years of service (1841). In 1842, he was compromised by implication in the Yabe Sadakata affair. (Yabe Sadakata, who had succeeded Tsutsui as Edo *machi-bugyo*, had refused to cooperate with *Roju* Mizuno Tadakuni. He was relieved from office and confined to his house, where he starved himself to death.)

Pardoned, Tsutsui was appointed to receive, together with Kawaji, the members of the Russian expedition. (Heki Shoichi, *Nihon rekishi jimmei jiten* [Biographical Dictionary of Japanese History] [Tokyo, 1938], p. 600.)

Kawaji Toshiakira (1801-1868). Also known as Sanzaemon and Saemon-no-jo. Served as coastal defense officer. A man of staunch loyalty, who would not transfer his allegiance to another master. When Edo castle was pressed upon (April 7, 1868) and the cause of his lord, the Tokugawa Shogun, was lost, he disemboweled himself, having written down: "I am the retainer of the Tokugawa Shogun. When I think of the man who picked up ferns to still hunger, even though I act against heavenly Deity. . . ." [Classical reference to Chinese who refused to live under a new dynasty, went into voluntary exile, and died after subsisting for a while on wild ferns.] (Heibonsha, *Shinsen dai-jimmei jiten,* II, 204.)

Koga Kinichiro (1816-1884). Also known as Masaru, Josen, Chakei, and Kindo. Followed in the footsteps of his father (Koga Doan) as Confucian official of the Shogunate. He was at the same time, however, an ardent student and well-known authority on Western learning. (*Ibid.,* 579.)

There is no biographical information about Arao Tosa-no-kami Narimasa at the disposal of this writer.

48. Nakamura Tameya (d. 1865), Dewa-no-kami. Conferred with members of both the Russian and the American expeditions. Promoted in 1857 from financial examiner to Shimoda *bugyo.* (Tokutomi, XXXIII, Appendix, 16.)

49. Goncharov, *Fregat Pallada,* p. 195; Koga, 240.

50. Goncharov, *Fregat Pallada,* p. 195.

51. One *sun* equals about 1.19 inches.

52. *Go* is an intricate Japanese game played on a checkered board with round, button-like stones.

53. Kawaji, 49.

54. Goncharov, *Fregat Pallada,* p. 197.

55. *Ibid.*

56. *Ibid.*

57. Koga, 240.

58. Kawaji, 35.

59. Goncharov, *Fregat Pallada,* p. 200; Koga, 240. Several of the officers, among them the admiral, "rested" in the conference room.

60. Goncharov, *Fregat Pallada,* p. 200.

61. Kawaji, 36; Koga, 240; Goncharov, *Fregat Pallada,* p. 200.

62. Kawaji, 36.

63. Goncharov, *Fregat Pallada,* p. 202.

64. Kawaji, 37.

65. *Ibid.;* Goncharov, *Fregat Pallada,* p. 202.

66. Goncharov, *Fregat Pallada,* p. 206.

67. Koga, 243.

68. Goncharov, *Fregat Pallada,* p. 206.

69. *Ibid.,* pp. 206-207.

70. Koga, 240; Goncharov, *Fregat Pallada,* p. 207.

71. Goncharov, *Fregat Pallada,* p. 207. "*Nichevo*" — spelled actually "nichego" but pronounced "nichevo" — can be translated as "nothing" or "it does not matter," the implication being in this sentence "but this is all right."

72. Koga, 240.

73. Goncharov, *Fregat Pallada*, p. 207.

74. *Tanabata-dake*: A bamboo pole on which poems are hung on the seventh day of the seventh month to celebrate the meeting of the Weaver (the star Vega) with his love on the Milky Way.

75. Kawaji, 37.

Chapter 4

1. Goncharov, *Fregat Pallada*, pp. 208-209.

2. Sansom, p. 279.

3. Goncharov, *Fregat Pallada*, pp. 209-210.

4. *Ibid.*, p. 183; Koga, 246.

5. "The Japanese have no woolen cloth," wrote Goncharov, "and not all know its use. It was purposely given to them as a gift so that they would learn what it was and would become accustomed to wearing it. There is a need: in winter they wear three or four flaxen robes, which do not take the place of even one woolen one. The common people go completely naked when the sun radiates warmth; when it gets cold they throw some rags over their shoulders." He pitied the men who, with their uncovered chest, shoulders, and legs, waited some three hours at a time, blue with cold and shaking all over, while the officials were being entertained in the cabin. (Goncharov, *Fregat Pallada*, pp. 183-184.)

6. *Ibid.*, p. 183.

7. Kawaji, 38-39. As will be seen in Chapter X, the Russians desired clarification of Japan's northern frontiers.

8. Yakibune: *yaki* from *yaku* (to burn); *bune* from *fune* (boat).

9. Kawaji, 38-39. Koga states that this plan was proposed by a feudal chief from Fukuoka. (Koga, 241.)

10. Kawaji, 38-39.

11. *Ibid.*

12. *Ibid.*

13. *Ibid.*

14. Neither Russian nor Japanese sources at our disposal indicate the content of these questions.

15. Goncharov, *Fregat Pallada*, p. 210.

16. *Noshi*: thin strip of dried sea-ear folded up in paper. Serving *noshi* personally, Kawaji made a gesture of respect toward Matsudaira.

17. One *cho* equals about 119 yards.

18. One *koku* equals 4.9629 bushels. Daimyo were rated by the number of *koku* of rice their fiefs yielded. Kawaji admired the fact that Matsudaira himself had gone to so much trouble, even though he was a wealthy lord.

19. Kawaji, 40.

20. Goncharov gives January 16 (January 4, Russian style) as the date of meeting, but both Kawaji and Koga agree on January 15. Putiatin does not give the exact date. Russia, "Otchet" agrees with Goncharov, but, compiled from "official reports," it may be based on records kept by Goncharov. Subsequent dates differ correspondingly by one day.

21. Koga, 241.

22. Goncharov, *Fregat Pallada*, pp. 212-213.

23. *Ibid.*, p. 213.

24. Kawaji, 45-46.

25. Goncharov, *Fregat Pallada*, p. 213.

26. Putiatin, "Vsepoddaneishii otchet," 59; Goncharov, *Fregat Pallada*, pp. 213-214.

27. Putiatin, "Vsepoddaneishii otchet," 59. This sword had been made by Jiro Taro, and bore the inscription "sword worn by Kawaji Saemon-no-jo." A certificate stated that it was a "hipbone-cutting sword." Both Putiatin and Goncharov record that they were told the sword had chopped off three heads at one time. But as the certificate and other references indicate, it had actually cut through three hips. Kawaji's diary states that he had informed the Russians through an interpreter that the sword had been tested on three men put next to each other. It had cut their hips like a melon. Some people might fear that it was too heavy to handle, reflected Kawaji. "Don't think so. I used one twice as heavy." Having practiced with it three thousand times daily, he could swing it like a dried vegetable stalk. How could the Japanese test it on human beings? "One cuts the corpses of criminals." "In Japan this is called '*tameshi-giri*' [sword test]." "Because the Westerners have not had the training," he added as an afterthought, "the sword may not cut [like this]. Nevertheless, it will certainly chop off one arm and one leg. . . ." (Kawaji, 46; Putiatin, "Vsepoddaneishii otchet," 59; Goncharov, *Fregat Pallada*, pp. 213-214.)

28. Goncharov, *Fregat Pallada*, pp. 217-218.

29. Kawaji, 41-44.

30. *Ibid.;* Goncharov, *Fregat Pallada*, pp. 217-218.

31. Koga, 242.

32. Kawaji, 41-44.

33. Goncharov, *Fregat Pallada*, pp. 217-218.

34. Kawaji, 41-44.

35. Koga, 243.

36. Kawaji, 43.

37. Koga, 243.

38. Goncharov, *Fregat Pallada*, p. 218.

39. Kawaji, 41-44.

40. *Ibid.*, 43.

41. Goncharov, *Fregat Pallada*, p. 218.

42. Koga, 243.

43. Goncharov, *Fregat Pallada*, pp. 218-219.

44. Koga, 243.

45. Kawaji, 42.

46. *Ibid.* Koga writes that the "Japanese white and black official flag and barbarian two-headed eagle flag flew from the middle mast as an expression of friendship." (Koga, 244.)

47. Kawaji, 42. The *sankin-kotai* system of alternate residence required feudal lords to spend part of the year in Edo. A person on duty was referred to as a *kimban.*

48. Goncharov, *Fregat Pallada*, p. 219.

49. Koga, 244.

50. Goncharov, *Fregat Pallada*, pp. 219-220.

51. Koga, 245.

52. Kawaji, 43.
53. Goncharov, *Fregat Pallada,* pp. 219-220.
54. Kawaji, 43.
55. *Ibid.,* 44.
56. Goncharov, *Fregat Pallada,* pp. 219-220.
57. *Ibid.,* p. 220.
58. *Ibid.*
59. Kawaji, 43.
60. Goncharov, *Fregat Pallada,* p. 221.
61. Koga, 353-354.
62. Goncharov, *Fregat Pallada,* p. 221.
63. *Ibid.,* p. 222; Koga, 245.
64. Goncharov, *Fregat Pallada,* p. 222.
65. Kawaji, 44.
66. The vermillion seal was the official seal. Before visiting the Russians, the plenipotentiaries would always deposit it in the Western Government Office. Conference completed, they would pick it up again.
67. Koga, 246; Kawaji, 144.
68. Putiatin, "Vsepoddaneishii otchet," 59.
69. *Ibid.,* 60.

Chapter 5

1. Goncharov, *Fregat Pallada,* p. 222.
2. *Ibid.,* p. 223.
3. *Ibid.,* p. 224; Koga, 246; Kawaji, 46.
4. Goncharov, *Fregat Pallada,* p. 224.
5. Putiatin, "Vsepoddaneishii otchet," 59; Kawaji, 46.
6. Putiatin, "Vsepoddaneishii otchet," 60-61.
7. Goncharov, *Fregat Pallada,* pp. 226-227. A similar situation existed during World War II. Americans taken prisoner by the Japanese did not have enough to eat, even when given the same rations as Japanese soldiers.
8. *Ibid.,* p. 227.
9. Koga, 247.
10. *Ibid.*
11. Kawaji, 50, 94; Goncharov, *Fregat Pallada,* pp. 227-228.
12. Putiatin, "Vsepoddaneishii otchet," 60; Koga, 253.
13. Goncharov, *Fregat Pallada,* p. 229.
14. *Ibid.,* pp. 227-228.
15. Koga, 251.
16. Literally "Green Duckweed" (name of a famous sword).
17. Koga, 251.
18. *Ibid.* "One or two ships," according to Mitsukuri Gempo. (Mitsukuri, 461.)
19. Koga, 251.
20. *Ibid.*
21. Kawaji, 49.
22. Goncharov, *Fregat Pallada,* pp. 229-230.
23. Koga, 252.

24. Goncharov, *Fregat Pallada,* p. 231.

25. *Ibid.*

26. *Ibid.,* p. 233; Kyozawa Kiyoshi, *Gaiko-shi* (History of Foreign Relations), Vol. III of *Gendai Nihon bummei-shi* (History of Japanese Civilization in Modern Times) (Tokyo, 1941), p. 59.

27. Koga, 247.

28. Goncharov, *Fregat Pallada,* p. 229.

29. Koga, 253.

30. Goncharov, *Fregat Pallada,* p. 229.

31. Koga, 253.

32. *Ibid.,* 254.

33. Goncharov, *Fregat Pallada,* pp. 232-233.

34. The Chinese and Dutch had traded with Japan throughout the Seclusion Period.

35. Italics in entire conversation are mine.

36. "The two old men [Tsutsui and Kawaji] said that they have the Russian letter to prove in writing the demands of opening harbors and trade. But as for sending soldiers they had never heard of it before." (Koga, 259.)

37. *Bakumatsu,* IV, 38-40; Koga, 259.

38. Koga, 260.

39. *Ibid.,* 260-262.

40. Goncharov, *Fregat Pallada,* p. 237.

41. *Ibid.,* p. 238; Koga, 261; Kawaji, 44.

42. Goncharov, *Fregat Pallada,* pp. 239-240.

43. *Ibid.,* p. 240.

44. *Ibid.,* p. 241; Koga, 263. According to Koga, Tsutsui received a leopard skin, said to have been obtained by Pos'et, and two timepieces; Kawaji, woolen materials and three timepieces. Lesser gifts were given to the other officials. (*Ibid.,* 264.)

45. Koga, 262-263.

46. *Ibid.,* 263.

47. Goncharov, *Fregat Pallada,* p. 241; Koga, 263.

48. Goncharov, *Fregat Pallada,* p. 241.

49. *Bakumatsu,* IV, 54.

50. Goncharov, *Fregat Pallada,* p. 242; Koga, 265.

51. Goncharov, *Fregat Pallada,* p. 242.

52. *Ibid.,* pp. 242-243.

53. Koga, 265.

54. *Ibid.,* 266.

55. Putiatin, "Vsepoddaneishii otchet," 60. "Not earlier than spring" according to Goncharov; "in summer" according to Koga. (Goncharov, *Fregat Pallada,* p. 243; Koga, 265.)

56. Putiatin, "Vsepoddaneishii otchet," 60-61; Goncharov, *Fregat Pallada,* p. 243; Russia, "Otchet," 160.

57. Koga, 265.

58. *Taikun,* or tycoon (Great Lord): term applied by Japanese to the Shogun, partly to conceal from the Westerners the fact that he was not the legitimate ruler of the country. Used by Koga in his diary.

59. Koga, 266-304.

Chapter 6

1. Putiatin, "Vsepoddaneishii otchet," 60.
2. Goncharov, *Fregat Pallada*, p. 243.
3. Putiatin, "Vsepoddaneishii otchet," 61.
4. Spalding, p. 210; Putiatin, "Vsepoddaneishii otchet," 61.
5. Putiatin, "Vsepoddaneishii otchet," 61. Commodore Perry "had arranged, provided the Japanese government refused to negotiate, or to assign a port of resort" for American merchant or whaling ships, "to take under surveillance of the American flag the island Great Lew Chew [Great Liu Ch'iu], a dependency of the Empire of Japan." Although this was to have been accomplished, if necessary, "on the ground of reclamation for insults and injuries well known to have been committed upon American citizens," these "measures of precaution" "seemed justified by the wily policy of the Japanese, which forbade any confident reliance upon its justice, and by the probability of the Russians, French, or English, in their eagerness to anticipate the Americans, stepping in before them and seizing a dependency like Lew Chew, which might so greatly further their purposes in regard to Japan...." (Hawks, p. 375.) We must add, however, that, as is known, the United States did not annex the Liu Ch'iu Islands but, on the contrary, concluded a Compact of Friendship and Commerce (July 11, 1854). (See William M. Malloy [comp.], *Treaties, Conventions, International Acts, Protocols and Agreements, Between the United States of America and Other Powers 1776-1909* [Washington, 1910], I, 1048-1049.)
6. Putiatin, "Vsepoddaneishii otchet," 61. The king of Liu Ch'iu recognized Japanese suzerainty through the daimyo of Satsuma. At the same time, with the full knowledge of Japan, he sent tribute to the Chinese court and received his investiture from the Chinese imperial throne. All real power in Liu Ch'iu was in the hands of a Satsuma resident, who retired into the mountains on the rare occasion that a Chinese envoy appeared. (Kuno, 21-22; Murdoch, 534.)
7. Putiatin, "Vsepoddaneishii otchet," 62. For a more detailed account of the Russian stay on the Liu Ch'iu Islands, see Goncharov, *Fregat Pallada*, pp. 244-282.
8. Putiatin, "Vsepoddaneishii otchet," 62-63. For a detailed coverage of the expedition at Manila, see Goncharov, "Manilla," *Otechestvennye zapiski* (Fatherland Journal) (October, 1855), 241 ff.; Goncharov, *Fregat Pallada*, pp. 283-360.
9. Putiatin, "Vsepoddaneishii otchet," 63; *Morskoi Sbornik*, XIV, No. 2, Hydrographic Sect. (February, 1855), 36.
10. Putiatin, "Vsepoddaneishii otchet," 63-64; Wilhelm Heine, *Reise um die Erde nach Japan an Bord der Expeditions-Escadre unter Commodore M. C. Perry in den Jahren 1853, 1854 und 1855, unternommen im Auftrage der Regierung der Vereinigten Staaten* (Voyage Around the World to Japan Aboard the Expeditionary Squadron under the Command of Commodore M. C. Perry in the Years 1853, 1854 and 1855, Undertaken by Orders of the Government of the United States) (Leipzig, 1856), II, 87.
11. Heki Shoichi, *Kokushi dai-nempyo* (Chronological Table of Japanese History) (Tokyo, 1935), III, 511.
12. *Ibid.* "In the third month of this year [April, 1854], the Russian ambassador Putiatin came again to Nagasaki and asked for the reply. He sent another letter

and said: 'If your country delays further, we shall decide the determination of the boundaries [ourselves].' " (Koga, 308.)

13. As will be recalled, the American vice-consul at Shanghai was also the official agent of the Russian government. (Walworth, p. 127.)

14. Putiatin, "Vsepoddaneishii otchet," 64.

15. For an account of Krusenstern's visit to Japan (1803-1805), see Lensen, *"Early Russo-Japanese Relations,"* 24-29.

16. Putiatin, "Vsepoddaneishii otchet," 65.

17. *Ibid.*

18. *Ibid.,* 66.

19. *Ibid.,* 67.

20. *Ibid.*

21. *Ibid.,* 68.

22. *Ibid.*

23. *Ibid.,* 69.

24. For an account of the voyage of the *Diana* from Kronstadt to De Kastri Bay, see Russia, "Otchet," 163-173.

25. Putiatin, "Vsepoddaneishii otchet," 69.

26. Goncharov, *Fregat Pallada* (abridged), pp. 655-666.

27. Putiatin, "Vsepoddaneishii otchet," 70.

28. *Ibid.,* 71.

Chapter 7

1. We do not know what circumstances caused this change of plans. As will be remembered, Putiatin had designated Southern Sakhalin as meeting place.

2. For text of treaty, see Appendix III. For an interesting illustrated English and Japanese account of Commodore Perry's visit, see Kojima Matajiro, *Amerika ichijo utsushi. Commodore Perry's Expedition to Hakodate May 1854* (Hakodate, 1953).

3. Putiatin, "Vsepoddaneishii otchet," 72.

4. *Ibid.*

5. Schilling, pp. 146-147.

6. Putiatin, "Vsepoddaneishii otchet," 73.

7. Schilling, p. 147; Putiatin, "Vsepoddaneishii otchet," 73; Koga, 308.

8. Schilling, p. 148; Putiatin, "Vsepoddaneishii otchet," 73.

9. Schilling, pp. 148-149.

10. Putiatin, "Vsepoddaneishii otchet," 73.

11. *Ibid.,* 74.

12. See Chapter IX.

13. Putiatin, "Vsepoddaneishii otchet," 75.

14. *Ibid.,* 75-76; Koga, 308.

15. Putiatin, "Vsepoddaneishii otchet," 76.

16. *Ibid.,* 77; Schilling, p. 149.

17. Probably the eastern shore of Awaji Island.

18. Putiatin, "Vsepoddaneishii otchet," 77-78.

19. *Ibid.,* 77.

20. Putiatin writes "Linskhoten Strait." Judging from the account of the

activities of the Russian boats and frigate on November 23, this must be Yura Strait.

21. Putiatin, "Vsepoddaneishii otchet," 78.
22. Illustrated London News, "British Expedition at Japan," *The Nautical Magazine and Naval Chronicle for 1855* (London, 1855), pp. 94-99.
23. *Ibid.*
24. Koga, 367.
25. Putiatin, "Vsepoddaneishii otchet," 78; Putiatin, "Raport General-Adiutanta Putiatina Velikomu Kniaziu General-Admiralu (O zemletriasenii i krushenii fregata *Diana*)" (Report of Adjutant-General Putiatin to the Grand Duke Lord High Admiral [Concerning the Earthquake and Shipwreck of the Frigate *Diana*]) [hereinafter cited as Putiatin, "Raport"], *Morskoi Sbornik*, XVII, No. 7, Part 2 (July, 1855), 231; Koga, 314.
26. Koga, 318.
27. Muragaki Yosaburo (1813-1880), better known as Muragaki Tanso; also known as Norimasa. Diplomat of the Shogunate. Appointed finance inspector in 1854, he served in Matsumae and Ezo, managing coastal defenses. Returning to Edo, he was ordered to accompany Tsutsui and Kawaji to Shimoda. Appointed governor of Hakodate in 1856, commissioner of foreign affairs in 1858. As governor of Kanagawa (1859) responsible for the opening of that port. Left for America aboard the *Powhatan* (1859) as a member of Japan's first embassy to the United States. (Heibonsha, *Shinsen dai-jimmei jiten*, VI, 175.)
28. Tokutomi, XXXIII, 62.
29. Kawaji, 114; Koga, 310.
30. Kawaji, 114-115; Koga, 312. Putiatin states that the plenipotentiaries arrived "not before December 14." (Putiatin, "Vsepoddaneishii otchet," 79.)
31. Koga, 313.
32. Putiatin, "Vsepoddaneishii otchet," 79; Schilling, p. 150.
33. Koga, 316.
34. Putiatin, "Raport," 232.
35. Koga, 316.
36. *Ibid.*
37. Kawaji refers to the temple as Gyokusen Temple. Townsend Harris was to reside in it a year and a half later.
38. Koga, 317.
39. Putiatin, "Vsepoddaneishii otchet," 79.
40. Koga, 317.
41. *Ibid.*
42. *Ibid.;* Putiatin, "Vsepoddaneishii otchet," 79.
43. One *ken* equals 1.99 yards.
44. Koga, 317-318.
45. *Ibid.*, 318.
46. *Ibid.*
47. Egawa Hidetatsu (Tarozaemon) (1801-1855). Shogunate official. Learned Dutch in his youth. Studied artillery under Takashima Shuhan. Built a cannon foundry and firing range. Helped fortify Nagasaki Harbor and Shinagawa (Edo Bay). Appointed coastal defense officer in 1853. Favored opening of country. (Martin Ramming [ed.], *Japan-Handbuch* [Handbook of Japan] [Berlin, 1941], p. 129; Lensen, "History," p. 160.)

48. Koga, 319.
49. Putiatin, "Vsepoddaneishii otchet," 79; Putiatin, "Raport," 232; Kawaji, 119.
50. Koga, 320.
51. *Ibid.*
52. Putiatin, "Vsepoddaneishii otchet," 79; Putiatin "Raport," 232; Kawaji, 119; Koga, 320.
53. Koga, 320.
54. Schilling, p. 151; Putiatin, "Vsepoddaneishii otchet," 79.
55. Kawaji, 119; Tokutomi, XXXIII, 68.

Chapter 8

1. Putiatin, "Raport," 233.
2. *Ibid.*
3. *Ibid.*, 234; Schilling, p. 152.
4. Spalding, p. 360.
5. Putiatin, "Raport," 235.
6. *Ibid.;* Schilling, p. 155.
7. Putiatin, "Raport," 236.
8. Schilling, p. 155.
9. Koga, 323; Schilling, p. 153.
10. Putiatin, "Raport," 234.
11. *Baba*: used both in Russian and Japanese with a somewhat similar meaning. Russian: "countrywoman," "peasant's wife"; Japanese: "old woman," "a grandmother," "a hag."
12. Putiatin, "Raport," 234; Schilling, p. 154.
13. Putiatin, "Raport," 234.
14. Koga, 328.
15. Out of the seventy-four households at Kakizaki, some had been partially damaged, others completely destroyed; but nobody had drowned. (*Ibid.*)
16. Putiatin, "Raport," 236.
17. There remained 80 feet of keel, 90 of false keel; 4½ feet high in the stern end, 2 feet in the bow.
18. Koga, 325.
19. The Shogunate also sent foodstuffs and gold. Funds were distributed among families whose dwellings had been damaged, additional sums being made available for the burial of each victim. (*Ibid.*, 328-329.)
20. *Ibid.*, 325.
21. *Ibid.*, 329.
22. *Ibid.*, 325.
23. *Ibid.*, 324-325.
24. *Ibid.*, 323-324.
25. Putiatin, "Raport," 236.
26. Schilling, p. 157.
27. See next chapter.
28. Koga, 335.
29. *Ibid.;* Putiatin, "Raport," 237.
30. Putiatin, "Raport," 237; Schilling, pp. 157-253.

31. Koga, 370.

32. Putiatin, "Raport," 237; Schilling, pp. 157-253.

33. A makeshift rudder; for full description, see Schilling, p. 254.

34. Putiatin, "Raport," 237; Koga, 330-331.

35. Putiatin, "Raport," 238.

36. Koga, 344.

37. Kawaji, 134; Putiatin, "Raport," 238.

38. Koga, 347.

39. Kawaji, 134; Putiatin, "Raport," 238; Koga, 346, 349; Putiatin, "Vsepodda-neishii otchet," 85.

40. Koga, 349.

41. *Ibid.*, 350.

42. Putiatin, "Raport," 238.

43. *Ibid.*, 239; Putiatin, "Vsepoddaneishii otchet," 85-86; Schilling, p. 225; Koga, 353. Schilling's account is the most detailed one.

44. This is of little importance during calm weather, but when there are fresh winds and high seas it prevents the vessel from hugging the wind.

45. Putiatin, "Vsepoddaneishii otchet," 86-87; Putiatin, "Raport," 239-240.

46. Putiatin, "Vsepoddaneishii otchet," 86-87; Putiatin, "Raport," 240.

47. Putiatin, "Vsepoddaneishii otchet," 86-87. Koga records that this occurred on January 13. He notes that there were more than twenty persons aboard the boat. He writes that nobody got killed, but that the ambassador fell into the water. (Koga, 353.) It seems that Koga combined or mixed up two different incidents, one of which occurred during the night of January 14 to 15, the other one on January 16.

48. Vasilii Makhov, *Fregat Diana* (The Frigate *Diana*) (St. Petersburg, 1867), p. 46.

49. Putiatin, "Vsepoddaneishii otchet," 87; Putiatin, "Raport," 240. According to Schilling, the gig was sent across without personnel, but with only a lit lantern and a list of the conventional lantern signals. (Schilling, p. 257.)

50. Putiatin, "Vsepoddaneishii otchet," 87.

51. Putiatin's report reads: "First to be taken off were the sick with the doctor, the priest and the church utensils; then the government money with the laced books, the journal etc., were moved across." (Putiatin, "Raport," 241.) According to Schilling, however, all these were not landed until afternoon, "when already half the crew was ashore." (Schilling, p. 259.)

52. Schilling, p. 259.

53. *Ibid.;* Koga, 353.

54. Putiatin, "Raport," 241.

55. Putiatin, "Vsepoddaneishii otchet," 88-89; Schilling, p. 259.

56. Putiatin, "Raport," 241; Putiatin, "Vsepoddaneishii otchet," 89.

57. Schilling, p. 261; Koga, 356-357.

58. Koga, 355.

59. Koga mentions only about forty-five vessels, but the other sources, Russian and Japanese, point to the larger figure.

60. Koga, 356.

61. Putiatin, "Raport," 242.

62. *Ibid.;* Putiatin, "Vsepoddaneishii otchet," 89-90; Schilling, pp. 261-263.

63. Koga, 356-357.

64. *Ibid.*, 356.
65. Putiatin, "Raport," 242.
66. Koga, 325.
67. *Ibid.*

Chapter 9

1. Koga, 362.
2. Allan B. Cole (ed.), *Yankee Surveyors in the Shogun's Seas* (Princeton, 1947), p. 61.
3. Koga, 357.
4. Schilling, p. 264.
5. *Ibid.*, p. 265; Koga, 360.
6. Schilling, p. 265.
7. See Chapter X.
8. Schilling, p. 265.
9. Koga, 368.
10. Schilling, p. 266.
11. Koga, 368-369.
12. *Ibid.*, 364.
13. *Ibid.*, 366.
14. *Ibid.*, 369.
15. *Ibid.*, 366.
16. Putiatin, "Vsepoddaneishii otchet," 91; Schilling, p. 266. Koga records that the whaler arrived on January 29, Kawaji, on January 28. (Koga, 367-368; Kawaji, 147.)
17. Koga, 371.
18. Schilling, p. 266. Schilling states that the admiral arrived on January 31; Kawaji and Koga, that he came the night before (January 30). The whaler departed on January 29. (Kawaji, 147; Tokutomi, XXXIII, 153.)
19. Schilling, p. 150.
20. Kawaji dates this January 31; Schilling, February 1.
21. Putiatin, "Vsepoddaneishii otchet," 92; Schilling, p. 266.
22. Koga, 375.
23. Kawaji, 147. For further detail, see Tokutomi, XXXIII, 162-167. Tokutomi Iichiro cites a letter from Kawaji to *Kanjo bugyo* Ishikawa Tosa-no-kami and Matsudaira Kawachi-no-kami, dated January 31, dealing with this venture, as well as a report about this from Matsudaira Jurobee.
24. Schilling, p. 266.
25. Koga, 372.
26. *Ibid.*, 364.
27. *Ibid.*, 365.
28. Schilling, p. 266.
29. Koga, 370.
30. *Ibid.*, 379.
31. Putiatin, "Vsepoddaneishii otchet," 93.
32. *Ibid.*
33. A. K. (Aleksandr Kolokol'tsov?), "Postroenie shkuny *Kheda* v Iaponii" (Construction of the Schooner *Heda* in Japan), *Morskoi Sbornik*, XXIII, No. 8, Part 3 (June, 1856), 279. There is no "h" in Russian, and "Heda" thus is called "Kheda." We shall use the proper Japanese spelling. For the article in the

Morskoi Sbornik used by Putiatin as guide, see Russia, Morskoe Ministerstvo, Morskoi Uchenyi Komitet, Technical Committee, "Shkuna Opyt, iakhta g. glavnago komandira Kronshtatskago porta" (The Schooner *Opyt*, Yacht of the Top Commandant of Kronstadt Harbor), with a sketch by *Leitenant* Bessarabskii, *Morskoi Sbornik*, I, No. 2, Part 1 (1849), 46-57, sketch facing 46. See also *Kontr-Admiral* Ivan I. von Shants (Schanz?), "Voennaia shkuna *Opyt*" (The War Schooner *Opyt*), *Morskoi Sbornik*, I, No. 2, Part 1 (1849), 117-128.

34. A. K., 280.

35. *Ibid.*, 281-283.

36. *Ibid.*, 282.

37. *Ibid.*, 283.

38. *Ibid.*, 284.

39. *Ibid.*, 288.

40. The crew usually worked from 5:30 A.M. to 11:30 A.M. and 1:30 P.M. till late in the evening. (*Ibid.*, 286-287.) "They work as fast as *kami* [gods, supermen], Koga had noted. (Koga, 369.)

41. A. K., 285.

42. The three American families were: Captain and Mrs. A. J. Worth, Mr. and Mrs. William C. Reed and their two children, and Mr. and Mrs. H. H. Doty. (Cole, *Yankee Surveyors*, p. 15; Putiatin, "Vsepoddaneishii otchet," 94.)

43. Later on, Reed and Dougherty reassured the governor in writing that "our object is not to mingle or trade with the Japanese, but to trade and assist our own people and ships that visit Japan," and Mr. Doty emphasized that they had landed only because they had not wanted to sail to Russia. He promised to leave Shimoda as soon as the *Caroline E. Foote* returned. "If the vessel should not return after a reasonable time for making the voyage has elapsed, I shall avail myself on the first opportunity that offers to sail direct for the United States of America." (Letter of Reed and Dougherty to the governor of Shimoda, dated April 22, 1855, and letter of Doty to the authorities of Shimoda, dated April 23, 1855, as cited in Hawks, p. 454.)

44. Putiatin, "Vsepoddaneishii otchet," 94; Cole, *Yankee Surveyors*, p. 15; Hawks, p. 453.

45. Hawks, p. 454.

46. A. K., 289; Putiatin, "Vsepoddaneishii otchet," 94; Cole, *Yankee Surveyors*, p. 15; Hawks, p. 453; Schilling, p. 269.

47. Putiatin, "Vsepoddaneishii otchet," 94; Schilling, p. 269.

48. Putiatin, "Vsepoddaneishii otchet," 95; Schilling, p. 269; A. K., 290; Cole, *Yankee Surveyors*, p. 15.

49. Putiatin, "Vsepoddaneishii otchet," 96; Schilling, pp. 271-272.

50. Schilling, p. 271. Putiatin gives the sum as 3,500 pounds sterling. (Putiatin, "Vsepoddaneishii otchet," 96.)

51. A. K., 291; Putiatin, "Vsepoddaneishii otchet," 96; Schilling, pp. 272-273.

52. Suzuki Riichiro, "Tachibana Kosai," unpublished sixteen-page Japanese manuscript by the present (1954) mayor of Kakegawa-*machi* (Ogasa-*gun*, Shizuoka-*ken*, pp. 1-2; Ramming, "Über den Anteil der Russen," 28-29; Watanabe Shujiro, *Sekai ni okeru Nihonjin* (Japanese in the World) (Tokyo, 1942), pp. 359-360; Schilling, p. 272.

53. A. K., 290.

54. *Ibid.*, 292.

55. For measurements and cost of *Heda*, see *ibid.*, 280, 294-296.

56. *Ibid.,* 292.

57. *Ibid.,* 293; Schilling, p. 273. As a Japanese naval officer was to write some seventy-five years afterwards: "These workmen were the first to learn the art of occidental shipbuilding. Later on, they were employed to build foreign-style ships at Kimizawa, near Toda [Heda]. . . . These workmen were later attached to the Shogun's navy and became the fathers of the shipbuilding industry in modern Japan." (Captain Hironori Mizuno, "The Japanese Navy," in Inazo Nitobe and others, *Western Influences in Modern Japan* [Chicago, 1931], p. 417.) Musin-Pushkin reported in a letter that the Japanese built three vessels in Heda after the model of the Russian schooner. (Ivan I. von Shants, "Vozrazhenie na stat'iu: Postroika shkuny *Kheda*" [In Reply to the Article: Construction of the Schooner *Heda*], *Morskoi Sbornik,* XXIV, No. 1, Part 4 [August, 1856], 1-2.)

58. A. K., 293.

Chapter 10

1. Although the signing of the treaty of Kanagawa between the United States and Japan on March 31, 1854, assured the conclusion of at least a similar convention between Japan and Russia, we believe that it was not until the Russians and Japanese became partners in misfortune and suffering that a truly new phase in their relations began.

2. *Bakumatsu,* II, 141.

3. *Ibid.; Tokutomi,* XXXI, 341-342.

4. Putiatin, "Vsepoddaneishii otchet," 42.

5. Tokutomi, XXXI, 349.

6. Putiatin, "Vsepoddaneishii otchet," 43-44.

7. Goncharov, *Fregat Pallada,* p. 49.

8. *Ibid.*

9. *Ibid.,* p. 214.

10. Putiatin, "Vsepoddaneishii otchet," 43.

11. *Ibid.,* 46.

12. *Ibid.,* 45-46. As we have seen (Chapter II), Putiatin at one time actually decided to proceed to Edo.

13. Goncharov, *Fregat Pallada,* p. 42.

14. *Bakumatsu,* III, 53; Tokutomi, XXXI, 411.

15. *Bakumatsu,* III, 53-54.

16. The Imperial Court was in Kyoto. Not since the Mongol invasion had the Shogunate consulted the Imperial Court in matters pertaining to foreign relations; in fact, the only justification for the Shogun's existence lay in his unqualified protection of the country from outsiders. His title "Seii-taishogun" meant "Barbarian-Subduing-Generalissimo."

17. *Bakumatsu,* III, 54. This Japanese reply was less uncompromising than that first sent to Perry. While the Russians were told that the Japanese government only wished to delay the opening of the country, the Americans had been informed that no answer whatsoever could be given, the question of trade not having been mentioned at all. (Inobe, p. 508; Lensen, "History," p. 98.)

18. Tokutomi, XXXI, 413.

19. Koga, 251.

20. *Bakumatsu,* IV, 38-40.

21. *Ibid.*, 54.
22. *Ibid.*, 38-40.
23. Ramming, "Über den Anteil der Russen," 25.
24. Goncharov, *Fregat Pallada,* pp. 238-239.
25. Koga, 331.
26. *Ibid.*, 258.
27. *Ibid.*, 365-366.
28. *Ibid.*, 322.
29. Schilling, p. 158.
30. Koga, 321.
31. *Ibid.*
32. *Ibid.*, 332-333.
33. Goncharov, *Fregat Pallada,* p. 214.
34. Tokutomi, XXXIII, 173.
35. Conversely, a threat by Tsutsui and Kawaji to discontinue the negotiations and return to Edo and request that different officials be sent to deal with Putiatin was equally effective. The Russians exclaimed: "If they send somebody else, we shall not stand it, we shall not stand it," and modified their attitude. (Koga, 332.)
36. *Ibid.*, 327.
37. Kawaji, 148.
38. Koga, 355.
39. Inazo Nitobe, *Bushido, the Soul of Japan* (New York and London, 1905), p. 23.
40. Putiatin, "Vsepoddaneishii otchet," 94.
41. Koga, 377.
42. The treaty was to be Japan's third treaty of amity and friendship, Admiral James Sterling of the British Navy having concluded one in August, 1854. Sterling's request to enter Japanese ports freely in pursuit of Russian ships had been rejected by the Shogunate. (See Yanaga, p. 23.)
43. There seem to have been two copies of each. When the treaty of Kanagawa was signed (March 31, 1854), the Japanese had retained three copies in Japanese, one in Dutch, one in Chinese; the Americans three in English, one in Dutch, one in Chinese. (Williams, 152.)
44. According to Koga, Tsutsui and Kawaji put their seals to the Japanese copies, Koga to the Chinese ones, the interpreters to the Dutch ones. Putiatin signed the Dutch copies, Goshkevich the Chinese ones. (Koga, 380-381.) Putiatin's main assistant, and the author of the Dutch draft, had been Pos'et. (Schilling, p. 268.)
45. Spelled "Euphimius Poutiatine" in the Dutch text.
46. Note difference in spelling in Russian text in introductory paragraph, signature after treaty, and signature after explanatory articles.
47. Treaty between Russia and Japan, concluded in Shimoda on February 7, 1855, and exchanged by ratifications at Shimoda on December 7, 1856. The text of the treaty, as given above, is based on the Russian and Dutch versions. The Japanese text differs at several points. "His Highness the Emperor, Autocrat of all Russia" and "His Highness the Great Sovereign of all Japan" are simply referred to as "Russian Kaiser [Roshiya Keidzuru]" and "Japanese Great Lord [*Nihon Taikun*]," respectively. Tsutsui and Kawaji are called "chief vassals [*chushin*]." The Dutch and Russian copies state: "Henceforth, let there be con-

tinuous peace and sincere friendship between Russia and Japan." Curiously enough, the Japanese text only says: "Henceforth the two countries being forever friendly...." *There is no mention of continuous peace.* The Japanese version mentions the ports to be opened, leaves out their principalities. The Russian and Dutch copies permit compensation with goods "from their store"; no qualification is given in the Japanese version. The Russian and Dutch texts note that only in cases of "extreme exigency" can Russian vessels go to ports other than the three opened. The Japanese version is somewhat more emphatic in its prohibition. Russian vessels not in distress can "never" (*kesshite*) go to other ports. (Japan, Foreign Office, *Treaties and Conventions Between the Empire of Japan and Other Powers Together with Universal Conventions, Regulations, and Communications since March, 1854* [Tokyo, 1884], pp. 585-589.)

48. Literally: "as for a private house, they must not enter it."

49. Literally: "crown house."

50. The explanatory articles are cited in Japan, Foreign Office, *Treaties and Conventions*, pp. 590-592. The Russian copy states that the Russians can visit "shrines"; the Japanese one, "temples and shrines."

51. Koga, 381.

52. *Ibid.*, 380.

53. *Ibid.*, 381.

54. Putiatin, "Vsepoddaneishii otchet," 92; Koga, 394.

55. Koga, 393-394.

Chapter 11

1. Hawks, p. 57.

2. *Ibid.*, pp. 78-79.

3. *Ibid.*, pp. 56-57.

4. *Ibid.*, p. 78.

5. Tsar Nicholas I had specifically ordered that Perry be shown "friendly attention and courtesy within due limits of reason and discretion." ([Admiral] G. I. Nevel'skoi, *Podvigi russkikh morskikh ofitserov na krainem vostoke Rossii 1849-1855* [Exploits of Russian Naval Officers in the Far East of Russia, 1849-1855], [Posthumous Memoirs Edited by His Wife (Ekaterina Ivanovna Nevel'skoi)] [St. Petersburg, 1878; reprinted edition, Moscow, 1947], p. 201.)

6. Hawks, pp. 78-79.

7. Walworth, p. 24.

8. Hawks, p. 89.

9. From a paper read before the American Geographical and Statistical Society by Commodore Perry in 1855 (pp. 28-29), as cited by Walworth, p. 129.

10. In a communication to the governor of Uraga, dated July 12, 1853, Perry wrote: "... if this friendly letter of the President to the Emperor is not received and duly replied to, he [Perry] will consider his country insulted, and will not hold himself accountable for the consequences." (Hawks, p. 282.) And one of the Shogunate officials recorded in his diary: "Perry said that he would enter into negotiations, but if his proposals were rejected, he was prepared to make war at once; that in the event of war he would have fifty ships in nearby waters and fifty more in California, and that if he sent word he could summon a command of one hundred ships within twenty days." (D. Hayashi [unsigned], "Diary

of an Official of the Bakufu," TASJ, Second Series, VII, 101.) "We are fully prepared to engage in a struggle for victory," Perry warned. "Our country has just had a war with a neighboring country, Mexico, and we even attacked and captured its capital. Circumstances may lead your country also into a similar plight. It would be well for you to reconsider." (Hayashi, 104.)

11. Walworth, p. 241.
12. *Ibid.*
13. Williams, 114.
14. Goncharov, *Fregat Pallada*, pp. 52-53.
15. *Ibid.*, pp. 56-57.
16. Koga, 368.
17. *Ibid.*, 366.
18. *Ibid.*, 371.
19. *Ibid.*, 401.
20. Heine, II, 81.
21. Basil Hall Chamberlain, *Things Japanese* (London, 1905), pp. 364-365.
22. *Ibid.*
23. They finally made peace and concluded an agreement whereby Unkovskii remained the commander of the *Pallada*, while Putiatin obligated himself not to meddle in affairs directly within the jurisdiction of the commander. When Putiatin transferred onto the *Diana*, he asked Unkovskii to be captain, but the latter refused, partly because he did not wish to deprive Lesovskii — whom he respected very much — of the position, partly because he wished to return to Russia. (Istomin, 129.) Discussing Putiatin and Unkovskii, Istomin writes that it is difficult to imagine two persons who are more different. Unkovskii was "an idealist, energetic, devoted to his duties to the extent of self-neglect, and high-strung," Putiatin "good-natured, religious to the extreme, inclined to monastic discipline, honest, but stubborn and small minded." *(Ibid.*, 121-122.)
24. Goncharov, *Fregat Pallada* (abridged), pp. 23-24.
25. Hawks, p. 79.
26. Philipp Franz von Siebold, "Deistviia Rossii i Niderlandov k otkrytiiu Iaponii dlia torgovli vsekh narodov" (Actions of Russia and the Netherlands toward the Opening of Japan for the Trade of All Nations), trans. from the German ("Urkundliche Darstellung der Bestrebungen von Niederland und Russland zur Eröffnung Japans für die Schiffahrt und den Seehandel aller Nationen" [Bonn, 1854]), *Morskoi Sbornik*, XV, No. 3, Part 4 (March, 1855), 3.
27. Townsend Harris was to admit that the constant conversations Pos'et held with the Japanese before and after the conclusion of the treaty of Shimoda "will help to prepare the way for me to make a treaty which shall at once open Japan (at different dates for different ports) to our commerce." (Mario Emilio Cosenza [ed.], *The Complete Journal of Townsend Harris, First American Consul General and Minister to Japan* [Garden City, 1930], p. 269.)

An interesting example of Russo-American cooperation (after the completion of Perry's mission in Japan) can be found in the fact that when the Russo-Japanese *Sbornik*, XIX, No. 11, Part 2 [November, 1855], 8-10.) Tachabana Kosai was entrusted to Commander Adams, as the *Heda* had not yet been completed and threat of capture by the Allies was great. (Putiatin, "Vsepoddaneishii otchet," p. 92.)

28. Hawks, p. 452.

29. For text of the Russo-Japanese treaty, see Chapter X; for text of the Japanese-American treaty, see Appendix I.

30. "Perry had asked for no extraterritorial rights whatever. It has been claimed and there is no reason to question the assertion that the absence of such a provision was due to Dr. S. Wells Williams, who accompanied the expedition as Chinese interpreter.... It is in the omission of this provision in the Japanese treaty that the true character of Perry is to be read. He would bluster, threaten, even intimidate, but he would not assume the responsibility of inflicting a possible evil on the Japanese." (Dennett, p. 269.) The Russo-Japanese treaty was an equal one, however, the privileges of extraterritoriality being extended to the subjects of both empires.

Chapter 12

1. A.K., 297.

2. *Ibid.*, 298. Pos'et, Losev, Peshchurov, Kolokol'tsov, Semenov, Lazarev, and Kornilov sailed aboard the *Heda*. The schooner had first gone out with 52 men, but limited space had required a reduction to 40.

3. *Ibid.*, 296.

4. Putiatin, "Vsepoddaneishii otchet," 96; Russia, Morskoe Ministerstvo, Morskoi Uchenyi Komitet, Technical Committee, "O plavanii v vostochnom okeane general-adiutanta Putiatina i kontr-admirala Zavoiki" (About the Sailing of Adjutant-General Putiatin and Rear-Admiral Zavoika on the Pacific Ocean) [hereinafter cited as Russia, "O plavanii"], *Morskoi Sbornik*, XX, No. 1, Part 3 (January, 1856), 174-187.

5. Putiatin, "Vsepoddaneishii otchet," 96-103; A. Peshchurov, "Shkuna Kheda v Tatarskom prolive" (The Schooner *Heda* in the Straits of Tartary), *Morskoi Sbornik*, XXII, No. 6, Part 4 (April, 1856), 1-4.

6. Russia, "O plavanii," 184.

7. Russia, Morskoe Ministerstvo, Morskoi Uchenyi Komitet, Technical Committee, "Dopolnitel'nye svedeniia ob ekipazhe fregata *Diana*" (Supplementary News about the Crew of the Frigate *Diana*), *Morskoi Sbornik*, XVII, No. 8, Part 2 (August, 1855), 282-285.

8. Cole, *Yankee Surveyors*, pp. 13-14, 63-65.

9. *Ibid.*, pp. 63-64.

10. *Ibid.*, pp. 65-66.

11. *Ibid.*, p. 16; Putiatin, "Vsepoddaneishii otchet," 95; Schilling, p. 275.

12. Schilling, p. 276.

13. *Ibid.*, p. 288.

14. *Ibid.*

15. Captain Sterling, son of Admiral James Sterling, commanding.

16. A list of the officers taken prisoner was attached. The officers were: Musin-Pushkin, Schilling, Zelenyi, Kovalevskii, Urusov, Mikhailov, Iolkin, Gosh-kevich, Pribylov (Japanese language specialist). Two hundred and forty-six men of lower rank had also been taken prisoner. Of these, 89 had been put on the *Sybille*, 62 on the *Spartan*, and 95 on the *Barracouta*. Dr. Krolevetskii, Father Makhov, and 21 sailors were released. (Letter reprinted in *Morskoi Sbornik*, XIX, No. 11, Part 2 [November, 1855], 8-10.) Tachibana Kosai was also in the group. It was during this captivity that he and Goshkevich compiled,

Notes to Pages 140-145 191

or began compiling, the first real Japanese-Russian dictionary. (See Lensen, *Report from Hokkaido*, pp. 66-72.)

17. Schilling, p. 317.
18. Russia, Inspector's Department, Circular No. 318, dated January 1, 1857, as reprinted in *Morskoi Sbornik*, XXXIII, No. 1, Part 1 (January, 1858), xxv-xxvi.
19. Russia, Morskoe Ministerstvo, Morskoi Uchenyi Komitet, Technical Committee, "Vysochaishii ukaz o pozhalovanii vitse-admiralu Putiatinu grafskago dostoinstva" (Imperial Ukase about Conferring the Dignity of a Count on Vice-Admiral Putiatin), *Morskoi Sbornik*, XX, No. 1, Part 1 (January, 1856), lxiv. A literal translation would read: "... having made out a patent ... to present ..."
20. Schilling, p. 318. For a photograph of some of these guns and a brief discussion of their disposition, see Lensen, *Report from Hokkaido*, pp. 59-60.

Chapter 13

1. Sansom, p. 277.
2. Ramming, *"Über den Anteil der Russen,"* 23. For text of parable, see *The Works of Mencius*, Book 1, Part 1, Chap. 3 (James Legge, *The Chinese Classics*, Second Edition, Revised [Oxford, 1895], II, 129-130).
3. Goncharov, *Fregat Pallada*, p. 32. Goncharov admitted, however, that underneath this apathy, the Japanese were "very lively" and "natural." "They have few such absurdities as the Chinese as for example that weighty pedantic obsolete and unnecessary learning from which people become stupid.... The Japanese are categorically the French, the Chinese the Germans of these places." (*Ibid.*, p. 59.)
4. *Ibid.*, p. 68.
5. *Ibid.*, p. 61.
6. *Ibid.*, p. 68.
7. *Ibid.*, p. 24.
8. *Ibid.*, p. 55.
9. *Ibid.*, p. 222.
10. *Ibid.*, p. 51.
11. *Ibid.*, p. 197.
12. *Ibid.*, pp. 229-230.
13. Kawaji, 37.
14. Goncharov, *Fregat Pallada*, p. 50.
15. *Ibid.*, p. 61.
16. *Ibid.*, pp. 87-88.
17. *Ibid.*, p. 208.
18. *Ibid.*, p. 78.
19. *Ibid.*, p. 201.
20. *Ibid.*, p. 21.
21. *Ibid.*, p. 18.
22. *Ibid.*, p. 104.
23. *Ibid.*, p. 24.
24. *Ibid.*, pp. 67-68.
25. *Ibid.*, p. 56.
26. *Ibid.*, p. 196.
27. *Ibid.*, p. 56.
28. *Ibid.*, pp. 210-211.

29. *Ibid.*, p. 187.

30. *Literaturnaia gazeta* (Literary Gazette), No. 62 (May 18, 1934), as cited by Muraveiskii in his introduction to Goncharov, *Fregat Pallada* (abridged), p. 4.

31. Kawaji, 44.

32. *Ibid.* As Dr. Nitobe points out: "We think praising one's own wife is praising a part of one's own self, and self-praise is regarded, to say the least, as bad taste among us,— and I hope among Christian nations too! . . . The polite debasement of one's consort was a usage most in vogue among the samurai." (Nitobe, pp. 154-155.)

33. Kawaji, 44.

34. *Ibid.*

35. *Ibid.*, 37. Kawaji was probably referring to M. M. (Misha) Lazarev, son of Admiral Lazarev. According to Engel'gardt, the thirteen-year-old Misha was taken along as naval cadet by Putiatin upon the request of Admiral Lazarev's widow. Although Misha displayed no particular attraction to the sea, he showed great musical talent and frequently entertained the mariners by playing on a piano in Unkovskii's cabin. (Engel'gardt, 368.)

36. Kawaji, 42.

37. *Ibid.*, 43.

38. Koga, 375.

39. Kawaji, 44.

40. Goncharov, *Fregat Pallada*, p. 232.

41. *Ibid.*, p. 238. Aleksandr Sergeevich Griboedov (1795-1829) satirized contemporary Russian society in his comedy *Gore ot uma*, "Misfortune from Intellect" or "The Mischief of Being Clever," as Sir Bernard Pares translates it. (Pares, p. 330.)

42. Kawaji, 44. Koga's diary differs somewhat from Kawaji's: "Kawaji said Tsutsui had a daughter the preceding year. The ambassador replied: 'In Russia there is a proverb: At fifty and sixty few children, at seventy none at all, at eighty on the contrary many.' How true it is." (Koga, 245.)

43. Goncharov, *Fregat Pallada*, pp. 52-53.

44. Kawaji, 42-43.

45. *Ibid.*, 43.

46. Koga, 361.

47. *Ibid.*, 335.

48. *Ibid.*, 368.

49. *Ibid.*, 253.

50. Kawaji, 46.

51. Koga, 341.

52. Instead of *Puchyachin*. *Futei* means "audacious [in a derogatory sense]," *yatsu* means "[rude] fellow."

53. Literally "universe."

54. Kawaji, 145-146.

Chapter 14

1. W. G. Aston, TASJ, First Series, I, Part 1, (Tokyo, 1882).

2. In 1945, I. V. Stalin declared ". . . the defeat of the Russian armies in the year 1904 during the Russo-Japanese war left in the conscience of the people painful memories. It was a black mark on our country. Our people believed and

waited that the day would come when Japan would be crushed and the stain liquidated. For forty years we, the people of the old[er] generation, have waited for this day. And here, this day has come. Today Japan has acknowledged herself defeated and has signed an unconditional surrender document." (Iosif Vissarionovich Stalin, "Obrashcheniia tovarishcha I. V. Stalina k narodu" [Speech of Comrade I. V. Stalin to the People], as cited in B. A. Romanov, *Ocherki diplomaticheskoi istorii russko-iaponskoi voiny, 1895-1907* [Sketches of the Diplomatic History of the Russo-Japanese War, 1895-1907] [Moscow, 1947], p. 3.)

3. One possible exception is S. I. Novakovskii's *Iaponiia i Rossiia* (Japan and Russia), a two-volume survey published in Japan. The work is very scarce, however, and not generally known. The first volume (Tokyo, 1918) carries the story only through the 1850's. According to the National Diet Library of Japan, the second volume has never been published. There are a number of brief Japanese studies.

4. First atomic bomb (Hiroshima): August 6, 1945; Russian entry into the war: August 9, 1945; Imperial Rescript bringing war to an end: August 14, 1945. (See Foreign Affairs Association of Japan, *Contemporary Japan,* XIV, Nos. 4-12 [April-December, 1945], 266-267.)

5. Putiatin maintained the dignity of his position. He refused to receive minor officials. He conformed with Japanese custom only when consistent with the honor of his country. He did not squat during negotiations as Rezanov had done, fired gun salutes whenever he saw fit, and took orders from no one in Japan. He readily sailed to Nagasaki, but he insisted on freedom of movement and negotiations.

6. See Chapter V.

7. See Chapter V.

8. See chapters V and X.

9. For reproductions of the nautical charts (drawn by the officers of the *Pallada*) of the bays of Osaka, Tago, Arari, Heda, Enoura, Shimoda, and others, see *Morskoi Sbornik,* XXIV, No. 10, Part 2 (August, 1856), between 104 and 105.

10. Putiatin, "Vsepoddaneishii otchet," 42-43.

11. *Ibid.,* 104.

Appendix 1

• *Sources*: Russia, Morskoe Ministerstvo, *Obzor zagranichnykh plavanii sudov russkago voennago flota s 1850 po 1868 god* (Survey of Foreign Voyages of Vessels of the Russian Navy from 1850 to 1868) [hereinafter cited as Russia, *Obzor*] (St. Petersburg, 1871), II, 708-709; and Russia, "Otchet," 132-133, 163-173.

Appendix 2

1. We have four official Russian tabulations at our disposal. No two are in agreement. Putiatin's report states that the *Pallada* departed with 23 officers, 3 civilians, and 439 men of lower rank. Of these, 6 officers and 37 men sailed as complement for the *Vostok.* Total left for the *Pallada:* 422. Putiatin, "Vsepoddaneishii otchet," 22-23.) Russia, "Otchet," places the total at 408. (Russia, "Otchet," 132-133.) The Navy Ministry's survey of foreign voyages of Russian vessels sets it at 426. (Russia, *Obzor,* II, 742-743.) The table above has been extracted from data that appeared in the appendix of the Russian Naval Ministry's

official account of its own activities during the years 1853-1854. (Russia, Morskoe Ministerstvo, *Kratkii otchet po morskomu ministerstvu za 1853 i 1854 god* [Brief Account of (the Activities of) the Ministry of the Navy During the Years 1853 and 1854], p. 56.) It is presented here to give the reader a general (not 100 per cent exact) idea of the number of men aboard the Russian vessels.

2. The *Kniaz' Menshikov* was a Russo-American Company vessel. We have no information at our disposal about the size of her crew.

Appendix 3

1. William M. Malloy (comp.), *Treaties, Conventions, International Acts, Protocols and Agreements, Between the United States of America and Other Powers 1776-1909*, I (Washington, 1910), 996-998.

2. Commodore Perry signed the English drafts, the plenipotentiaries the Japanese drafts. Dutch and Chinese translations were certified by interpreters of both sides. (Hawks, p. 440.)

Bibliography

I. *Primary Sources*

A. PRINTED SOURCES: OFFICIAL DOCUMENTS, ETC.

BOLTIN, ALEKSANDR. "Shtorm v vostochnom okeane vyderzhennyi fr. *Pallada"* (The Storm in the Pacific Ocean Weathered by the Frigate *Pallada), Morskoi Sbornik,* XVII, No. 7, Part 5 (July, 1855), 7-10.

GONCHAROV, IVAN ALEKSANDROVICH. "Russkie v Iaponii v kontse 1853 i v nachale 1854 goda (Ekspeditsiia grafa Putiatina)" (Russians in Japan at the End of 1853 and Beginning of 1854 [The Expedition of Count Putiatin]), *Morskoi Sbornik,* XVIII, No. 9, Part 1, Sect. 4 (September, 1855), 14-84; and Part 2, Sect. 4, 127-162; No. 10, Part 1, Sect. 4 (October, 1855), 299-327; and Part 2, Sect. 4, 417-453; No. 11, Sect. 4 (November, 1855), 63-128.

GRIMM, E. D. (ED.). *Sbornik dogovorov i drugikh dokumentov po istorii mezhdunarodnykh otnoshenii na Dal'nem Vostoke* (1842-1925) (Collection of Treaties and Other Documents Pertaining to the History of International Relations in the Far East [1842-1925]). Moscow, 1927.

HAWKS, FRANCIS L. (COMP.). *Narrative of the Expedition of an American Squadron to the China Seas and Japan, Performed in the Years 1852, 1853, and 1854 under the Command of Commodore M. C. Perry, United States Navy, by Order of the Government of the United States.* New York, 1856.

HEINE, WILHELM. *Reise um die Erde nach Japan an Bord der Expeditions-Escadre unter Commodore M. C. Perry in den Jahren 1853, 1854 und 1855, unternommen im Auftrage der Regierung der Vereinigten Staaten* (Voyage Around the World to Japan Aboard the Expeditionary Squadron under the Command of Commodore M. C. Perry in the Years 1853, 1854 and 1855, Undertaken by Orders of the Government of the United States). 2 vols. Leipzig, 1856.

IOLKIN, PETR. "Zametki o gidrograficheskikh zaniatiiakh, vo vremia krugosvetnago plavanii na fregate *Diana* s 1853 po 1855 god" (Notes about Hydrographical Exercises during the Round-the-World Voyage Aboard the Frigate *Diana* from 1853 to 1855), *Morskoi Sbornik,* XXIV, No. 10, Part 2 (August, 1856), 105-131.

Ishin shiryo hensan-kai (Society for the Compilation of Restoration Material) (comp.). *Dai-Nihon ishin shiryo* (Historical Material Concerning the Meiji Restoration). 18 vols. Tokyo, 1938-1943.

IVANOVSKII, I. (ED.). *Sobranie deistvuiushchikh dogovorov zakliuchennykh Rossieiu s inostrannymi derzhavami, Dogovory otnositel'no interesov promyshlennosti* (Compilation of Effective Treaties Concluded by Russia with Foreign Powers, Treaties Concerning Industrial Interests). Odessa, 1890.

Japan, Foreign Office. *Treaties and Conventions Between the Empire of Japan and Other Powers Together with Universal Conventions, Regulations, and Communications since March, 1854.* Tokyo, 1884.

K. A. (Kolokol'tsov, Aleksandr?). "Postroenie shkuny *Kheda* v Iaponii" (Construction of the Schooner *Heda* in Japan), *Morskoi Sbornik,* XXIII, No. 8, Part 3 (June, 1856), 279-299.

LESOVSKII, STEPAN STEPANOVICH. "Vypiska iz shkanechnago zhurnala fregata *Diana*" (Extract from the Logbook of the Frigate *Diana*), *Morskoi Sbornik*, XVII, No. 7, Part 2 (July, 1855), 244-257.

LOSEV KONSTANTIN. *"O Nagasakskikh ukrepleniiakh"* (Concerning the Nagasaki Fortifications), *Morskoi Sbornik*, XXIII, No. 8, Part 3 (June, 1856), 300-306.

MALLOY, WILLIAM M. (COMP.). *Treaties, Conventions, International Acts, Protocols and Agreements, Between the United States of America and Other Powers 1776-1909*. Washington, 1910.

MUSIN-PUSHKIN, ALEKSANDR. "Pis'mo Leit. Musina-Pushkina" (Letter of Lt. Musin-Pushkin), *Morskoi Sbornik*, XIX, No. 11, Part 2 (November, 1855), 8-10.

PESHCHUROV, A. "Shkuna Kheda v Tatarskom prolive" (The Schooner *Heda* in the Straits of Tartary), *Morskoi Sbornik*, XXII, No. 6, Part 4 (April, 1856), 1-4.

PESHCHUROV, A. (? unsigned). "Opisanie Nagasakskago Porta" (Description of Nagasaki Harbor), *Morskoi Sbornik*, XX, No. 1, Part 3 (January, 1856), 202-215.

POS'ET, KONSTANTIN NIKOLAEVICH. "O plavanii iz Anglii na mys Dobroi Nadezhdy i v Zondskii proliv v 1853 godu" (Concerning the Sailing from England to the Cape of Good Hope and Sunda Strait in the Year 1853), *Morskoi Sbornik*, X, No. 9 (1853).

POS'ET, KONSTANTIN NIKOLAEVICH (here given as Capitaine Ponsset). "Opisanie zemletriaseniia v Simode i krusheniia fregata *Diana*" (Description of the Earthquake in Shimoda and the Shipwreck of the Frigate *Diana*), *Morskoi Sbornik*, XV, No. 4, Part 4 (April, 1855), 293-296.

PUTIATIN, EVFIMII VASIL'EVICH. "Raport General-Adiutanta Putiatina Velikomu Kniaziu General-Admiralu (O zemletriasenii i krushenii fregata *Diana*)" (Report of Adjutant-General Putiatin to the Grand Duke Lord High Admiral [Concerning the Earthquake and Shipwreck of the Frigate *Diana*]), *Morskoi Sbornik*, XVII, No. 7, Part 2 (July, 1855), 231-243.

———. "Vsepoddaneishii otchet general-adiutanta grafa Putiatina, o plavanii otriada voennykh sudov nashikh v Iaponiiu i Kitai, 1852-1855 god" (Most Devoted Report of the Adjutant-General Count Putiatin about the Sailing of a Detachment of Our Warships to Japan and China, 1852-1855), *Morskoi Sbornik*, XXIV, No. 10, Part 1 (August, 1856), 22-104.

Russia, Inspector's Department. Circular No. 318 (January 1, 1857), as reprinted in *Morskoi Sbornik*, XXXIII, No. 1, Part 1 (January, 1858), xxv-xxvi.

Russia, Morskoe Ministerstvo (Ministry of the Navy). *Kratkii otchet po morskomu ministerstvu za 1853 i 1854 god* (Brief Account of [the Activities of] the Ministry of the Navy During the Years 1853 and 1854). St. Petersburg, 1860.

———. *Letopis' krushenii i drugikh bedstvennykh sluchaev voennykh sudov russkago flota* (Annals of Shipwrecks and Other Calamities [Suffered] by Men-of-War of the Russian Navy). St. Petersburg, 1874.

———. *Obzor zagranichnykh plavanii sudov russkago voennago flota s 1850 po 1868 god* (Survey of Foreign Voyages of Vessels of the Russian Navy from 1850 to 1868). 4 vols. St. Petersburg, 1871.

Russia, Morskoe Ministerstvo, Morskoi Uchenyi Komitet (Naval Scientific Section), Technical Committee. *Morskoi Sbornik* (Nautical Collection). St. Petersburg, 1849-   .

———. "Dopolnitel'nye svedeniia ob ekipazhe fregata *Diana*" (Supplementary

News about the Crew of the Frigate *Diana*), *Morskoi Sbornik*, XVII, No. 8, Part 2 (August, 1855), 282-285.

————. "Iaponskaia ekspeditsiia pod nachal'stvom kommodora M. C. Perri, v 1852 godu" (The Japanese Expedition under the Command of Commodore M. C. Perry in the Year 1852), *Morskoi Sbornik*, VII, No. 4 (1852), 417-419 and No. 5, 519-520.

————. "Izvlechenie iz pisem morskikh ofitserov: Zarubina, Peshchurova i Boltina, nakhodiashchikhsia na eskadre Vitse-Admirala Putiatina" (Extracts from Letters of the Naval Officers Zarubin, Peshchurov, and Boltin, Serving with the Squadron of Vice-Admiral Putiatin), *Morskoi Sbornik*, XII, No. 7, Part 3 (July, 1854), 319-332.

————. "Komand fregatov: *Pallada, Diana, Avrora,* shkuny *Vostok* i dr., nakhodivshikhsia vo vremia krymskoi voiny u beregov Sibiri" (The Crew of the Frigates *Pallada, Diana, Avrora,* the Schooner *Vostok* and Others, [that] Were at the Shores of Siberia During the Crimean War), *Morskoi Sbornik*, XXIII, No. 1, Part 1 (January, 1858), xxv-xxvi.

————. "O plavanii fregata *Pallada* iz Anglii k mysu Dobroi Nadezhdy (Iz doneseniia general-adiutanta Putiatina)" (Concerning the Sailing of the Frigate *Pallada* from England to the Cape of Good Hope [From a Report of Adjutant General Putiatin]), *Morskoi Sbornik*, IX, No. 6 (1853), 494-499.

————. "O plavanii v vostochnom okeane general-adiutanta Putiatina i kontradmirala Zavoiki" (About the Sailing of Adjutant General Putiatin and Rear-Admiral Zavoika on the Pacific Ocean), *Morskoi Sbornik*, XX, No. 1, Part 3 (January, 1856), 174-187.

————. "Otchet o plavanii fregata *Pallada,* shkuny *Vostok,* korveta *Olivutsa* i transporta *Kniaz' Menshikov,* pod komandoiu General-Adiutanta Putiatina, v 1852, 53 i 54 godakh, s prilozheniem otcheta o plavanii fregata *Diana,* v 1853, 54 i 55 godakh" (Account of the Sailing of the Frigate *Pallada,* the Schooner *Vostok,* the Corvet *Olivutsa,* and the Transport *Kniaz' Menshikov,* under the Command of Adjutant General Putiatin, in the Years 1852, 1853, and 1854, with a Supplementary Account of the Sailing of the Frigate *Diana,* in the Years 1853, 1854, and 1855), *Morskoi Sbornik*, XX, No. 1, Part 3 (January, 1856), 132-173.

————. "Plavanie eskadry general-adiutanta Putiatina, sostoiashchei iz fregata *Pallada,* korveta *Olivutsa,* shkuny *Vostok,* i transporta Amer. kompanii *Kniaz' Menshikov*" (Sailing of Adjutant-General Putiatin's Squadron, Consisting of the Frigate *Pallada,* the Corvet *Olivutsa,* the Schooner *Vostok,* and the Transport of the American Company *Kniaz' Menshikov*), *Morskoi Sbornik*, X, No. 12 (1853), 168-171; XI, No. 3 (1854), 150-152; No. 4 (1854), 265-267; XIII, No. 9 (1854), 55 ff.

————. "Shkuna *Opyt,* iakhta g. glavnago komandira Kronshtatskago porta" (The Schooner *Opyt,* Yacht of the Top Commandant of Kronstadt Harbor), with a Sketch by *Leitenant* Bessarabskii, *Morskoi Sbornik*, I, No. 2, Part 1 (1849), 46-57.

————. "Vysochaishii ukaz o pozhalovanii vitse-admiralu Putiatinu grafskago dostoinstva" (Imperial Ukase about Conferring the Dignity of a Count on Vice-Admiral Putiatin), *Morskoi Sbornik*, XX, No. 1, Part 1 (January, 1856), lxiv-lxv.

Russia, Morskoe Ministerstvo. "Zamechaniia o shtorme, vyderzhannom fregatom *Pallada* v 1853 godu" (Observations about the Storm Weathered by the Frigate *Pallada* in the Year 1853), *Morskoi Sbornik*, XX, No. 2, Part 3 (February, 1856), 459-468.

VON SHANTS (SCHANZ?) IVAN I. "Otvet g. Musinu-Pushkinu" (Reply to Mr. Musin-Pushkin), *Morskoi Sbornik*, XXVI, No. 14, Part 4 (December, 1856), 6-10.

——. "Voennaia shkuna *Opyt*" (The War Schooner *Opyt*), *Morskoi Sbornik*, I, No. 2, Part 1 (1849), 117-128.

——. "Vozrazhenie na stat'iu: Postroika shkuny *Kheda*" (In Reply to the Article: Construction of the Schooner *Heda*), *Morskoi Sbornik*, XXIV, No. 1, Part 4 (August, 1856).

VON SIEBOLD, PHILIPP FRANZ. "Deistviia Rossii i Niderlandov k otkrytiiu Iaponii dlia torgovli vsekh narodov" (Actions of Russia and the Netherlands Toward the Opening of Japan for the Trade of All Nations), translated from the German ("Urkundliche Darstellung der Bestrebungen von Niederland und Russland zur Eröffnung Japans für die Schiffahrt und den Seehandel aller Nationen" [Bonn, 1854]), *Morskoi Sbornik*, XV, No. 3, Part 4 (March, 1855), 1-41.

SUMIDA MASAICHI (ED.). *Kaiji shiryo sosho* (Collectanea of Historical Material on Maritime Affairs). 20 vols. Tokyo, 1929-1931.

Tokyo teikoku daigaku (Tokyo Imperial University) (ed.). *Bakumatsu gaikoku kankei monjo* (Documents [Pertaining to] Foreign Relations [during] the Last Days of the Shogunate), Series C of *Dai-Nihon ko-monjo* (Ancient Documents of Japan). Tokyo, 1901- .

B. DIARIES, MEMOIRS, LETTERS, AND RECORDS

BARSOV, N. "Vospominanie ob I. A. Goncharove" (Recollections about I. A. Goncharov), *Istoricheskii Vestnik* (Historical Messenger), XLVI (1891), 628.

COLE, ALLAN B. (ED.). *Yankee Surveyors in the Shogun's Seas*. Princeton, 1947.

COSENZA, MARIO EMILIO (ED.). *The Complete Journal of Townsend Harris, First American Consul General and Minister to Japan*. Garden City, 1930.

ENGEL'GARDT, B. (ED.). "Putevye pis'ma I. A. Goncharöva iz krugosvetnago plavaniia" (Travel Letters of I. A. Goncharov from [the] Around-the-World-Expedition), *Literaturnoe Nasledstvo* (Literary Heritage), XXII-XXIV (Moscow, 1935), 309-426.

GONCHAROV, IVAN ALEKSANDROVICH. *Fregat Pallada* (The Frigate *Pallada* [Pallas]), Vol. VII of *Polnoe Sobranie Sochinenii* (Complete Works). St. Petersburg: Glazunov, 1884.

——. *Fregat Pallada*, abridged edition, with introduction and commentary by S. D. Muraveiskii, Moscow: Gosudarstvennoe Izdatel'stvo Geograficheskoi Literatury, 1949.

——. "Manilla" (Manila), *Otechestvennye zapiski* (Fatherland Journal). St. Petersburg, October, 1855.

HAYASHI, D. (unsigned). "Diary of an Official of the Bakufu," *The Transactions of the Asiatic Society of Japan* [abbr. TASJ], Second Series, VII (Tokyo, 1930), 98-120.

KAWAJI SAEMON-NO-JO (Toshiakira). "Roshia osetsu-kakari Kawaji Saemon-no-jo (Toshiakira) nikki" (Dairies of Kawaji Saemon-no-jo [Toshiakira], Charged with the Reception of [the] Russia[ns]), *Bakumatsu* [see Tokyo teikoku daigaku], Suppl. 1 (1913), 1-193.

KOGA KINICHIRO (Masaru). "Roshia osetsu-kakari Koga Kinichiro (Masaru) seishi nikki" (Diaries of the Western Mission of Koga Kinichiro [Masaru], Charged with the Reception of [the] Russia[ns]), *Bakumatsu*, Suppl. 1, 194-413.

MAKHOV, VASILII. *Fregat Diana* (The Frigate *Diana*). St. Petersburg, 1867.

MITSUKURI GEMPO (Kenju). "Roshia osetsu-kakari tsuke Tsuyama hanshi Mitsukuri Gempo (Kenju) seisei kiko" (Journal of the Western Travel of the Tsuyama Clansman Mitsukuri Gempo [Kenju], Attached [to those Charged with the] Russian Reception), *Bakumatsu*, Suppl. 1, 414-527.

NEVEL'SKOI, G. I. *Podvigi russkikh morskikh ofitserov na krainem vostoke Rossii 1849-1855* (Exploits of Russian Naval Officers in the Far East of Russia, 1849-1855), (Posthumous Memoirs Edited by His Wife [Ekaterina Ivanovna Nevel'-skoi]). St. Petersburg, 1878; reprinted edition, Moscow, 1947.

PILKIN, KONSTANTIN PAVLOVICH. "Zaniatie v 1862 g. russkimi sudami ostrova Tsu-sima" (The Occupation of Tsushima Island by Russian Vessels in 1862), extract from the journal of *Kapitan 2-go ranga* Konstantin Pavlovich Pilkin, commander of the clipper *Abrek, Morskiia Zapiski* (Naval Records), VIII, No. 1 (New York, March, 1950), 2-7.

SCHILLING, NIKOLAI G. II. "Iz vospominanii starago moriaka" (Memoirs of an Old Mariner), *Russkii Arkhiv* (Russian Archives) (St. Petersburg, 1892), pp. 126-159, 247-276, 287-318.

———. *Vospominaniia Starago Moriaka* (Memoirs of an Old Mariner). Moscow, 1892.

SPALDING, J. W. *Japan and Around the World.* New York, 1855.

STALIN, IOSIF VISSARIONOVICH. "Obrashcheniia tovarishcha I. V. Stalina k narodu" (Speech of Comrade I. V. Stalin to the People), as cited by B. A. Romanov, *Ocherki diplomaticheskoi istorii russko-iaponskoi voiny, 1895-1907* (Sketches of the Diplomatic History of the Russo-Japanese War, 1895-1907) (Moscow, 1947), p. 3.

WILLIAMS, SAMUEL WELLS. "A Journal of the Perry Expedition to Japan (1853-1854)," TASJ, First Series, XXXVII, Part 2 (Tokyo, 1910), 1-259.

II. *Secondary Sources*

A. BOOKS AND ARTICLES

AKAGI ROY HIDEMICHI. *Japan's Foreign Relations.* Tokyo, 1936.

CHAMBERLAIN, BASIL HALL. *Thinks Japanese.* London, 1905.

DENNETT, TYLER. *Americans in Eastern Asia.* New York, 1941.

ECKEL, PAUL E. "The Crimean War and Japan," *The Far Eastern Quarterly*, III, No. 2 (Menasha, February, 1944), 109-118.

FUJII JINTARO. *Bakumatsu ishin-shi* (History of the Bakumatsu Period and the Restoration), Vol. IX of *Dai-Nihon shi koza* (Lecture Series on Japanese History). Tokyo, 1928-1930.

HIRANO MASAHIDE. *Nichiro kosho shiwa* (History of Russo-Japanese Relations). Tokyo, 1944.

IAZYKOV, DMITRII. "Literaturnaia deiatel'nost I. A. Goncharova" (Literary Activity of I. A. Goncharov), *Istoricheskii Vestnik* (Historical Messenger), XVIII (1884), 139-140.

Illustrated London News. "British Expedition at Japan," *The Nautical Magazine and Naval Chronicle for 1855* (London, 1855), pp. 94-99.

INOBE SHIGEO. *Ishin zenshi no kenkyu* (Historical Study of the Pre-Restoration Period). Tokyo, 1935.

ISTOMIN, V. K. "Admiral I. S. Unkovskoi. Razskazy iz ego zhizni" (Admiral I. S. Unkovskoi. Stories Out of His Life), *Russkii Arkhiv* (1887), Part 1, pp. 129-145; Part 2, pp. 280-288; Part 5, pp. 117-129.

KATSU YASUYOSHI. *Kaikoku kigen* (How Japan Was Opened Up). 3 vols. Tokyo, 1893.

KAWAKAMI, K. K. *Japan in World Politics*. New York, 1917.

KEMUYAMA, S. "Nichiro no gaiko" (Russo-Japanese Diplomatic Relations), in Japan, Department of Education, *Rokoku kenkyu* (A Study of Russia) (Tokyo, 1917), pp. 399-443.

KOBAYASHI SHOJIRO. *Bakumatsu* (End of Shogunate), Vol. XI of *Nihon jidai-shi* (Japanese History by Periods). Tokyo, 1927.

KRUPINSKI, KURT. *Japan und Russland, Ihre Beziehungen bis zum Frieden von Portsmouth* (Japan and Russia, Their Relations till the Peace of Portsmouth). Königsberg and Berlin, 1940.

KUNO, YOSHI S. *Japanese Expansion on the Asiatic Continent*, II (Berkeley and Los Angeles, 1940).

KURITA MOTOTSUGU. *Sogo kokushi kenkyu* (Synthetic Study of Japanese History). 3 vols. Tokyo, 1935-1936.

KYOZAWA KIYOSHI. *Gaiko-shi* (History of Foreign Relations), Vol. III of *Gendai Nihon bummei-shi* (History of Japanese Civilization in Modern Times). Tokyo, 1941.

LENSEN, GEORGE ALEXANDER. "Early Russo-Japanese Relations," *The Far Eastern Quarterly*, X, No. 1 (November, 1950), 2-37.

——. "One Hundred Years Ago: Commodore Perry in Japan," *Florida State University Studies*, X (1953), 41-47.

——. "The Historicity of *Fregat Pallada*," *Modern Language Notes* (November, 1953), 462-466.

——. "The Russo-Japanese Frontier," *Florida State University Studies*, XIV (1954), 23-40.

——. *Report from Hokkaido: The Remains of Russian Culture in Northern Japan*. Hakodate, 1954.

——. "Russians in Japan, 1858-1859," *The Journal of Modern History*, XXVI (June, 1954), 162-173.

MAINOV, V. "Uspekhi geograficheskikh znanii v Rossii (1855-1880)" (Progress of Geographical Knowledge in Russia [1855-1880]), *Istoricheskii Vestnik*, III (1880), 74.

MARUYAMA KUNIO. *Nihon hokuho hatten-shi* (History of Developments in Japan's Northern Regions). Tokyo, 1942.

MORSE, HOSEA BALLOU. *The International Relations of the Chinese Empire*, I (London, 1910).

MIZUNO, CAPTAIN HIRONORI. "The Japanese Navy," in Inazo Nitobe and others, *Western Influences in Modern Japan* (Chicago, 1931), 408-446.

MURDOCH, JAMES. *A History of Japan*, III (London, 1926).

NITOBE, INAZO. *Bushido, the Soul of Japan*. New York and London, 1905.

NUMATA, ICHIRO. *Nichiro gaiko-shi* (History of Russo-Japanese Foreign Relations). Tokyo, 1943.

OKUDAIRA, T. "Kurimiya senso to kyokuto" (The Crimean War and the Far East), *Kokusai-ho gaiko zasshi* (The Journal of International Law and Diplomacy). Tokyo, 1936.

OKUMA SHIGENOBU. *Kaikoku taisei-shi* (History of the Opening of Japan). Tokyo, 1913.

OSTEN-SAKEN, BARON F. R. "Pamiati grafa Evfimiia Vasil'evicha Putiatina pochetnago chlena imperatorskago russkago geograficheskago obshchestva" (Remembrances of Count Evfimii Vasil'evich Putiatin, Honorary Member of the Imperial Russian Geographical Society), *Izvestiia Imperatorskago russkago geograficheskago obshchestva* (News of the Imperial Russian Geographical Society), XIX (St. Petersburg, 1883), 383-397.

OTA SABURO. *Nichiro Karafuto gaiko-sen* (Russo-Japanese Diplomatic Intercourse [Concerning] Karafuto [Sakhalin]). Tokyo, 1941.

PARES, SIR BERNARD. *A History of Russia*. New York, 1948.

PETROVA, O. P. "Admiral E. V. Putiatin v bukhte Kheda" (Admiral E. V. Putiatin in Heda Bay), Akademiia Nauk (Academy of Sciences), Institut Vostokovedeniia (Institute of Eastern Studies), *Sovetskoe Vostokovedenie* (Soviet Eastern Studies), VI (Moscow and Leningrad, 1949), 368-382.

RAMMING, MARTIN. "Über den Anteil der Russen an der Eröffnung Japans für den Verkehr mit den Westlichen Mächten" (Concerning the Role of the Russians in the Opening of Japan to Intercourse with the Western Powers), *Mitteilungen der Deutschen Gesellschaft für Natur- und Völkerlunde Ostasiens*, XXI, Part B (Tokyo, 1926).

SANSOM, SIR GEORGE B. *The Western World and Japan*. New York, 1950.

SATOW, ERNEST MASON (trans.). *Japan 1853-1864 (Genji yume monogatari)*. Tokyo, 1905.

SHIBUSAWA EIICHI. *Tokugawa Yoshinobu ko den* (Biography of Prince Tokugawa Yoshinobu [Keiki]). 8 vols. Tokyo, 1918.

SIEMERS, BRUNO. "Japans Eingliederung in den Weltverkehr 1853-1869" (Japan's Inclusion into International Intercourse 1853-1869), *Historische Studien*, Pamphlet No. 316 (Berlin, 1937).

TABOHASHI KIYOSHI. *Kindai Nihon gaikoku kankei-shi* (History of Japan's Foreign Relations in Recent Times). Tokyo, 1930.

TOKUTOMI IICHIRO. *Kinsei Nihon kokumin-shi* (History of the Japanese People in Modern Times), XXXI (*Peri raiko oyobi sono toji* [Perry's Visit to the Shores of Japan and Those Times]), XXXII (*Kanagawa joyaku teiketsu-hen* [Conclusion of the Treaty of Kanagawa]), XXXIII (*Nichiro-eiran joyaku teiketsu-hen* [Conclusion of Treaties between Japan and Russia, England and Holland]). Tokyo, 1929-1930.

TREAT, PAYSON JACKSON. *The Early Diplomatic Relations Between the United States and Japan, 1853-1865*. Baltimore, 1917.

TSUJI ZENNOSUKE. *Kaigai kotsu shiwa* (Story of the History of [Japanese] Intercourse with Foreign Countries). Tokyo, 1930.

WALWORTH, ARTHUR. *Black Ships off Japan*. New York, 1946.

YANAGA, CHITOSHI. *Japan since Perry*. New York, 1949.

B. REFERENCE WORKS

BEZOBRAZOV, V. (PUBL.). *Entsiklopediia voennykh i morskikh nauk* (Encyclopedia of Military and Naval Sciences). St. Petersburg, 1893.

HEIBONSHA (PUBL.). *Dai-hyakka jiten* (Great Encyclopedia). 28 vols. Tokyo, 1931-1935.

——. *Shinsen dai-jimmei jiten* (Revised Large Biographical Encyclopedia). 9 vols. Tokyo, 1937-1941.

HEKI SHOICHI. *Kokushi dai-nempyo* (Chronological Table of Japanese History). 6 vols. Tokyo, 1935.

——. *Nihon rekishi jimmei jiten* (Biographical Dictionary of Japanese History). Tokyo, 1938.

PAPINOT, E. *Historical and Geographical Dictionary of Japan*. Yokohama, 1910.

POLOVTSOV, A. A. (ED.) *Russkii biograficheskii slovar'* (Russian Biographical Dictionary). St. Petersburg, 1910.

RAMMING, MARTIN (ED.). *Japan-Handbuch* (Handbook of Japan). Berlin, 1941.

TSUJI ZENNOSUKE. *Dai-Nihon nempyo* (Chronological Table of Japan). Tokyo, 1943.

YOSHIDA TOGO (ED.). *Dai-Nihon chimei jisho* (Encyclopedia of Japanese Geographical Names). 7 vols. Tokyo, 1911-1913.

C. UNPUBLISHED MANUSCRIPTS

LENSEN, GEORGE ALEXANDER. "A History of Russo-Japanese Relations, 1700-1860" (Master's Essay, Department of Chinese and Japanese, Faculty of Philosophy, Columbia University, 1947).

SUZUKI RIICHIRO, "Tachibana Kosai," unpublished sixteen-page manuscript by the present (1954) mayor of Kakegawa-*machi* in Ogasa-*gun*, Shizuoka-*ken*. Undated.

III. *Books and Articles Mentioned*

ASTON, W. G. "Russian Descents into Saghalin and Itorup," TASJ, First Series, I, Part 1 (1882).

BAER, K. E. *Die Verdienste Peter des Grossen um die Erweiterung der geographischen Kenntnisse* (Peter the Great's Part in the Widening of Geographical Knowledge), Vol. XVI of *Beiträge zur Kenntnis des russischen Reiches*. St. Petersburg, 1872.

BARROWS, EDWARD MORLEY. *The Great Commodore, The Exploits of Matthew Calbraith Perry*. Indianapolis, 1935.

BARTHOLD, W. *Die geographische und historische Erforschung des Orientes mit besonderer Berücksichtigung der russischen Arbeiten* (The Geographical and Historical Investigation of the Orient with Special Reference to Russian Works), Vol. VIII of *Quellen und Forschungen zur Erd- und Kulturkunde*. Leipzig, 1913.

BERG, L. S. *Ocherki po istorii russkikh geografischeskikh otkrytii* (Essays Concerning the History of Russian Geographical Discoveries). Moscow, 1946.

COLE, ALLAN B. (ED.). *A Scientist with Perry in Japan, The Journal of Dr. James Morrow*. Chapel Hill, 1947.

——. *With Perry in Japan, The Diary of Edward Yorke McCauley*. Princeton, 1942.

DALLIN, DAVID J. *The Rise of Russia in Asia*. New Haven, 1949.

FALK, EDWIN A. *From Perry to Pearl Harbor*. Garden City, 1943.

Foreign Affairs Association of Japan, *Contemporary Japan* (Quarterly). Tokyo, 1933- .

GOLOWNIN, CAPTAIN [V. M. GOLOVNIN]. *Narrative of My Captivity in Japan During the Years 1811, 1812, and 1813*. London, 1818.

GRAFF, HENRY F. (ED.). *Bluejackets with Perry in Japan; A Day to Day Account Kept by Master's Mate John R. C. Lewis and Cabin Boy William B. Allen*. New York, 1952.

GRIFFIS, WILLIAM ELLIOT. *Matthew Calbraith Perry: A Typical American Naval Officer*. Boston, 1887.

HARRISON, JOHN A. *Japan's Northern Frontier*. Gainesville, 1953.

KOJIMA MATAJIRO. *Amerika ichijo utsushi. Commodore Perry's Expedition to Hakodate May 1854*. Hakodate, 1953.

LEGGE, JAMES. *The Chinese Classics*. Second Edition, Revised, II (Oxford, 1895).

MATTICE, HAROLD ALLISON. *Perry and Japan, An Account of the Empire and an Unpublished Record of the Perry Expedition*. New York, 1942.

NOVAKOVSKII, S. I. *Iaponiia i Rossiia* (Japan and Russia), I (Tokyo, 1918).

OGLOBLIN, N. N., "Pervyi Iaponets v Rossii" (The First Japanese in Russia), *Russkaia Starina* (Russian Antiquity), St. Petersburg, October, 1891.

OKAMOTO RYUNOSUKE. *Nichiro kosho Hokkaido shiko* (Hokkaido Historical Documents Concerning Russo-Japanese Relations). Tokyo, 1898.

POZDNEEV, D. M. *Materialy po istorii severnoi Iaponii i eia otnoshenii k materiku Azii i Rossii* (Material Concerning the History of Northern Japan and Her Relations to the Asiatic Mainland and Russia). Tokyo, 1909.

RIUMIN. *Zapiski kantseliarista Riumina po prikliucheniakh ego s Beniovskim* (Memoirs of the Chancery Clerk Riumin Concerning His Adventures with Benyovszky). St. Petersburg, 1822.

SAKAMAKI, SHUNZO. "Japan and the United States, 1790-1853," TASJ, Second Series, XVIII (1939).

SGIBNEV, A. "Istoricheskii ocherk glavneishikh sobytii v Kamchatke v 1772-1816 g." (Historical Sketch of the Most Important Events in Kamchatka from 1772 to 1816), *Morskoi Sbornik*, July-August, 1869.

——. "Popytki Russkikh k zavedeniiu torgovykh snoshenii s Iaponieiu (v XVIII i nachale XIX stoletii)" (Attempts of the Russians to Establish Trade Relations with Japan [in the Eighteenth and in the Beginning of the Nineteenth Centuries]), *Morskoi Sbornik*, January-February, 1869.

SWISCHER, EARL. "Commodore Perry's Imperialism in Relation to America's Present-Day Position in the Pacific," *Pacific Historical Review*, XVI, No. 1 (February, 1947), 30-40.

VINACKE, HAROLD M. A History of the Far East in Modern Times. New York, 1941.

WALLACH, SIDNEY (ED.). Abridged edition of Francis L. Hawks (comp.), *Narrative of the Expedition of an American Squadron to the China Seas and Japan under the Command of Commodore M. C. Perry, United States Navy*. New York, 1952.

WATANABE SHUJIRO. *Sekai ni okeru Nihonjin* (Japanese in the World). Tokyo, 1942.

Index